CAST OF ONE

CAST OF ONE

One-Person Shows
from the Chautauqua Platform
to the Broadway Stage

JOHN S. GENTILE

UNIVERSITY OF ILLINOIS PRESS
Urbana and Chicago

Library of Congress Cataloging-in-Publication Data

Gentile, John Samuel, 1956–
    Cast of one: one-person shows from the Chautauqua platform
to the Broadway stage / John S. Gentile.
    p. cm.
Originally presented as the author's thesis (doctoral—
Northwestern University, 1984) under title: The one-person show in
America.
Bibliography: p.
Includes index.
ISBN 0-252-01584-3 (alk. paper)
    1. Oral interpretation.   2. Multiple role acting.   I. Title.
PN4145.G45 1989
808.5′4—dc19   88-29553
                                                            CIP

To Dana

CONTENTS

ACKNOWLEDGMENTS

The years spent in research and writing were made more pleasant by many individuals who graciously contributed their time and expertise to this study. To these people, I express deep gratitude.

Foremost among those who helped shape this book during its early stages are Professors Leland H. Roloff, Dwight Conquergood, Lilla A. Heston, and Frank Galati of the Department of Performance Studies at Northwestern University. Dr. Roloff's careful guidance as my dissertation advisor during a very difficult year will always be kindly remembered, as will Dr. Conquergood's inspirational encouragement years earlier in a graduate seminar in performance history that ultimately lead to my interest in the present topic. I am also grateful for the helpful comments by Dr. Galati and the late Dr. Heston made during the initial writing of this study.

I am indebted to many artists who have been willing either to speak with or to write to me. Deserving special mention is the late Emlyn Williams, who spoke with me at length about his own rich experience as a solo performer. Other artists whose comments enrich this study are Spalding Gray, Alec McCowen, Quentin Crisp, Mark Stevenson, Arthur Peterson, Steven Rumbelow, William Norris, Charles Busch, and Emily Ellison.

The staffs of many special collections at libraries across the country have been of great assistance. I am particularly grateful to Robert A. McCown of the Redpath Chautauqua Collection at the University of Iowa; Todd Gustavson, Barbara B. Haug, and Alfreda L. Irwin of the Chautauqua Collection at the Chautauqua Institution; Mary Ellen Brooks of the Hargrett Rare Book and Manuscript Library at the University of Georgia; Margaret Goostray of the Special Collections at Boston University; and Dorothy L. Swerdlove of the Billy Rose Theatre Collection at the Library and Museum of the Performing Arts at Lincoln Center; and the staffs of the Theatre Collection at the Museum of the City of New York and of the Berg Collection at the New York Public Library.

Along with many individuals, several institutions deserve mention for their support of my research. I thank the National Endowment for the Humanities for awarding me two travel-to-collections grants, Kennesaw State College for three faculty development grants, the Graduate School of Northwestern University for a dissertation grant, and the College of Humanities and Fine Arts at the University of Northern Iowa for a research grant. Without the generous financial assistance from these institutions, I would not have been able to complete this study.

Other individuals continue to merit my gratitude. George Beggs of Kennesaw State College approved special funding to assist in manuscript preparation and supported my request for released time from teaching to allow me to concentrate on research. Mary Frances HopKins of Louisiana State University, Philip Collins of the University of Leicester, Gerald Kahan of the University of Georgia, Everett Albers of the North Dakota Humanities Council and the Great Plains Chautauqua, Evy Nordley of the Minnesota Chautauqua, Lou Burton of the Wyoming Chautauqua Society, Brian C. Crockett of the Utah Humanities Resource Center, and Penny Hummel of the Oregon Committee for the Humanities and the Oregon Chautauqua, John Starr of Kolmar-Luth Entertainment, Inc., Harvey Elliott of Arthur Cantor, Inc., and Ken Yellis and Linda Currie of the National Portrait Gallery at the Smithsonian Institution have all supplied me with valuable information. The staff of the reference department at Kennesaw State College's library has been consistently helpful. Lisa Betts and Jo Dilbeck, my student assistants during the last years of my research, greatly facilitated bringing this study to completion. Louise Hayes graciously typed the revised manuscript under unpleasant time constraints. Joseph R. Kelly helped us through many problems in manuscript preparation. The staff at the University of Illinois Press has been a pleasure to work with, particularly Richard L. Wentworth, whose interest in this book was immediate, and Barbara E. Cohen, whose assistance as copyeditor was invaluable.

Finally, on a personal level, I have been fortunate to have several people who have consistently showed interest in my progress. I thank John Logan, who never seems to tire of my ramblings about one-person shows; Katharyn Machan Aal, who is always willing to share her knowledge with me about poetry readings and the tension between writing and performance; Samuel and Marie Gentile, who have always been supportive of me; Nathaniel Gentile, who has brought so much joy into my life; and, most of all, Dana Gentile, who cheerfully assisted me in the preparation of the manuscript and who has endured the tumultuous years spent in research and writing. To her, I dedicate this book.

CAST
OF ONE

Introduction

> At their worst (which is most of the time) one-person shows are as
> much fun as watching paint dry. It is cruelly difficult for a group of
> performers to hold an audience enthralled, and for one person to do
> it requires enormous skill, concentration and magnetism.
>
> But at their best, one-person shows are magnificent theatre: here is
> the stage, here is the actor, here is the audience; there are no obstacles
> to the connection, and when the connection is made, there is pure
> theatre.
>
> —Tom Topor

One-person shows have grown enormously in popularity over the
last forty years. So startling is this theatrical phenomenon that it
may seem to have sprung uncontrollably from some new artistic
innovation. Research reveals, however, that one-person shows—
quite contrary to a naive initial assumption—have long been a
vital part of our American performance history. As an entertainment event, the one-person show is as old as humankind, dating
back to the ancient oral poets and storytellers. It is true, however,
that only within the twentieth century has our critical perspective
shifted away from viewing one-person shows as a form of entertainment distinct from theatre to one integral to theatre. Why has
our critical perspective undergone such a radical transformation?
What are the roots of the contemporary one-person show? Why
have certain periods been more receptive to the one-person show
as a theatrical experience? Which cultural forces encourage the
proliferation of this performance modality? Which cultural forces
hinder it? These are among the questions examined in this study
of the evolution of the professional one-person show as a theatrical and cultural phenomenon in the United States since the second
half of the nineteenth century, a time during which platform entertainments enjoyed a golden age of unprecedented popularity.

I

"[O]ur present lack of information," a theatre historian recently wrote, "would make it foolish to posit a tradition of solo perform-ance" (Ridgman 1981:35). A 1985 exhibit by the Museum of the City of New York has dramatically proven otherwise.[1] While no study could possibly cover every one-person show produced in our country, and I know that some readers may find a favorite per-formance missing from these pages, this book does offer an ex-amination of representative performances of various kinds of pop-ular one-person shows. In doing so, it provides solo performers and the one-person show genre with the kind of consideration that their significant contributions to American culture have war-ranted.

NOTE

1. Cast of One: One-Person Shows on the New York Stage, exhibit, organized by Mary C. Henderson, Theatre Collection of the Museum of the City of New York, New York, 20 Nov. 1985–30 June 1986. The present book in its original form as a doctoral dissertation pre-dates the exhibit (Gentile 1984). Only in its choice of title was this book inspired by the exhibit. The cover of the exhibit catalog is reproduced below.

1

The One-Person Show in Late Nineteenth-Century America: The Golden Age of Platform Performances

One-person shows enjoyed an unprecedented artistic and commercial vogue in the United States during the second half of the nineteenth century. Of course, the origins of this performance genre reach much further back in time; the nineteenth-century solo performers were, in fact, inheritors of a tradition already possessing a rich history. The rhapsodes of classical Greece, the scops of Anglo-Saxon England, and the jongleurs of medieval France are all part of the tradition of solo performance. Important contributions were also made by soloists in the eighteenth century. Samuel Foote delighted London audiences at the Little Theatre in the Haymarket in the mid-1700s with his entertainments in mimcry called *The Diversions of the Morning*. Foote's *Diversions*, which he opened in 1747 and continued to perform for the next thirty years, inspired George Alexander Stevens's durable *A Lecture on Heads* and John Collins's *Brush for Rubbing Off the Rust of Care*.[1] Actors subsequently performed these later two solo entertainments in America and effectively established the tradition of the professional one-person show in our country.

Although nineteenth-century performers cannot be credited with originating the one-person show, theirs was the age that witnessed its unprecedented rise to popularity as a form of public entertainment. Cultural forces that allowed platform performances, as one-person shows were then commonly called, to become commercially viable had converged by the middle of the cen-

3

tury. Chief among these forces was the pervasive prejudice against the theatre inherited by Victorian Americans from their Puritan ancestors.[2]

Attacked as a corruptor of morals in public sermons, speeches, newspapers, and published tracts, the theatre—"a place of vain amusement"—appealed to "the lovers of pleasure" and not to "the lovers of God" (Thompson 1847:6). Considered "a polluter of public taste," a contributor to the "unhealth of this country," and "the enemy of domestic life" (Talmage 1875:32, 37, 38), the theatre's very roots in Dionysian rites made it suspect. "To a troop of bacchanalians belongs the honor of originating this great intellectual, social, and as some say, moral entertainment!" said the pastor of New York's Broadway Tabernacle Church in 1847. "The theatre has never parted company with Bacchus in whose orgies it originated" (Thompson 1847:11, 35). Actors were assumed to be people of low morals; likewise, audience members were thought to be degenerates. In 1875 T. DeWitt Talmage categorized those whom many felt were the typical theatregoers:

Husbands who have lost all love of home go there. Horse-jockeys go there. Thieves go there. The lecherous go there. Spendthrifts go there. Drunkards go there. Lost women go there. The offscourings of society go there by scores and by hundreds. They block up the doorway. They hang over the gallery, and ogle, and smirk, and shout aloud in the applause that greets a brilliant passage, or one that caricatures religion, or sneers at virtue as prudery or over-niceness, or hints at indecency, and makes the pure-hearted wife or mother turn away her head and say, "God forgive us for ever coming to such a place as this." An institution that nightly draws together from the lowest haunts of vice so many of the leprous, and unwashed, and abandoned, must have in it a moral taint (1875:20–21).

Thus the theatre was believed to be corrupt for its origins, for the character of those attracted to its employ, for the people who regularly attended it as audience members, and for its very nature.

The antitheatre sentiments among the righteous were not altogether unfounded. The nineteenth-century American playhouse was a notorious haven for prostitutes, who frequented the "guilty third tier" of the gallery to meet their clientele. While ensuring the box office manager of ticket sales to one segment of society, the presence of prostitutes in the theatre repulsed potential patrons of another, more respectable segment. As Claudia D. Johnson points out in her examination of prostitution in the Victorian American theatre, "[t]he highly influential clerical stand against the theater, based in large measure on its relationship with prostitutes, kept many would-be theatergoers away and prevented any broad-based support from developing" (1976:119). The antipathy for the theatre prevailed at midcentury and did not subside until the end of the Victorian age. "Attendance upon the theater," wrote Albert M. Palmer in 1895, "was looked upon even fifty years ago by at least seven tenths of the people of the United States as almost a sin. The fashionable ungodly and the lowest and most depraved made up the audiences" (1895, vol. 1:165). It was only toward the end of the Victorian period that attitudes began to relax in relation to the theatre.

The prejudice against the theatre was a great benefit to platform performances for the simple reason that the resistance to the stage was not held against the platform. The theatre was considered dangerous not only for the company of depraved men and the allurements of lecherous women but also for the stage's use of illusionistic devices such as scenery, make-up, and costuming, all of which aimed at seducing the unwary away from reality into a false world of fantasy. "Religious periodicals," David Grimsted explains in *Melodrama Unveiled*, "pointed to the example of Alsypius, an early Christian whom pagan pranksters forced to a gladitorial show where he became so fascinated with blood and splendor that he left the church for the amphitheater" (1968:24). Young men were particularly warned against the perils of the theatre, for they were believed to be "particularly exposed to its temptations" (Thompson 1847:39). The platform with its lectures and solo readings of literature traditionally used no gaudy illusionistic devices and was esteemed as genteel, dignified, and thoroughly respectable. The very tracts that most vehemently attacked the theatre upheld the platform as an edifying force in American culture. The work of platform speakers and readers was accredited for "setting this country fifty years further in advance than it would have been without the lecture platform" (Talmage 1875:93). As Lewis A. Erenberg states, "Certain types of amusements were considered too fast, and hence too lower class . . .

while others of a higher and more refined stamp fit more securely into a set of familial and class values" (1981:5). The theatre and the drama, in short, fell among the former kinds of amusements, whereas the platform and solo readings fell among the latter.

After the Civil War, when intolerance for the stage was prevalent, Americans needed a release from the preceding years of political and military strife. Returning soldiers, grown accustomed to the excitement of battle, sought amusements to escape the routine of civilian life. The demand at this time among the prosperous middle-classes for a nontheatre form of entertainment was immense (Bode 1956:248). Coupled with this demand was the national attainment of widespread literacy, which increased as the nineteenth century progressed. In the Victorian age (often labeled by literary historians as "the age of the novel"), reading was a favorite national pastime. With a wide public familiar with the works of such writers as Irving, Dickens, Scott, and Shakespeare, authors and performers could rightfully assume an interest in platform readings by a general audience. In our own age of electronic media entertainment, the very notion of a general public avidly awaiting an author's reading seems absurd. Authors' readings, while common today, tend to appeal to a specialized elite—the literati. What we are experiencing today is the effect of the split between "mass" and "high" culture, a division that is now sadly gaping but that was nearly nonexistent during the Victorian era. In his essay "Victorian Culture in America," Daniel Walker Howe explains:

Some divisions that we take for granted within our own cultural system did not yet fully exist in America during the Victorian age. One of these is the dichotomy between "mass" and "high" culture. It was 1915 when Van Wyck Brooks complained that American culture was bifurcated into "lowbrow" and "highbrow." Victorian authors with large readership like Longfellow, Horace Bushnell, and Harriet Beecher Stowe, however, had defied this classification, as had performers like Edwin Booth and the European visitor Jenny Lind. Nor did only a few great individuals transcend the categories; many long-since obscure writers like Lydia Sigourney and William Ware did too (1976:13).

As the nation's level of literacy improved, the lower classes impressed their tastes on national culture. Such a situation, while inherently democratic, raised fears among the gentry regarding the potential influence on society by the newly literate. Richard D. Altick discusses these fears in nineteenth-century England:

> The fear was that the traditional culture would be vulgarized, leveled down to the lowest common denominator of taste. . . .
>
> The demand for simply written books and papers suited to the semi-literate mind began, about mid-century, to prove that much money could be made in publishing for this audience. A new branch of the trade was established, shrewdly attuned to the unsophisticated tastes and limited capacities of these multitudes of readers. Dedicated to giving the people what they wanted, most entrepreneurs of cheap print cared nothing for its effects on the general level of culture. They were simply out to sell their merchandise. As the volume of their product increased year by year, the prospect grew that the mass audience, by sheer exercise of purchasing power, would eventually dominate the taste of the whole nation. A new version of Gresham's law was often cited: in the free operation of the cultural market, mediocrity and vulgarity always tend to drive out superior goods. Side by side with old-established book shops, where gentlemen of substance always dealt, sprang up innumerable neighborhood news agents' cubicles with their lurid assortment of penny and shilling thrillers. It was an ominous development. Could the culture of the drawing room and study compete with the culture of the pavement? Mill, writing in the late fifties, when the issue had not yet reached its full magnitude, presented by inference the specter of a whole society—its moral values, its intellectual life, its fine arts—succumbing to the tyranny of the majority (1973:241–42).

The situation was similar in the United States. Slowly a mass culture did come into being, but it only reached its full development towards the end of the era we refer to as Victorian. Of America, Howe writes:

> A distinctive "mass" culture emerged gradually and against the opposition of the gentry; one of its earliest forms was the minstrel show. That which we would regard as "high" culture was characteristically undifferentiated in the Victorian world; the specialized "expert" had not yet become prominent. College professors taught what seems to us a bewildering variety of subjects; ladies and gentlemen of letters felt free to pontificate on all topics. Only recently—mainly in the twentieth cen-

tury—did scholarship and some of the arts become so recondite and specialized, so consciously exclusive, as to be inaccessible to all but a handful of initiates. When this happened, it was a symptom of the disintegration of Victorian culture (1976:14).

During the Victorian period, the divisions in culture were just then emerging and literature we now consider elite enjoyed a truly popular audience. Howe continues his discussion by quoting W. L. Burn's comment on the English reading public in the nineteenth century; Burn had said, "I have no doubt but that there was a higher proportion of the population who had read and were prepared to discuss the novels of Dickens and the poems of Tennyson than could be found to discuss the works of any particular novelist or poet today" (Burn 1964:7, quoted in Howe 1976:13–14). Arguing that the same could be said of Americans, Howe adapts Burn's statement: "Substitute Longfellow for Tennyson and the same could be said of the Victorian United States" (1976:14).

The Victorian interest in literature extended beyond solitary silent reading. Home reading-aloud circles were common family events. Children would gather together at the family hearth to hear father or mother read aloud from *David Copperfield* or *Rip van Winkle*.[3] So universal was this practice that authors felt compelled to write texts appropriate for family consumption and were restricted from explicit handling of adult themes; a novel read aloud in the home had to be pure enough for a young girl's ears. Platform readings by authors and elocutionists were, therefore, fully accepted as wholesome entertainment; they represented nothing less than the professional extension of a favorite family activity. Celebrity readers, in turn, through the glamour of their public appearances on the platform, lent a prestige and heightened credibility to home oral readings and schoolroom elocution lessons. Reading aloud, to use Philip Collins apt phrase, was truly "a Victorian métier" (1972).

The American enthusiasm for reading in the nineteenth century was indistinguishable from a kindred enthusiasm for speaking. The vitality in nineteenth-century America was reflected in the tremendous growth of American vernacular. American English became differentiated from British English through the coinage of new words and new names for new places, from the adaptation and adoption of words from the Amerindian, French, Dutch, Spanish, German, Nordic, and African tongues, and through the development of colloquialisms and slang. Americanisms in language became so predominant, in fact, as to cause a reaction against the new vernacular.[4] Daniel J. Boorstin addressed this issue in *The Americans: The National Experience:* "[W]hen American speech was acquiring its new vitality many American academic students of language and American literary writers were trying to keep the language 'pure.' These Mrs. Grundies, the self-appointed censors of linguistic morality, never worked harder" (1965:277). The elocutionary movement and, by extension, platform readings were manifestations, in part, of the reaction against the epidemic of American vernacular. "The golden age of American oratory," then, came into being counterbalancing the coarseness of the speech of a pioneer country. The American preoccupation with language and speech eventually influenced the literature of the age, giving birth to a declamatory literature, described by Boorstin: "Much of it [declamatory literature], at its best and most characteristic, would be the *spoken* word cast into print. It was a self-conscious literature—self-conscious in the sense that it was aware of its *sound*, of its *audience*, of its effect as a stirrer primarily of common sentiments between a speaker (rather than a writer) and a listener (rather than a reader)" (1965:307). Anthologies of declamatory literature, known as "readers" or "speakers," dominated the teaching of reading. These books, filled with the great American orations (such as Patrick Henry's "Give me liberty or give me death" and Daniel Webster's "Against Hayne") and literature emphasizing the oral/aural qualities (such as Longfellow's "Psalm of Life" and Poe's poem "The Raven"), could be found in schoolhouses and homes across the country. McGuffey *Readers* were preeminent among this class of textbooks in the nation's schoolrooms for over seventy-five years after their initial publication in 1836. "It is sometimes forgotten," writes Boorstin in his discussion of American oratory, "that these books, out of which generations of American schoolchildren learned to read, aimed to teach boys and girls how to read *aloud*" (1973:463).

The conflicting attitudes that Americans held towards their language and speech mirrored their feelings towards their country. Proud of their freedom from Great Britain, they nonetheless feared being culturally inferior. They seemed to revel in their Americanisms in speech at the same time that they worked diligently to maintain the purity of literary British English. This peculiar conflict was also seen in the American taste in platform performers. Indeed, a survey of popular platform celebrities ranges from precise British authors to colloquial American humorists and poets.

All of these cultural forces—the prejudice against the theatre, the subsequent demand for a nontheatre form of entertainment, the solidity of a culture not divided into highbrow and lowbrow, and the intertwined interests in language/literature/reading/speech—contributed to the upsurge in popularity of the one-person show in Victorian America. And yet without adequate means of rapid transportation even the most devoted performers would have been thwarted in their aspirations for a career on the platform. It was the railroad transporting the solo performer on tour that made the one-person show commercially viable in the nineteenth century. William M. Thackery, during his 1855–56 American lecture tour, wrote home after a wintry journey: "What a blessing to be able to come 500 miles through the driving snow. . . . 20 years ago that journey wd. have taken a fortnight. Oughtn't I for one to be thankful for railroads, who never could have made all these dollars without 'em?" (1946, vol. 3:531).

If Thackery sounded somewhat mercenary, he was not alone; the lure of financial gain was the primary motivating force for writers to go on a lecture or reading tour. The monetary rewards for British literary figures in this country far exceeded what they could reap at home, and so nineteenth-century America saw on the platform, along with Thackeray, Charles Dickens, Edwin Arnold, Matthew Arnold, Hall Caine, Wilkie Collins, Arthur Conan Doyle, Anthony Hope, Charles Kingsley, George MacDonald, Martin Tupper, Oscar Wilde, and Edmund Yates. Their talents as performers and lecturers varied widely but the greatest of these was Charles Dickens.

CHARLES DICKENS

The reading tours of Charles Dickens in Britain and America between the years 1858 and 1870 created a sensation. His American tour of 1867–68 was unparalleled until the arrival of the Beatles in the early 1960s. "The excesses of his [Dickens's] public would today be more associated with a pop star than with a writer reading extracts from his own works," writes Raymund Fitzsimons in his account of Dickens's reading tours. "The readings appealed, as did the books, to all ages and to all tastes, cultivated and simple. It was this universal appeal that put the Readings into a different category from all other entertainments" (1970:15). The combination of his literary fame and his considerable histrionic gifts made Dickens not only a superlative example of the Victorian dramatic reader but also the exemplary solo performer of his century. "The Public Readings of Charles Dickens," continues Fitzsimons, "were the greatest one-man show of the nineteenth century" (1970:15).

Platform performances were already growing in popularity in both Britain and the United States when Dickens began his career as a professional public reader, and the study of elocution flourished at the time. Dickens's own background was closely allied to the theatre, for in his youth he had aspired to be an actor. He enjoyed the theatre immensely and admired the work of Albert Smith and Charles Mathews, two British solo performers of the nineteenth century. Dickens shared a personal friendship and an enjoyment of a writer's bohemian lifestyle with Albert Smith, a versatile and indefatigable showman who was also a journalist, a playwright, and a novelist (although hardly of the same caliber as Dickens). It was Smith's work as an entertainer, however, that brought him his greatest fame. He presented one-person travelogues of his own exotic adventures, illustrated with dioramas, humorous character sketches, and original comic songs. He performed his most popular entertainment, "Mr. Albert Smith's Ascent of Mount Blanc," for seven seasons and 2,000 performances.[5] In his biography, Fitzsimons credits Smith for being the one who "set the fashion of literary men appearing on the lecture platform" (1967:104). When Dickens decided to launch his own professional platform career, he turned to Smith for advice and consultation, the result of which was that Smith's brother Arthur served as Dickens's business manager for several years.

While Albert Smith directly influenced Dickens with regard to the practical matters of touring, an even greater role model as a performing artist was the actor-comedian Charles Mathews, whose talents Dickens deeply admired as a youth. Each of Mathews's solo "At Homes" and "Trips to . . . (various places)" was a *tour de force*. The actor impersonated living and fictitious characters, frequently with minimal or no facial make-up. He had an "inexhaustible repertoire of voices and mannerisms, male and female, and an expert command of dialects" (Fawcett 1952:7). One scholar wrote of Mathews:

> In his "At Home" presentations Mathews had a showcase of his talent, and took advantage of this opportunity by broadening his act. He generally opened with a short monologue and then quickly began telling the audience of an eccentric character he knew. Each character was given an individual trait, and was allowed to exhibit his peculiarities for several minutes before the next character was introduced. This could go on until as many as five characters were carrying on conversations with one another at the same time, Mathews, of course, impersonating their voices as well as [using] his own (Zambrano 1972:236).

As well as in his native England, Mathews toured his solo shows in the United States during the early nineteenth century. His first American tour, in 1822–23, resulted in his highly successful "A Trip to America" solo show, written in collaboration with playwright James Smith, in which he burlesqued various American character types. Despite his initial misgivings about performing the show in the United States, his English success, along with his needs for money and fresh inspiration for the show's sequel, convinced him to tour "A Trip to America" in this country, which he did successfully in 1834.

Like the rest of Mathews's solo shows, "A Trip to America" proved the commonly accepted axiom that what works well in performance does not always work well as literature. His outstanding success in spite of chronically weak scripts gives credit to his talents as an actor. Walter Blair has noted that:

> More impressive evidence of Mathews' greatness than rhapsodies of contemporaries is furnished by surviving accounts and partial scripts of his one-man marathons. . . . They were horrible—hazy characterizations, weak jokes, dingy lyrics, meandering monologues. . . .
> Clearly no one but a very talented actor—perhaps no one but a genius—could metamorphose such wretched stuff into the great per-

formances acclaimed by the perceptive critics of Mathews' day (1976:2, 4).

Young Charles Dickens was one of those "perceptive critics" who thoroughly esteemed the actor-comedian's work. Mathews's solo shows, with their lightening changes of character, "appealed to Dickens as the highest form of dramatic talent" (Fawcett 1952:7). So impressed was young Dickens that he "set himself to memorize Mathews's various roles" (Fawcett 1952:7). Ultimately, Dickens's early self-directed lessons in Mathews's roles shaped his public readings from his novels and stories.[6] Dickens's performances, which emphasized his ability to embody a large number of diverse characters, were clearly reminiscent of Mathews's impersonations. One New York critic wrote:

His characters are real to him, and he makes them real to his readers: and therein consists the spell that he wields, no less as an actor than as a writer. . . . His reading, last night, was full of excellence. As on the first occasion he perfectly personated Bob Crachit, the Little Judge, Windle, Weller and Old Scrooge—in the later case even to so slight a detail as the habit of putting the hand to the mouth when speaking—so, on the second occasion, he omitted no characteristic of the unctuous humor and stately bombast of the heroic Micawber, nothing of Mrs. Micawber's sweetly insinuating gabble, not a particle of Mrs. Crupp's garrulity, nor the doleful drawl of "lorn" Mrs. Gummidge, not the shrill, vixenish, spitefulness of Mrs. Raddle, not the bland benevolence and childlike simplicity of Mr. Pickwick. Hard work was evident at every point; but it was work that had been done, and now told only in its perfect results ("Charles Dickens: His Second Reading" 1867:4).

Dickens's strength as a performer, like Mathews's, arose from his talent in assuming a multitude of different characters in quick succession. Time and again reviews comment in terms of this kind: "Dickens displays his marvellous faculty for effacing himself in whatever character he is personating, whether it be pompous Mr. Dombey . . . or any other creation with which he has peopled our memory" ("Charles Dickens: The Story of Little Dombey and the Trial from Pickwick" 1867:4).

Each program was customarily comprised of two lengthy segments from different works that could stand independent from their sources. The two selections were divided in performance by an intermission. Although Dickens did not indulge in conversation with his audiences, he did occasionally interject a brief commentary during the readings. For the most part, however, Dickens's readings were memorized pieces, meticulously rehearsed to the subtlest gesture and constantly "subject to further abbreviation, rephrasings, and extempore improvements" (Collins 1975: xxxvi). His performance scripts consisted of carefully edited selections from his early novels and Christmas books and Christmas stories. Among his most successful readings were "Bardell and Pickwick" from *The Pickwick Papers,* an abridged version of *A Christmas Carol,* and "Little Dombey," the pathetic deathbed sequence from *Dombey and Son,* which regularly reduced the audience to tears. After *Pickwick* and *A Christmas Carol,* the most frequently performed items were the Christmas stories *Boots at the Holly-Tree Inn* and *Doctor Marigold.* Neither are well remembered today although both were popular favorites in Dickens's lifetime. The complete list of Dickens's readings is curious for its omission of his major works of social criticism, works such as *Our Mutual Friend* and *Bleak House,* upon which his literary reputation now rests. Instead, the list represents, as Philip Collins states, the novelist's "writings at their second-best—effective scripts filled out by Dickens's histrionic abilities, and making a special appeal to the laughter-and-tears predilection of his audiences" (1975: lxiv-lxv). Collins continues with a valuable speculation (Dickens has left us no statement of his philosophy of the art of platform reading) regarding Dickens's rationale for script selection, concluding with two major points concerning the readings:

First . . . he evidently judged that public readings were not the occasion for social criticism. . . . [T]he Readings were conscientiously prepared and presented, were fully professional and defensible manifestations of his art, but were "entertainments" from which some graver notes and larger pretensions had to be excluded. . . . My second point is that the novels from which he gave Readings (and indeed those from which he prepared Readings which were never performed, *A Tale of Two Cities* and *Great Expectations*) were, as they still are, the essential "popular" Dickens. During his lifetime, the earlier novels were also more esteemed, as well as more loved (1975: lxv-lxvi).

"Direct appeal," as Paul Schlicke states "was of the essence in his public readings" (1985:230). That Dickens's estimation of his public's taste was accurate is validated by the scores of elocutionary anthologies published for years afterwards in which the Dickens selections typically corresponded to the author's own reading texts.

The strenuous rehearsal process that preceded any public performance of a reading eventually undermined Dickens's health. The rigors of his rehearsals, the emotional exhaustion of his performances, and the strains of his travel schedule all suggest that the act of performance fulfilled in Dickens something much deeper than simply an added income, an escape from domestic unhappiness, or a realization of a simple boyhood wish. Some scholars maintain that Dickens's public reading tours were indications of a dark, suicidal drive.[7] The present author rejects that suggestion, believing instead that the performances were manifestations, as healthy and as legitimate as his writings, of Dickens's creative genius.[8]

For Dickens, the enactment of scenes served not only as a preparation for a public performance but also as a mode of original composition. In her memoirs, Mamie Dickens related a fascinating incident in which she fortuitously witnessed her father's method of composition: while working on a new novel Dickens would suddenly jump up from his desk to perform pantomimes in front of a mirror. The purport of these curious exercises—which included vocalizations—at first escaped the understanding of the young girl. Years later, however, she came to realize that "he had thrown himself completely into the character he was creating and . . . had actually become in action, as in imagination the character of his pen" (Dickens n.d.: 48). Here we see that performance for Dickens, far from being merely a quick way to make a fortune, was the essence of his creativity and the fullest expression of his unique genius. The fire of his imagination forced expression in performance—both solitary and public. His public appearances were simply one extension of the Dickensian creativity that required realization in the performance act.[9]

Dickens's readings were deliberately staged to enhance the virtuosity of the performer. His years of experience enabled him to hone his setting to achieve maximum theatrical effect; by his

1867–68 American tour, the stage setting consisted of a large maroon screen and a reading table covered in a matching cloth. The reading table was specifically designed to supply a block for a hand rest (he held a book during his performances) and a shelf for a tumbler and his white evening gloves, while at the same time revealing the entire figure of the performer (Collins 1978:8–16). In front of a plain maroon backdrop, Dickens stood, illuminated by gaslight. Both the dark screen and the light served to distinguish the gestures of his body and the expressions of his face, which was noted as being "capable of wonderfully varied expression" (Field 1871:21). No drapery concealed the table legs, the significance of which was that no gesture would be hidden from the audience.

Gesture, indeed, played an important part in Dickens's performances. Kate Field stated that "what Dickens *does* is frequently infinitely better than anything he says, or the way he says it. . . . It is pantomime worthy of the finest actor" (1871:8). Dickens's use of character gesture was in contrast to the graceful elocutionary posing of the period: "He laughs the 'Rules' [of elocution] to scorn. . . . He makes what gestures he has mind to. He even defies propriety time and again by making gestures with his legs. Viewed from the conventional standpoint his reading is quite shocking" ("Mr. Dickens's Third Reading" 1867:4). His penchant for vocal and physical characterization at the expense of elocutionary grace may well have made his readings "shocking" to an audience. Yet for Dickens to delete the mannerisms of his characters—many of which are loved for their unique quirks—and to perform always with perfect pronunciation and elegant movement would have resulted in the distortion of his texts. Indeed Dickens may have had a personal dislike for the study of elocution and of those who held themselves up as exemplars of the art, as his comic depiction of Mr. Turveydrop and his "Deportment" in the chapter of that name in *Bleak House* suggests. Ultimately Dickens as a reader was not without his detractors: he was described as monotonous in narrative passages, lacking in articulation, limited in vocal power, and unpleasantly husky at times. One critic in the *New York Times* denounced Dickens as a performer quite thoroughly: "To recite *properly* is quite as difficult as to write well . . . it rarely happens that a man can do two things equally well. We are of the opinion that Mr. Dickens forms no exception to the rule" ("Mr. Dickens as a Reader" 1867:5). Reviewers often noted Dickens's inclination toward acting rather than elocution,[10] generally agreeing that "Mr. Dickens succeeds in dialogue more than in recitation, which shows that he is a better actor than elocutionist in the highest sense of that term" ("Dickens' Readings—Fifth Night" 1867:5). Despite conflicting reports, Dickens's reading tour was a major event in the performing arts of nineteenth-century America. His stature as a platform performer remains unrivaled, as one British reviewer wrote:

Hear Dickens and die; you will never live to hear anything of its kind so good. There has been nothing so perfect, in their way, ever offered to an English audience. Great actors and actresses—Mrs. Siddons herself among them—have read Shakespeare to us, smaller actors, like the Mathews, elder and younger, John Parry, and others, have given "entertainments" of a half-literary, half-histrionic order; eminent authors, like Coleridge, and Hazlitt, and Sydney Smith, and Thackeray, have read lectures—and many living authors lecture still—but all those appearances, or performances, or whatever else they may be called, are very different from Mr. Dickens' appearances and performances as a reader. He is a story-teller; a prose *improvisatore;* he recites rather than reads; acts rather than lectures ("Mr. Charles Dickens's Farewell Readings" 1868:2).

This review is obviously enthusiastic. Yet, along with the excited hyperbole, the reviewer reveals his confusion in placing Dickens's one-person show in a suitable category. Apparently even in the nineteenth century, an age noted for solo performances, critics were bewildered when they confronted solo "appearances, or performances, or whatever else they may be called."

The review raises intriguing questions. Can Dickens's performances of prose fiction be rightfully compared to Sarah Siddons's solo performances of Shakespearean drama? Should Dickens be classed along with Charles Mathews, who performed from unpublished scripts and impersonated historic figures? Can lectures such as those given by Thackeray be considered, as Erving Goffman suggests, performances? (1981:160–96). What is meant by the reviewer's statement that Dickens "recites rather than reads"? Under the pressure of such questions, the critic's own confusion in genre classification becomes apparent, as does his inability to successfully describe the performance act in his available language. What remains is a highly emotional reaction to the performance—in this case a very favorable one, but one that lacks careful consideration of the complex range of possible solo performances, which cannot be rightfully compared because of differences in generic aesthetics. Such critical confusion plagues discussions of the one-person show into our own time.

THE LYCEUM

During Dickens's American reading tour, the novelist performed at Boston's Tremont Temple on a cold December evening in 1867. In the audience sat "a bearded crusader, pamphleteer, war correspondent and shrewd promoter"—James Redpath (Harrison 1958:31). The event was propitious. Dickens had experienced difficulties dealing with the practicalities of the reading tour and was quite disgusted with the discomforts of life on the road. James Redpath, prior to the Boston performance, had already spoken to Dickens's manager, George Dolby, about the frustrations encountered while on tour. But it was after actually hearing Dickens in Tremont Temple that Redpath "put his agile mind to work overnight and at breakfast next morning he outlined to his family an idea that had come to him in the night" (Harrison 1958:32). The remembrance by Redpath's daughter, Caroline M. Morse, of that breakfast conversation is recorded by Charles F. Horner: "On the following morning at our breakfast table James said to my mother and me, 'there should be a general headquarters, a bureau for the welcome of literary men and women coming to our country for the purpose of lecturing. They should be made to feel at home among us, and the business of arranging routes of travel and dates for lectures and so forth be in charge of competent workers, and an established fee agreed upon'" (1926:128–29). This was the beginning of the Boston Lyceum Bureau, later known as the Redpath Bureau, which soon became the most prominent lyceum booking agency in the country.

The lyceum bureau as a professional booking organization "served as agent between the lecturer [or reader] and the contracting party, usually for a ten per cent commission" (Martin 1953:554). The bureau functioned in three ways: it organized courses of lectures and performances from among their "attractions" and operated as managers of the course themselves, they coordinated an entire course for a sponsoring group (which paid a set fee for the full program of appearances), and they rented the services of single platformists, usually for high fees.

Although the development of lyceum bureaus was a relatively new phenomenon when Redpath had his inspiration, the American lyceum was not new. In various forms, this sturdy national institution had thrived since the second quarter of the nineteenth century. Its roots in America go much further back than Redpath and the lyceum booking agencies.

In November 1826 Josiah Holbrook had begun the "early lyceum," which lasted until 1845–50. As Robert C. Martin (1953) points out, its purpose as Holbrook conceived it was the promotion of "Associations of Adults for Mutual Education." Holbrook's early lyceum revolved around the concept of local discussion groups and lectures given by local citizens. Holbrook had no intention of initiating a policy that brought in invited specialists from outside the local community. It was only years later, when the inherent limitations of Holbrook's "local lecturer policy" caused a disintegration of interest, that an actual lecture system blossomed. The change in lyceum policy was, of course, dependent on the midcentury development of adequate rail transportation.

The history of the nineteenth-century platform lectures and performances can be divided into three periods: the early lyceum (1826–50), the lecture system (1851–74), and the Chautauqualyceum (1874–1925).[11] By 1851, once the early lyceum's "local lecturer policy" had given way to a system based on guest appearances by noted specialists, touring platform performances were becoming common. The improvements in transportation, the growing desire for educational and cultural activities, and the antislavery movement contributed to the upsurge in platform activity that lasted into the early 1860s. Major platformists of this period included Ralph Waldo Emerson, Henry David Thoreau, Alexander Graham Bell, James Russell Lowell, Oliver Wendell Holmes, Bronson Alcott, Daniel Webster, and Henry Ward Beecher. During this period, as today, the platform also served as a means for celebrated writers to publicize their works and supplied novelists and poets with a much-needed second income (Bode 1956:224). For these reasons, Edgar Allan Poe began his platform career.

EDGAR ALLAN POE

Poe's career as a platform performer spans the years 1843 to 1849, the transition years between the early lyceum and the lecture system. Because the practice of visiting lecturers and performers was becoming more and more common during these years, Poe was able to tour the eastern cities and acquire an income to alleviate his financial difficulties. His performances consisted of literary lectures and demonstrations of poetic principles illustrated by performing poetry. For the great majority of his appearances, Poe drew upon two lectures: "The Poets and Poetry of America," in which he attacked the writings of popular contemporaries such as William Cullen Bryant and Henry Wadsworth Longfellow, and "The Poetic Principle," in which he defined poetry and stated its purpose.

Although Poe's one-person shows were strongly lecture-centered, he was also a poetry performer of considerable talent. Like the young Dickens, Poe in his youth was drawn to the theatre but his stepfather, believing that theatrical activities were unsuitable for a gentleman, thwarted any professional aspirations in that direction (Fagin 1949:36). In later life, Poe became the editor of New York's *Broadway Journal* and often associated with actors and elocutionists. During this time, Poe was particularly close with James E. Murdoch, a well-known actor and author of texts on elocution. Murdoch was probably influential in the formation of Poe's own performance style, which displayed elocutionary qualities. After Poe's delivery of "The Poetic Principle" in Lowell, Massachusetts, on 10 July 1848, one audience member remarked that:

Everything was rendered with pure intonation, and perfect enunciation, marked attention being paid to the rhythm. He almost sang the more musical versifications. I recall more perfectly than anything else the undulations of his smooth baritone voice as he recited . . . measuring the dactylic movement perfectly as if he were scanning it. The effect was very pleasing. He insisted upon an even, metrical flow in versification, and said that hard, unequal stepping poetry had better be done in prose. I think he made no selections of a humorous character either in his public or parlor readings. He smiled very seldom, and never laughed, or said anything to excite mirth in others. His manner was quiet and grave (quoted in Allen 1926, vol. 2:763–64).

Another account describes Poe's performance style as "cantilating": "When he read poetry, his voice rolled over the rhythm of the verse like silver notes over golden sands—rather monotonously and flute-like—so that, it may be said here that he rather cantilated than read" (Chivers 1952:63). These reviews make clear that while Poe could be classified along with Dickens as a writer-performer, such categorization is too simplistic: the two men's performances differed far too greatly to be considered of a kind. Dickens performed prose fiction with an actor's inclination for strong characterization; Poe lectured and performed poetry with an elocutionist's penchant for vocal resonance and musicality. One method of genre classification that offers a degree of reliability categorizes one-person shows according to the material performed and the performance style. Difficulties quickly arise, however, when a solo performer such as Poe merges literary genres or performance styles. Poe both lectured and recited poetry; his performances stand as a paradigm of the one-person show hybrid simply called "the lecture-recital." Faced with this sort of hybridization, we may easily imagine a confused critic unable to decide whether to evaluate the presentation as a lecture or as an entertainment.

JAMES E. MURDOCH

During the 1850s, an increasing number of writers, preachers, politicians, and scientists appeared on platforms across the country. As the Civil War approached, the platform was dominated by political figures making speeches on the great issues of the day. Once the war began, many performers chose to join the armed services. James E. Murdoch, a popular Shakespearean actor and elocutionist of the mid-nineteenth century, was unable to participate actively in the war. However, when his son enlisted in the Union troops, Murdoch was determined to serve his country; he suspended his acting career and publicly announced his plans to devote himself to the Union cause by appearing in benefit solo readings, the proceeds of which would aid the wounded men of the services while the literary selections would rouse patriotic pride in the audiences. Typical selections in Murdoch's wartime programs included John Greenleaf Whittier's "Barbara Frietchie," Joseph Drake's "American Flag," Thomas Buchanan Read's "Three Eras," and George H. Boker's "On Board the Cumberland." As well as offering benefit readings to the public, Murdoch also presented charity readings for the wounded soldiers in hospitals and in the camps close to the battlefront.

Murdoch's Civil War readings were very successful; his experience as a Shakespearean tragedian, as an elocutionist, and as a professor of elocution provided a thorough preparation for his career as a public reader in the service of his country, which reached a zenith on 20 January 1863, when he performed in the Senate chamber in Washington, D.C., before an illustrious audience including President and Mrs. Lincoln and the chief magistrate of the nation. Lincoln's assessment of Murdoch's influence over an audience may be judged by the president's personal request in 1864 that Murdoch perform an anonymous poem that expressed a sentiment disdaining an unhonorable peace. Murdoch eventually edited *Patriotism in Poetry and Prose,* a collection of his wartime readings and lectures. The volume was published in 1865 and included an introduction by Murdoch in which he wrote of his platform readings during the war and of their effect on the soldiers: "How often have I observed, in the bivouac or at the campfire, after reading a poem of which the soldier's suffering and the honor of his flag have been the theme, the hitherto separate groups of officers and men mingle together, while the silent tear, and the glow of patriotic pride, spoke in eloquent terms of the presence of that generous sympathy which binds man to man, and is indeed, the corner-stone of all nationality" (Murdoch 1865:16).

The end of the Civil War brought peace to an exhausted nation. And although the war's end released Murdoch from his pledge and allowed him to return to the stage as an actor, he continued periodically to present solo readings. A reading engagement in New York in 1868 brought the inevitable comparisons of Murdoch's performances with those of Charles Dickens, who was concurrently performing in American cities on his reading tour. One review in the *New York Leader* was particularly adept at citing the two men's differing strengths as solo readers:

The concluding scene from the "Pickwick Papers" brought Mr. Murdoch invariably into comparison with Mr. Dickens. Of course he is the better reader, and of course he yields to Mr. Dickens in that magic power of facial mimicry by which Mr. Dickens looks so wonderfully the character he reads. . . . Yet, as a reader, it must be confessed Mr. Dickens was a great disappointment. . . . His voice is poor and untrained. . . . Mr. Murdoch, on the other hand . . . is a magnificent elocutionist, and reads not only with mechanical skill, and an intellectual appreciation of the subject, but with an intense feeling that arouses a corresponding emotion in his audience. Every shade of meaning, every subtlety of passion that the text suggests, is conveyed in his changing intonations (quoted in Bowyer 1952:65).

The review is notable for its contrast of the two readers' performance styles: whereas Dickens appears to have presented a performance closer to an actor's reading, Murdoch displayed the virtuosity and craft of the very best elocutionary reading.

Into the last decades of his life, Murdoch continued to present platform readings. Even as old age approached, nothing indicated a diminution of his elocutionary talents. Such continued success remains strong testimony to Murdoch's ability as a reader. His contribution as a teacher and theorist was assessed by Garff Wilson:

Murdoch was a far less gifted actor than [Edwin] Booth, and his name does not retain the luster of his younger colleague's. Yet Murdoch was the more influential of the two in shaping the style of American acting. Whereas Booth wrote no treatise on the art of the stage, and left no successors or disciples, Murdoch recorded his theories in three different books; he became an eminent teacher of elocution; his methods and benefits influenced the course of dramatic instruction throughout the whole United States (1966:80).

In spite of such noteworthy exceptions such as Murdoch's wartime performances, the American Civil War was responsible for a general decrease in platform activity during the war years. The Civil War platform decline resulted from the public's weariness with the war's issues (which had so dominated the platform in the preceding years), the unsettled financial conditions of the nation, and the retirement or death of some of the major platformists. By the time Dickens came to America on his reading tour in the late 1860s, the country was ripe for one-person shows of a primarily entertaining, as opposed to political, nature. "A year or two after the war," commented James B. Pond (a successor of James Redpath's), "when over a million men had returned from military strife to civil pursuits . . . there came an unprecedented demand for entertainment and amusements" (quoted in Bode 1956:248). The public was ready for entertainment: the political issues of the war were decided, the economy had improved in the North, transportation had become easier, and the booking agencies, such as James Redpath's Boston Lyceum Bureau, greatly facilitated the touring process. By the early 1870s, the one-person show was enjoying a strong ascendancy in popularity. The last quarter of the nineteenth century was truly a golden age for platform performances.

Novelists, poets, preachers, and politicians saw in the platform a means of income supplement. Professional performers, too, recognized the potential rewards of touring in a one-person show and, indeed, some of the best remembered nineteenth-century British and American actors and actresses appeared as platform performers: Sarah Siddons, William Charles Macready, Edwin Forrest, George Vandenhoff, Henry Irving, Charles Mathews (both father and son), Ellen Terry, Charles Kemble, Anna Cora Mowatt, Fanny Kemble, and Charlotte Cushman. Their names are as much associated with the stage and the drama as with the platform and the one-person show.

WOMEN ON THE PLATFORM

The nineteenth-century platform provided an additional showcase for the great actors and actresses of the day. By appearing in a one-person show, these performers found an audience that, due to antitheatre sentiments, eluded them at play productions. A solo production offered actors and actresses the benefits of full artistic control, impossible in an ensemble production, as well as the attraction of appearing in an ultimate tour de force. The reason (or combination of reasons) behind an actor's or actress's choice to attempt a solo performance varied, of course, for each individual player. In most instances, nineteenth-century actors and actresses appeared as solo performers irregularly and only for special occasions, such as for charity benefits. Three great theatrical figures of the Victorian period, however, appeared as platform readers not as auxillary supplements to their stage work but as important centers of their professional careers. As artists and celebrities, Anna Cora Mowatt, Fanny Kemble, and Charlotte Cushman brought a prestige previously unknown to solo performance; as women, they brought a respectability and an acceptance that allowed women of a later age to enjoy professional platform careers.

Anna Cora Mowatt

When Anna Cora Mowatt stepped onto the platform of Boston's Masonic Temple for her debut as a public reader in October of 1841, she brought with her no prior public reputation or celebrity in solo performance or any other professional field. Her career remains one of the rare exceptions in the history of the American one-person show, because she debuted as a professional in a solo performance. In the great majority of cases, the performer came to the platform as a soloist only after achieving fame in a related field, most frequently as a writer or as an actor. The reasons for this are understandable when we consider how difficult it was (and still is) for an unknown to attract an audience and critical attention without prior celebrity. A preestablished public reputation not only offered a solo performer clout in financing and mounting a one-person show, but it often guaranteed an initial audience interest and served to enhance the performer-audience relationship during the performance.

Despite her lack of formal training and experience, as well as the prevailing hostility toward women performing in public, Anna Cora Mowatt announced her debut series of readings in the autumn of 1841. As she later recounted in her autobiography, the loss of her husband's fortune in speculations and his failing health moved her to seek a career for herself with which she could support her family (Mowatt 1854:139). Her wide literary reading and her early experience in private family theatricals suggested the stage, but her own morals would not permit such a career. "I had talents for acting," mused Mowatt, "I could go upon the stage; but that thought only entered my mind to be instantly rejected. The idea of becoming a professional actress was revolting" (Mowatt 1854:141).

Fortuitously, just at the time Mowatt was searching for a career, she attended a series of readings in New York by John Vandenhoff. The Vandenhoff example, along with her own experience in reading aloud in private family gatherings, gave Mowatt the courage to choose platform readings as a profession. Once resolved upon this new undertaking, she lost no time in carrying her intentions into execution. "Everyday I practised my voice," wrote Mowatt in her autobiography, "reciting aloud for hours in the vine-covered arbor, where I had cast aside the dark mantle of despair, and put on the life-giving robes of hope" (1854:141). She chose material from major poets, such as Byron and Scott, as well as selections by a host of minor American poets of the time including Epes Sargent, who composed two dramatic narratives expressly for the readings, "The Missing Ship" and "The Light of the Lighthouse." The Sargent poems, by Mowatt's own admission, were the highlights of her performance.

Through the invaluable assistance of a Boston friend, Mowatt was able to arrange her debut at the Boston Masonic Temple in October 1841. Favorable reviews followed her Boston performances, reviews that Mowatt later discounted as "eulogiums, not critiques. By common consent, it seemed to be decided that I was to be exempt from criticism" (Mowatt 1854:151). The warm reception in Boston did give her strength, however, as she traveled from Providence to New York to begin a series of readings at the Styvesant Institute. She had been apprehensive about performing in New York, her home, where she would likely have to face the ostracism of family and friends. Only too aware was Mowatt, when embarking on a platform career, of the risk involved as a woman of polite society performing in public for money:

From Providence we went to New York, and a course of readings for four nights was announced to take place at the Styvesant Institute. Curiosity drew me full audiences; but I did not feel as though Sympathy sat side by side with Curiosity, as she had done in Boston. I found it more difficult to read impressively than I had done before my indulgent New England audiences. The sphere seemed different, the recipients less impressible. I could not feel the same easy *abandon*—the utter freedom from constraint. I had too many personal friends constantly present, and I thought too much of what the Mrs. Grundies were saying (1854:152).

Although she received strong support from her father following her New York debut, Mowatt did indeed suffer the indignation of relatives and friends. "They were shocked at my temerity in appearing before the public," remembered Mowatt sadly. "They even affected not to believe in Mr. Mowatt's total loss of means. They tacitly proscribed me from the circle of their acquaintance" (1854:152). In several New York papers Mowatt received excellent notices, but in others she fared no better than she had with her friends and relatives: "I had not been treated by the New York press with the same courteous leniency as by that of Boston. Some of the leading papers were warm in their encomiums—others contained most just criticism, pointing out faults of style of which I was myself gradually becoming conscious. Others condemned *in toto* the bold and novel step I had taken, ignoring its motive" (1854:154). Despite such harsh criticism, her New York appearances brought favorable attention from the theatrical community, however unwanted. When approached with an offer to appear as an actress by a manager of the Park Theatre, Mowatt, still holding the stage suspect as immoral, rejected the proposal indignantly. The extreme tension of Mowatt's New York readings and their aftermath finally resulted in a severe respiratory illness that forced her to postpone her reading commitments at the Rutger's Institute for Young Ladies and at the Society Library and that ultimately ended her short platform career in 1842. Once recovered, Mowatt eventually became a playwright and, finally, an actress.

The brevity of Mowatt's solo career does not diminish its significance in the history of the one-person show in America. Anna Cora Mowatt—a lady from respectable society—had dared to appear as a professional platform reader. Her audacity paved the way for other women to follow. As Mowatt noted soon after her one season of readings: "My success gave rise to a host of lady imitators, one of whom announced 'Readings and Recitations in the Style of Mrs. Mowatt.' I was rather curious to get an idea of my own style, and, had my health permitted, would have gone some distance to have seen it illustrated. At one time there were no less than six advertisements in the papers, of ladies giving readings in different parts of the Union" (1854:157). Mowatt's work began a tradition in the United States of women on the platform as solo performers, a tradition enriched in later years by such great talents as Fanny Kemble and Charlotte Cushman.

Anna Cora Mowatt is notable in this history not only for her work as a platform reader but also for her personal history in respect to her changing attitudes towards the theatre, because her experience stands as an illustration of what proved to be a national phenomenon. As a young girl, she vehemently adhered to the religious teachings opposing the stage and adopted the opinions of her beloved pastor. Remembering her youth, Mowatt later wrote:

> I went to Sunday school with my sisters twice every Sunday—at first as pupil, and then as teacher. I had a species of enthusiastic admiration and reverence for Bishop E——n. I loved to see him enter the Sunday school; I loved to hear him in the pulpit; and was happier all day if he accidentally bestowed upon me a passing word. He disapproved of theatres; he pronounced them the "abodes of sin and wickedness." It never occurred to me to inquire what he *really knew* of theatres; but I trusted implicitly in his *supposed* information. I determined that I never would enter such a dreadful place. My sisters went now and then with our father; but, in spite of my decided passion for plays and for acting, the thought of the imaginary monsters of evil, which I was certainly to behold, kept me away (1854:37–38).

The devout young girl often scolded her family for their more liberal attitudes towards the theatre. However, when Fanny Kemble created a public sensation by her American theatre tour in the 1830s, young Anna was tempted to go and "see Fanny Kemble, just *once*" (1854:38). The result of her first theatre experience was everything her pastor would have feared. "All my prejudices against the theatre," wrote Mowatt, "melted 'into thin air' with this first night" (1854:40). Her complete conversion of attitude was years away; this first change of heart proved shallow. Years later, when she found herself searching for a profession, she instinctively rejected the stage, finding the idea, as we have seen, "revolting." Even after her New York readings, when she had experienced the work of a public performer, she violently spurned an offer to appear on the stage as an actress:

> My first course of readings in New York was accidentally attended by one of the managers of the Park Theatre, who, through a friend, made a highly lucrative proposal if I would appear upon the stage. I remember the indignant reply I gave the gentleman who communicated to me this offer. The recollection of that answer had often rendered me forbearing towards those who I have since heard violently denounce the stage, and who were as ignorant as I was at that period of every thing that related to a theatre (1854:157).

Only after writing her successful comedy *Fashion* and personally witnessing the rehearsal process was Mowatt convinced of the value of the theatre as an art form, the foibles of social misconceptions, and the propriety of becoming a member of the acting profession herself:

> My views concerning the stage, and my estimate of the members of dramatic companies, had undergone a total revolution. Many circumstances had proved to me how unfounded were the prejudices of the world against the profession as a body. The communication into which I had been brought, by the production of *Fashion,* with the managers and members of the Park company and the managers of the Walnut Street Theatre, added to all I heard of their private histories, convinced me that I had formed unjust conclusions. Rather, I had adopted the conclusions of those who were as ignorant on the subject as myself—who, perhaps, cared as little as I had done to ascertain the truth. . . .
> I pondered long and seriously upon the consequences of my entering the profession. The *"qu'en dira t'on?"* of Society had no longer the power to awe me. Was it right? was it wrong? were questions of higher moment. My respect for the opinions of "Mrs. Grundy" had slowly melted away since I discovered that, with that respectable representative of the world in general, *success* sanctified all things; nothing was reprehensible but *failure* (1854:215–16).

Anna Cora Mowatt was ahead of her time both in her willingness to appear on the public platform as a professional reader and, later, in her acceptance of the theatre as a respectable form of entertainment. In both instances, the country followed her lead. In relation to women on the platform, only a few years elapsed before members of polite society of either gender appeared in public on the platform without ridicule. In relation to the theatre as an accepted form of entertainment, a longer period of time was necessary. Indeed, the prejudice against the theatre did not relax for over half a century.

FANNY KEMBLE

Frances Anne (Fanny) Kemble, unlike Anna Cora Mowatt, was already a respected actress and a celebrity when she first appeared as a solo reader. The British actress had achieved her fame early in her youth as a member of the Kemble acting family. In America, her tour in 1832 with her father, Charles Kemble, introduced her to American audiences and established her as a star in this country as well as in her native Britain. Her dissatisfaction with her life and work as an actress in play productions lead her to seek escape in marriage to Pierce Butler, a wealthy American, in 1834. The marriage proved unhappy. Unknown to Kemble at the time of her wedding, Butler's family possessed extensive holdings in the South from which much of his wealth was derived. Thus it was only after marriage that Kemble found herself living on money earned through slavery, an institution she deeply abhorred. Her stay at Butler's plantation produced her *Journal of a Residence on a Georgia Plantation in 1838–39,* an eloquent account of her inner turmoil resulting from the conflicts between her moral beliefs and her position as a wife to a slaveholder. A dozen years later the marriage failed and Kemble returned to Britain.

Finding herself now entering middle age without the security of a husband, Kemble needed to return to her profession. Frustrated with her new ventures on the stage, Kemble determined not to repeat her early career as an actress in ensemble play productions; instead she chose to devote herself to platform readings of Shakespeare. Her own family history prepared her for such an endeavor. In her youth, she knew the success her aunt, Sarah Sid-

dons, enjoyed as a reader of Shakespeare and Milton; more recently her father had taken to giving Shakespeare readings. As if
providence lead her to the platform, just about the time Kemble
found herself seeking a new life, her father retired from the reading platform. Thus Kemble was able to reinvent her professional
persona, from actress to Shakespearean reader. Her new position
allowed her to support herself financially but, perhaps more im-
portantly, the new role also supported her spiritually by allowing
her to continue her link to the great Kembles as an acting family
and by permitting her to devote herself so completely and con-
tently to the poet she most admired.

Her father's performances exerted a great influence on her
own platform work. Although originally intending to present a
repertory of all of Shakespeare's plays in their entirety, she soon
found that such a "project of making her readings 'studies of
Shakespeare' for the public quite illusory" (Kemble 1882:632).
She turned to her father's edited reading versions as guides for her
own. Kemble's acceptance of the necessity of edited texts, however, did not mean she gave up her aspiration to present a repertory of Shakespeare's complete canon. Whereas her father only
read the most popular plays and her own business managers tried
to persuade her to see the practicality of her father's decision,
Fanny insisted on performing the lesser-known plays as well, in
order to avoid what she most dreaded, "becoming mechanical or
hackneyed . . . in their delivery by perpetual repetition of the same
pieces" (Kemble 1882:634). Ultimately Kemble's repertory of
Shakespeare readings included twenty-five of his plays, whereas
her father used only five or six plays. In her *Records of Later Life*,
Kemble noted the reception of her various readings:

> The public *always* came in goodly numbers to hear "Macbeth,"
> "Hamlet," "Romeo and Juliet," and "The Merchant of Venice"; and
> Mendlessohn's exquisite music, made an accompaniment to the reading
> of the "Midsummer Night's Dream," rendered that a peculiarly popular
> performance. But to *all* the other plays the audiences were considerably
> less numerous, and to some few of them I often had but few listeners. . . .
> My great reward has been, passing a large portion of my life in familiar
> intercourse with that greatest and best English mind and heart, and living
> almost daily in that world above the world, into which he lifted me
> (1882:634).

After her initial success as a public reader in Great Britain, Kemble came to the United States for a reading tour in 1849. Her lasting reputation from the 1832 theatre tour and the current scandal involving the divorce proceedings—which "showed a tendency to well up in Fanny's favor" (Furnas 1982:341)—made her American readings an event. Kemble began her American tour with a performance of *The Tempest* on Friday, 26 January 1849, at Boston's Masonic Temple, where Anna Cora Mowatt had begun her platform career eight years earlier. Kemble used the simple staging for her readings that she had developed in Britain: a chair (she sat during her readings) and a table covered with dark red cloth with volumes of Shakespeare's plays and two lamps. Opening night brought excellent reviews, the *Boston Herald* announcing her as "unquestionably *the* Shakespearian reader of the present age" ("The Palmy Days of Fanny Kemble" 1849:1), and her success as a public reader in America was assured. While in Boston, Kemble enjoyed friendships with members of the literary elite, including Ralph Waldo Emerson, James Russell Lowell, and especially Henry Wadsworth Longfellow and his wife. Longfellow's journals of January and February of 1849 provide a running commentary and testimony to Kemble's talents as a reader. He wrote on the night of her American premiere:

26th [January]. We went to hear Mrs. Butler read 'The Tempest.' A crowded house. A reading-desk covered with red, on a platform, like the gory block of the scaffold; upon which the magnificent Fanny bowed her head in tears and great emotion. But in a moment it became her triumphal chariot. What glorious reading! the spiritual Ariel, the stern Prospero, the lover Ferdinand, Miranda the beloved, Stefan, Trinculo, Caliban,—each had a voice distinct and separate, as of many actors (Longfellow 1891, vol. 2:142).

Longfellow's comments continue in the following entries, chronicling his attendance at Kemble's readings. Toward the end of the Boston engagement, the American poet exclaims:

16th [February]. "Hamlet," sublimely read; with the only true comprehension and expression of the melancholy Dane I have ever had the good fortune to hear. What nights these are!—with Shakespeare and such a reader (Longfellow 1891, vol. 2:145).

Longfellow was deeply affected by Fanny Kemble's interpretations of Shakespeare; his admiration moved him to compose a sonnet, "On Mrs. Kemble's Readings from Shakespeare":

> O PRECIOUS evenings! all too swiftly sped!
>   Leaving us heirs to amplest heritages
>   Of all the best thoughts of the greatest sages,
>   And giving tongues unto the silent dead!
> How our hearts glowed and trembled as she read,
>   Interpreting by tones the wondrous pages
>   Of the great poet who foreruns the ages,
>   Anticipating all that shall be said!
> O happy Reader! having for thy text
>   The magic book, whose Sibylline leaves have caught
>   The rarest essence of all human thought!
> O happy Poet! by no critic vext!
>   How must thy listening spirit now rejoice
>   To be interpreted by such a voice!
>   (Longfellow 1893:112).

Longfellow was not the only distinguished admirer of Fanny Kemble to write memorably of her work as a platform artist. Henry James wrote with great affection and respect of her *Readings from Shakespeare;* his essay gives a vivid testimony to the power of Kemble's interpretations:

The reader dressed in black velvet for *Lear* and in white satin for the comedy [*A Midsummer Night's Dream*], and presented herself to my young vision as a being of formidable splendor. I must have measured in some degree the power and beauty of her performance, for I perfectly recall the sense of irreparable privation with which a little later I heard my parents describe the emotion produced by her *Othello,* given at the old Hanover Square Rooms and to which I had not been conducted. I have seen both the tragedy and the "Dream" acted several times since then, but I have always found myself waiting vainly for any approach to the splendid volume of Mrs. Kemble's "Howl, howl, howl!" in the one, or the animation and variety that she contributed to the other. I am confident that the most exquisite of fairy-tales never was such a "spectacle" as when she read, I was going to say mounted, it (James 1893:91).

Fanny Kemble's first American reading tour was an outstanding success, but the illness of her father forced a sudden departure for Britain in the summer of 1850. She returned to the American platform in 1856 and performed regularly until the Civil War compelled her to return home once again. Once the war was over, Kemble came to America in 1866 and remained through 1869. The close of the 1868 season brought an end to Fanny Kemble's platform career in the United States, and although she did return once more and stayed from 1873 to 1877, by then she felt herself too old and her voice diminished in quality. Her last American reading tour in 1868 coincided with that of Charles Dickens. The excitement of two platform luminaries was unparalleled; in his chronicle of the 1867–68 season George C. D. Odell wrote: "Reader, I confess to a feeling of expanded breast even as I think of Dickens and Fanny Kemble; one breathes bigger, freer air in presence of that giant race before the flood of mediocrity which submerges the world of these our post-war days. . . . Summer heat brought a close to the 'entertainments' of 1867–68. But Dickens and Fanny Kemble—think of what the season had provided! With that season these two great historic figures left the platform in America" (1927–49, vol. 8:367–68).

CHARLOTTE CUSHMAN

When Charlotte Cushman first appeared as a solo reader in 1871, she followed a traditional already boasting the performances of Anna Cora Mowatt and Fanny Kemble. Like Kemble before her, Cushman brought to the platform her established reputation as a major actress. Her long and distinguished career in the theatre had won her public recognition as one of America's leading theatrical talents. Her fame was such that "at her last appearance on stage, a body of eminent citizens, with William Cullen Bryant as spokesman, presented her with a laurel wreath" (Horner 1926:149). As had been the case with Kemble, Cushman's pre-existing renown as an actress brought immediate critical and public attention to her platform performances.

Fanny Kemble's retirement from the American platform left a vacancy that Cushman was destined to fill. Cushman was considered a Shakespearean reader comparable to the incomparable Kemble: "In this department Miss Cushman has been equalled only by Fanny Kemble, and excelled by none" (Clement 1882:94).

Cushman's performances from Shakespeare included readings from *Hamlet, Macbeth, Henry VIII, Romeo and Juliet, The Merchant of Venice, As You Like It,* and *Much Ado About Nothing.* Selections from one of these seven Shakespeare plays usually comprised the first half of her program, whereas the second half was devoted to the poetic works of Browning, Tennyson, Rossetti, Burns, Southey, Longfellow, Macaulay, and Elizabeth Barrett Browning. Along with poems by major writers, Cushman included a variety of humorous and dialect poems to close her programs on a light note. Among the lighter verse Cushman performed were: "Miss Maloney on the Chinese Question," "The Bapteesement o' the Bairn," and "Betsy and I Are Out." References to Cushman's great personal charisma and her virtuosity as a dramatic reader characterize accounts of her performance; Emma Stebbins wrote of the platform readings in 1878, two years after Cushman's death:

She seemed to cast off, with grand ease, every influence, every suggestion of any other life but the one she was for the time to interpret. She identified herself with it, and after her graceful, self-possessed entrance, she seated herself at her table, and, with one comprehensive glance which seemed to gather in all her audience and hold them, as it were, by a spell peculiarly her own,—the spell of a potent and irresistible magnetism,—she set aside all feeling of personal identity, and lived, and moved, and acted the varied personages of the story as they each came upon the scene; they lived before us, each one distinctly marked as an individual, and never by any chance merging into the others, or losing its clearly marked character (1878:91).

In light of her remarkable success as a platform reader, Cushman's initial resistance to solo performance seems ironic. Even after illness curtailed her brilliant career as a stage actress in the late 1860s, Cushman still found little appeal in the prospect of appearing on the platform. In his biography of the actress, Joseph Leach indicates that the sensation surrounding Charles Dickens's public readings may have intimidated Cushman—at least temporarily. Cushman's return from Europe to New York in 1868 coincided with Dickens's American tour:

Too tired to think about acting, she had packed no costumes. Nor would she go in for public readings. Of late, Charles Dickens had all but preempted that stellar position in America. Last December, Dickens had created near-frenzy. By 8 A.M. the day of his Boston debut the ticket office queue had stretched nearly half a mile, and his farewell in New York in April had left a sweet taste in all America's mouth. . . . Not even Fanny Kemble could compare with Dickens on the platform. . . . Charlotte made herself clear about public readings. "I hate to read except to six people, and I won't read to a public if I can possibly help it" (Leach 1970:338–39).

It was not until 1871, after Dickens's death (brought on, at least in part, by the physical exertion of his readings and his tours) and Kemble's retirement, that Cushman sought solace in platform performance. By then her failing health had significantly restricted her work as an actress. Rather than choose retirement, Cushman with the encouragement of her doctor used platform readings as a creative outlet for her well-being. Thus through solo performance Charlotte Cushman was able to rechannel her great talents as a theatrical artist.

Cushman's "reinvention" of her public persona as a platform reader is reminiscent of the individual performers already examined. The performances of Dickens, Mowatt, Kemble, and Cushman were all products of personal crises in the lives of the performers. Although economic factors influenced their decisions to become soloists, deeper, more personal reasons appear to have attracted them to the platform. Dickens wanted to amass a fortune for the security of his children, but he also sought escape from marital difficulties and a release for his frustrated histrionic talents, which were central, not peripheral, to his genius. Mowatt, driven to the platform in response to her husband's financial failure, used solo performance to invent a professional persona. In doing so, she created a showcase for her innate talents and willingly risked ostracism by moving against societal norms. Fanny Kemble, separated from the support of her American husband, needed to carve out her own livelihood. But her *Readings from Shakespeare* not only supplied her living, they also allowed her to reassert herself triumphantly at a time of great personal anxiety and confusion as a rightful heir of the Kemble family acting dynasty. Cushman would have been economically secure without the earnings from her readings, but her platform work served as therapy, permitting her a creative outlet, a new kind of interaction with her adoring public, and a renewed fame as a leading American talent. The use of solo performance as a means for an individual to invent or "reinvent" a public persona is seen recurringly through the history of the one-person show, as we will see later in this study of solo art.

When Charlotte Cushman retired from professional life amid the adoration and fireworks of her farewell appearances in 1875, she left behind a legacy. Her platform performances, along with those of Fanny Kemble and Anna Cora Mowatt, have been credited for encouraging America's changing attitudes toward speech education. "[I]t became perfectly acceptable for young Americans," writes David W. Thompson, "to imitate their splendid speech skills and literary enthusiasms without, finally, any sense of betraying the political and cultural Revolution which gave Americans the precarious freedom to be themselves" (1983:648). It also had become quite acceptable for women to appear as public readers without ridicule or ostracism. Mowatt, Kemble, and Cushman helped change Victorian attitudes while they brought a prestige and a glamour hitherto unknown to solo performance.

THE FOUNDING OF THE CHAUTAUQUA ASSEMBLY

During the last years of Charlotte Cushman's platform career, two gentlemen formed a new institution that, in time, developed into a national movement that rivaled the lyceum as a popularizing influence of the one-person show in America. The two gentlemen were John Heyl Vincent and Lewis Miller, and the movement was Chautauqua. The origins of the institution were discussed by Vincent in his book *The Chautauqua Movement:*

> The Chautauqua Assembly opened as a Sunday-school institute,— a two weeks' session of lectures, normal lessons, sermons, devotional meetings, conferences, and illustrative exercises, with recreative features in concerts, fireworks, and one or two humorous lectures. It was called by some a "camp-meeting." But a "camp-meeting" it was not, in any sense, except that the most of us lived in tents. There were few sermons preached, and no so-called "evangelistic" services held. It was simply

a Sunday-school institute, a protracted institute held in the woods. We called it at the first "The Chautauqua Sunday-school Assembly" (1886:16).

The beginning of the Chautauqua movement was a single assembly on the shores of Chautauqua Lake in western New York. In his book Vincent pointed out the components upon which the entire Chautauqua movement was based. In summary, the components rested on two major propositions: that the "whole of life is a school" (that is, education is a life-long process not completed with graduation from compulsory education or college) and that the "true basis of education is religious" (1886:12–13).

The first signs of the future growth of Chautauqua from a single Sunday-school assembly in a bucolic setting to a national (indeed international) cultural phenomenon occurred at the original New York institution. What began as a two-week summer course in religious instruction expanded into a full summer of broad cultural education. Realizing the need to diversify their programming and increase their base of support, Vincent and Miller introduced various lectures and seminars on secular topics.[12] Ever since, and in fact right up to the present day, the direction of the Chautauqua Institution in New York has been toward comprehensive educational and cultural programming and nondemoninationalism.[13] By the time the New York assembly celebrated its tenth anniversary in 1884, Chautauqua had come to mean much more than religious instruction, as Victoria and Robert Case observed: "'Chautauqua' meant study, music, dramatic interpretation, lectures and oratory, stereopticon views and camping by the lake shore, the best in the cultural and educational world, with good food and fireworks, for a grand total of six to ten dollars a week" (Case and Case 1948:17).

Independent assemblies in imitation of the original institution sprang up across the country throughout the remainder of the nineteenth century. Within fifteen years of the opening of the New York Chautauqua, 100 independent local assemblies were operating nationwide. By the first years of the twentieth century, the number of independent Chautauquas had more than doubled. Chautauqua had become a national movement even before the advent of the twentieth-century phenomenon known as the tent Chautauqua.

Although expanded to include cultural events, Chautauqua's arts programming did not include theatre pieces or play productions. Vincent and Miller, like so many of their generation, were opposed to the stage, and as founders of a new institution with a religious foundation, they incorporated their attitude into the Chautauqua philosophy (Hadley 1956:85–87). The Chautauqua founders' influence was felt nationwide in the perpetuation of antitheatre sentiments by independent Chautauquas, which had adopted the original assembly's aims, ambiance, and philosophy. The Chautauqua hostility towards the theatre contributed to the continuing success of one-person shows. Unwilling to offer plays as part of their cultural program, the Chautauquas avidly subscribed to platform performances. Thus between the flourishing lyceums and the new Chautauqua assemblies, the one-person show enjoyed its golden age through the close of the nineteenth century.

Before discussing the nature of the one-person shows presented at the Chautauquas, perhaps a word of clarification is necessary to distinguish between the lyceum and the permanent Chautauquas, the differences between the two organizations being chiefly those of locale and season of operation.

The Lyceums and the *permanent* Chautauquas had no ... relation to each other. They operated in different worlds and different seasons. Lyceum attractions were presented in the winter, staged in comfortable auditoriums where the dress circle might glitter with diamonds. Chautauqua operated only in the summer and emphasized low prices, outdoor study and a selected "respectable" audience. Lyceum was strictly an urban movement, while Chautauqua reveled in the grove-of-trees idea, with physical culture, rowing on the lake, and singing around a bonfire as healthful if somewhat bucolic complements to its course of "uplift" and "inspiration" (Case and Case 1948:26).

Although the lyceums and the permanent Chautauquas were separate and distinct institutions, they shared a common pool of talent. Performers appearing on the lyceum circuit in the winter months could be seen on the platform at a Chautauqua come the summer.

Among the many performers who worked both the lyceum circuit and the permanent Chautauqua were John K. Gangs, Isabel Beecher, Helen Potter, Will Carleton, Edward P. Powers, Montaville Flowers, Leland Powers, S. H. Clark, and Robert McLean Cumnock.

PERFORMERS OF THE CHAUTAUQUA ASSEMBLIES

The entertainments of the Chautauqua performers varied in content and in style, but the majority would today be considered restrained readings of literature.[14] The permanent Chautauqua's dedication to education and morality demanded that the quality of the literature be kept at a high standard and that the style of performances avoid the broadly theatrical. It is hardly surprising, then, that the professional performers who tapped the Chautauqua market created one-person shows that were essentially readings of nondramatic (except Shakespearean) literature.

ROBERT MCLEAN CUMNOCK

Preeminent among the readers who appeared at Chautauqua and on the lyceum circuit was Robert McLean Cumnock. From 1883 to 1891, Cumnock held the position of head of the original Chautauqua Assembly's Department of Elocution. His work on the platform as a professional reader and at Northwestern University as a teacher of elocution had attracted the attention of John Heyl Vincent. The two men formed a close association, which continued after Cumnock left his post at Chautauqua; in 1895, when Cumnock opened the new Annie May Swift Hall to house his School of Oratory at Northwestern University, Vincent came to deliver the dedicatory address. During his tenure as head of its Department of Elocution, Cumnock brought special recognition to the art of platform reading previously unknown at Chautauqua. He appeared, as Vincent said in his dedicatory speech, "as a public reader before our great amphitheater at least thirty-five times, and no man could command a larger audience" (quoted in Mattern 1929:91). Cumnock also recommended other readers of talent to be invited to perform at the amphitheater and developed a program of elocutionary study for Chautauqua's students (Hadley 1956:29–51).

Today Robert McLean Cumnock is probably best remembered as an educator. The establishment of his School of Oratory marks a major achievement in the history of American speech education (Wallace 1954:198). During his lifetime, however, Cumnock's reputation was equally dependent on his brilliant career as a professional solo reader. He spent much of his professional life touring the nation and presenting literary readings on the lyceum circuit and at Chautauqua assemblies. In 1908 *The Lyceumite and Talent* (a professional magazine published for platformists, lyceum and Chautauqua bureau managers, and potential patrons) printed a full cover photograph of Cumnock on its October issue; within appeared a feature article that recognized Cumnock as a major performer in the field:

In these days when lyceum audiences put a premium on novelty and generally refuse to listen to the interpretation of literature for its own sake, it is worth while to pay tribute to a man who has compelled recognition for his work in this difficult field, where so few gain distinction. Such active bureau managers as the veteran Henry L. Slayton and his contemporary Alonzo Foster, and the hardly less venerable J. E. Brockway, all say that this country has hardly had a reader so capable, so successful, as Doctor Cumnock. All of the older lecture courses to be reached from such centers as Chicago, Pittsburg, New York and Boston have repeatedly booked his readings. And for a dozen years or so he was the most popular reader at Chautauqua Institution, where he was engaged every year for four or five recitals. The field[s] of interpretation in which he especially excels are Dickens, where he hardly has an equal, and Scotch literature, where he stands preeminent (Pearson 1908b:15).

Such recognition by the major professional publication in his field is a strong testimony to Cumnock's reputation as a solo reader. The same 1908 issue, paradoxically, bears witness to the low ebb to which circuit Chautauqua entertainments could sink: an advertisement appeared for Charlotte Chamberlain's one-person show "Ye Merry Birds." Chamberlain called herself a "bird warbler" and her platform entertainments promised "Trills," "Chirps," and "Whistles." [15] By many accounts in the lyceum and Chautauqua magazines of the period, public taste had shifted toward sensationalism in entertainment during the 1890s and after the turn of century. Cumnock did not succumb to the pressure of popular trends but resolutely maintained his own standards in public reading:

He had never run after fads in elocution, nor has he been as unlike others as to be peculiar or grotesque. The conservatism which has always dominated Doctor Cumnock's art and his business policy is both temperamental and a firm conviction. From the beginning of his career he abhorred the excesses that have brought the term elocution into disrepute. So he always avoids the elocutionary tricks and pretentions, aiming to be what Bishop John H. Vincent has well called him, "an interpreter of literature" (Pearson 1908b:15).

HELEN POTTER

Although Cumnock's readings are exemplary of the kind of platform entertainments usually offered at Chautauqua assemblies in the late nineteenth century, a few Chautauqua performers presented entertainments that tended toward the more theatrical. Throughout the 1870s and 1880s, Helen Potter appeared on the lyceum circuits and at the New York Chautauqua and independent assemblies around the country. Potter presented impersonations "of well-known actors and lecturers, giving extracts from their principal plays or lectures" (Wright 1906:150).

Beginning her platform career as a reader, she took the advice of James Redpath, who suggested that she consider impersonations. While she was studying at the Normal Art Training School in Boston in 1873, Redpath called on her and she recited for him. An account of the conversation appeared years later in *Talent* after Potter had achieved considerable fame:

"No one wants readings or recitations," [said Redpath] "but if some one could give what I call 'ten lectures in one,'—that is, take a ten-minute extract from the text of ten of our best lectures and give it one evening—it would make a hit. I have proposed it to several readers, but none of them seem to be able to 'catch on.'"

Nothing further was said on the subject, but Miss Potter "caught on" immediately. The suggestion opened up great possibilities to her. . . . It was presently borne in upon her that to give accurate imitations in costume of the people whose text she used would give added force to its presentation (Smith 1906:7).

She then worked diligently in creating her impersonations, giving much detailed consideration to the representation of the physical and vocal aspects of the subjects and to the selection and duplication of costumes, on which significant sums were spent. Her success after opening at the Lyceum Theatre in New York on 7 May 1874 was such that she eventually became known as "Queen of the Lyceum." Among the lecturers and actors impersonated by Potter were: Susan B. Anthony's speech "On Trial for Voting"; Henry Ward Beecher's sermon on Lincoln; Sarah Bernhardt as *Dona Sol* (French and English text); Edwin Booth as *Hamlet* and as *Richelieu;* Charlotte Cushman as *Queen Katharine, Katharine of Aragon,* and *Meg Merriles;* Anna Dickinson's lecture "For Your Own Sake"; John B. Gough's lectures "Blunders" and "Temperance"; Julia Ward Howe's lecture "American Art"; Fanny Kemble's readings from *The Tempest;* Abraham Lincoln's "Gettysburgh Speech"; Adelaid Ristori as *Queen Elizabeth* (Italian and English text); Tommaso Salvini as *Othello;* Mary F. Scott-Siddons's reading "Portia and Nerissa"; Elizabeth Cady Stanton's address "Declaration of Rights"; T. DeWitt Talmage's lecture "Newspapers"; Ellen Terry as *Portia;* George Vandenhoff in "Wolsey's Soliloquy"; and Oscar Wilde's lecture "Art." [16] Potter's choice of subjects is noteworthy for its variety and for the fact that she was credible in her impersonations of men as well as of women. In retrospect, Potter's impersonations are of special interest as examples of the kind of recycling or refertilization of inspiration that occurs throughout the history of the one-person show. Over a span of years, we can see one platform artist's work being recreated by another artist of a later generation. Helen Potter's work is a forerunner of the kind of solo re-creations of the mid-twentieth century; just as Potter re-created the platform performances of Fanny Kemble and Mary Scott-Siddons, in our time Emlyn Williams and Hal Holbrook re-create the platform appearances of Charles Dickens and Mark Twain.

Comments on the depth, range, and accuracy of Potter's impersonations were recurring in reviews of her work. Critics clearly made a distinction between Potter's performances and the coarser impersonations of the vaudeville houses: "The restrained and sustained fidelity of her impersonations was a theme of comment wherever she appeared. They were as unlike the 'jump-on-and-off-again' so-called impersonations common to vaudeville, and, alas! not unknown on the Lyceum platform, as a delicate rose is unlike a gaudy sunflower" (Smith 1906:8).

That Potter was in demand as a performer long after she retired from the platform in 1890 testifies to her talent. Her so-called retirement was, in fact, marked by sporadic return appearances, and in 1897 a lead article in *Talent* joyfully announced her formal return in several new series of character studies. In "Kinetescope of the Ages," Potter presented costumed sketches of "Social Types," such as "The Outlaw," "The Society Woman," "The Woman who wants the Ballot and the Woman who don't want the Ballot," and "The Puritan Fanatic." Her "National Points of View" series focused on majority political problems of the day "from the various standpoints of the nations or classes vitally interested. For instance, the present European difficulties will be explained respectively by an Armenian, a Turk, a Russian, a Greek and so on. A Cuban and a Spaniard will present the two phases of the problem at our own boundaries. A 'Populist,' a 'Gold Bug' and a 'Silverite' will discuss the campaign money question and the probable outcome of the campaign in 1900" ("Helen Potter Again!" 1897:1–2). By the turn of century, Helen Potter had become the grande dame of the lyceum and Chautauqua platforms.

LELAND POWERS

Leland Powers was perhaps the most influential performer in bringing a more favorable attitude toward the theatrical at Chautauqua. He appeared at the New York Chautauqua in the nineteenth century in 1889, 1890, 1892, 1894, 1896, and 1898, and unlike Helen Potter, he did not use theatrical effects such as costumes. Instead, he appeared we are told as "a distinguished, scholarly gentleman in evening clothes, who by simple change in voice and manner portrayed all characters" (MacLaren 1938:54). It was Powers's performance style (which emphasized full characterization), as opposed to the external accoutrements, that made his one-person shows theatrical. He is, in fact, credited in *Who's Who in the Lyceum* as the "originator of [a] special form of play-reciting" (Wright 1906:150). In her study of Chautauqua's solo performers, Hadley cites Powers's "special form" of performance and notes Powers's readings of plays and novels as significant in changing Chautauqua's attitude towards the stage:

It was Powers who invented the term "monacting" and made that technique his own. So jealous was he of his invention that it is said he thoroughly resented the use of the term by other readers. Powers's style of performance and popularity are both of special interest in a study of readers at Chautauqua during these early years. His performances seem decidedly to have leaned toward the theatrical, and, more nearly than most of the other Chautauqua performances of his day, to have approximated what today would be called play readings with a decided flavor of characterization. That this was true is not surprising when it is recalled that his school [Leland Powers School in Boston] specialized in the training of public performers rather than stressing an academic approach to elocution. His popularity thus seems to have fore-shadowed a more tolerant attitude toward the stage and a higher regard for the theatrical than had at first been the case at Chautauqua (1956:113).

Powers's platform innovations, however, did not at first meet with universal approval from the lyceum and Chautauqua audiences. A retrospective feature article on Power's career and contributions published in 1908 recounted the difficulties Powers had met in the early days of his platform career:

His work in interpreting characters in dramatic literature was an innovation upon the lyceum platform, and many a person of superfine religious sentiments was at first almost or entirely horrified by such "play-acting."

"I've been praying ever since to get back the blessing," said one old lady who heard him give his dramatization of "David Copperfield" in the early days of the mother Chautauqua. And this was the attitude of no inconsiderable number of those who composed his first audiences (Pearson 1908a:14).

Only Bishop Vincent's intervention brought Powers clear acceptance with those early audiences at Chautauqua. Scheduled to present his solo rendition of *David Garrick,* Powers anticipated audience disapproval particularly for a scene in which the character Garrick feigns intoxication. Fearing that members of the audience might be outraged by such a scene, Powers confided his anxiety to Vincent, who assured the young performer that his recital would be well received. We are told that:

As Powers finished this crucial scene in his recital, the Bishop himself led the applause from the platform, and as the impersonator left the stage the father of Chautauqua rose and said to the audience, "I propose that when this young man returns we give the Chautauqua salute for him."

It was given, and given with a will. Bishop Vincent had set the seal of his approval upon the work of Leland Powers (Pearson 1908a:14).

Thus through Vincent's intervention Powers won the acceptance and eventually the high regard of the Chautauquans.[17] We are left to wonder if Vincent ever realized the importance of his part in changing Chautauqua's attitudes toward the theatrical.

Ultimately Powers attained the enviable reputation as a major artist in his field, both as a performer and as the founder and principal of the Leland Powers School for the Study of the Spoken Word in Boston.[18] His influence was felt throughout the country as students and followers of his joined the growing ranks of professional platformists: "The art of Leland Powers is that of a master. He has many imitators, but I have never heard his equal. . . . The first to present modern plays as monologues, Mr. Powers has the ability, and the genius for hard work to keep him always in the lead of the many others who present the same art form" (Pearson 1908a:15).

Theatrical one-person shows, like those of Helen Potter and Leland Powers, were instrumental in changing the attitude against the theatre not only at the New York Chautauqua Assembly but also throughout the country. Potter, Powers, and the performers who imitated their innovations were seen throughout the nation on the platforms of the lyceum circuit and in the independent Chautauquas. Their work gradually helped to dissipate the anti-theatre sentiment nationwide. The effect of this change in attitude on the one-person show as a medium for public entertainment was profound: as theatre and play productions became accepted, the one-person show genre fell from vogue. Ironically, the one-person show actually helped cause its own fall from popular favor. Such changes in circumstances, however, were well into the future; the two decades surrounding the turn of the century mark the apogee in popularity of platform performances.

CHAUTAUQUA VERSUS VAUDEVILLE

In the 1890s, while Chautauqua was establishing itself as an important cultural movement, another mode of entertainment was enjoying a rise in popularity. Vaudeville—the very word was enough to make many Chautauquans cringe—was becoming increasingly popular as the nineteenth century drew to its close. With its roots in minstrel shows and variety acts, vaudeville's aims were at variance with those of Chautauqua. Chautauqua had begun as a Sunday-school institute; its aims were religious and educational. Even after the program was broadened to include cultural events and entertainment, the Chautauqua retained an air of respectability and continued to attract as patrons and audience members the middle classes, the families, the educated, and those with cultural aspirations. Vaudeville, on the other hand, grew out of popular (and often crude) variety acts. Its audiences were mostly male and mostly working-class people who were interested in hearty laughs and ribald and irreverent humor. Vaudeville in its early days was song-and-dance and comic monologues with an emphasis on physical slapstick. No one could accuse vaudeville of intellectual or cultural pretensions:

> Vaudeville was the entertainment of the masses and reflected the attitudes of the masses. . . . If any action on stage ever threatened to diminish attendance, it was removed. John Royal, a former manager of a part of the most powerful vaudeville circuit ever developed, made it clear that his boss, Benjamin F. Keith, subscribed to the motto, "Get the coin." Vaudeville thus tended to be anti-intellectual itself. . . . The patron's mind was not to be joggled by social questions or matters of import and challenge. It was presumed he had faced his pressures for the day by the time he came to the theatre. Now he was to relax, to be spoonfed his laughs and delights. . . . It was in reality, the vast intellectual wasteland of its day (DiMeglio 1973:6).

As long as Chautauqua and vaudeville remained true to their respective roots, they continued as separate institutions, distinct both in their audiences and in their performers. Cultural changes, however, eventually brought the Chautauqua and vaudeville toward a closer relationship. As we have already seen, Chautauqua gradually became more liberal in its approval forms of platform entertainment (this became even more true in regard to the tent Chautauqua in the next century). Simultaneously, as the 1890s progressed, vaudeville became more "refined." An article published in 1900 chronicled the new developments in vaudeville, stating that "[t]here is evidently an upward tendency of the vaudeville stage to-day which brings it more in line with the lyceum platform, that is, its entertainment novelties. There is a desire on the part of the vaudeville managers to attract refinement" ("Vogue of the Vaudeville" 1900:5). The article, a reprint in *Talent* from the *Brooklyn Eagle,* then continued:

Vaudeville, plain, vulgar variety stage vaudeville, once despised as something repulsive and immoral, is now having its vogue. It is practically the same old vaudeville, but it now wears robes of respectability, also all the better classes would not be swarming to it with their patronage. This washed and rehabilitated style of amusing people is now more genuinely popular than the legitimate drama. . . . Longing for something clean and light and refreshingly entertaining, the wearied public embraced vaudeville and made the despised variety stage the proper thing. This public did not stoop to the old level of vaudeville; it raised the old vaudeville to its own level, so that it might be enjoyed without the public losing caste. Canting conventionalities have all along cried out against this recognition of what was looked upon as common and vulgar; but its cries were vain, for vaudeville has a hold on America like unto an epidemic ("Vogue" 1900:5).

Why the sudden popularity of vaudeville among respectable society? The likely answer is the loosening of Victorian morality in the Gay Nineties, specifically concerning the theatre:

The reason for this marvelous development of the variety stage is that the American people persist in being natural. They have been smarting under the rigorous restrictions of conventionality a long time, and have at last rebelled. The vast majority of the Americans now try to be their normal selves, and if they chance to have a wicked desire to go to a music hall to listen to the catchy songs and watch the flying footed dancers, they usually gratify the desire and go, and do not lose their social position by so doing, for nearly all their friends go and do likewise ("Vogue" 1900:5).

Just as Chautauqua was changing under the press of shifting public attitudes, so too was vaudeville. In the case of vaudeville, the results was an upgrading of its entertainment fare from what was once "the lowest order . . . with cheap performers and claptrap songs . . . little to attract people of even average intelligence" to quality variety performances ("Vogue" 1900:5). The transformation of vaudeville was as swift as it was startling:

> The growth of the variety stage from the disreputable to the respectable has nearly all occurred within the last few years. Ten years ago a variety performance was avoided by even a man if the man had what he called a good character and wanted to keep it. It was regarded as a disgrace to mingle with the toughs and vulgar members of the lower classes who patronized such places. . . .
> Nowadays this has all changed ("Vogue" 1900:5).

As Chautauqua and lyceum entertainment became more theatrical and vaudeville acts became more refined, the distinctions blurred. Inevitably, Chautauqua/lyceum performers, eager for fame and fortune, appeared on the vaudeville circuits. The crossover by platform artists to what many Chautauquans continued to feel was a lower institution was not met with easy approbation. With its origins in the minstrel show, vaudeville was representative of the rising "mass" culture of the late nineteenth century, which, as Howe explained, "emerged gradually and against the opposition of the gentry" (1976:14). Chautauquans—most of whom were members of the gentry—expressed their disapproval of the sudden transition by their performers to the vaudeville stages in the issues of *Talent* at the turn of the century, as seen in this editorial entitled "The Lyceum Entertainer in Vaudeville":

> It is with keen regret the writer notes the increasing frequency with which lyceum entertainers are announced for appearance at the various vaudeville theatres throughout the country.

And inasmuch as a partial ostracism from the leading lyceum bureaus is sure to result from such extremely ill-advised action; the transition continues apace.

The execrable judgment indulged in by these artists is virtually abandoning a profitable field of amusement, which has created for their services a steady and positive demand, for a form of cheap theatrical enterprise, and catering to audiences wholly at variance with the entertainers' peculiar talents, which are best fitted for the platform and resulting mostly in disaster for the artists thus engaged (1899:2).

The writer continues his editorial by illustrating his argument with accounts of recent failures of lyceum performers who appeared in vaudeville. While maintaining that vaudeville is no more than "a form of cheap theatrical enterprise," he acknowledges that "refined audience[s] of theatre going people" do attend the better houses. He does not blame the audiences for the performers' failures nor does he hold that they are "insufficiently intelligent to properly recognize appreciative entertainment." Rather, he argues that the "logical conclusion then is, that an audience patroning vaudeville do [sic] not want platform favorites." The writer concludes with a statement of hope, believing that the recent failures will serve as "an object lesson" and so deter other lyceum and Chautauqua artists from the temptations of vaudeville glory:

The writer sincerely trusts that the artists who have thus vainly appealed for theatrical glory and lost, have been taught an object lesson, and will in the future confine themselves to their legitimate field of amusement and be content with the glory to be obtained therein.

In view of these attempts and failures, it is a source of inexplicable mystery and wonderment to the writer that there are still a number of lyceum artists willing to tempt the vaudeville "Goddess of Fortune" with their talents, which should be plainly manifest is fully appreciated only by those people attending lyceum entertainments (1899:2).

Many Americans remained convinced that the lyceum and Chautauqua audiences were more attentive than those in the vaudeville houses. To this there may be some truth. The sense of earnest duty that compelled the Chautauqua and lyceum people may have made them more decorous, if not more appreciative, than their vaudeville counterparts. Arguments continued in the pages of *Talent* as the nation entered the new century. Eventually articles appeared that supported the performers whose ambitions lead them to work in vaudeville as well as in the lyceum and Chautauqua. Platform reading as an art was a speciality of the lyceum and Chautauqua, not of vaudeville, and platform readers willing to try their luck on the vaudeville circuits had to broaden their appeal and include entertainments appropriate for vaudeville, such as character impersonations. After recounting the success in vaudeville of lyceum performer Henry Lee, an impersonator of famous figures, the March 1903 *Talent* concluded that the once seemingly impossible had become a reality: "There has been much discussion as to the lyceum talent entering vaudeville. . . . In many respects the refined vaudeville furnishes opportunities which the lyceum does not, but it requires the artists of broader public experience to sustain the dignity of the platform and meet the demands of a refined vaudeville audience. It is delicate ground, but it can be done. See Henry Lee" ("A Reverie" 1903:2). The tension between the Chautauqua/lyceum and vaudeville, although never fully resolved, did continue to diminish as the early decades of the twentieth century progressed. Once the tent Chautauqua opened and programs of novelty entertainment became common, distinctions from vaudeville were virtually in spirit only.

MARK TWAIN

Audiences of the last decade of the nineteenth century saw one of the most ambitious solo performance efforts of the Victorian era: Mark Twain's Tour Around the World of 1895–96. Beginning in Cleveland, Ohio, the tour moved westward across the United States; from there it continued into Canada and on to New Zealand, Australia, India, South Africa, and, finally, London. Twain's reputation as a platform celebrity had steadily increased throughout the last quarter of the century. By the time he began his world tour, he was one of the most popular platform artists in the country.

Although he read from his published works in the later portion of his platform career, Twain cannot be rightfully considered a "dramatic reader," for he was never best known, as Dickens had been, for his characterizations in performance. Twain's reputation as a major platform talent was based on the personality he projected—that of a lazy, drawling, southwestern gentleman and commentator on the lunacies of human life. The tradition with which Twain is most closely associated is that of the American humorist. This rich tradition in popular culture has roots that stretch back into the eighteenth century and the colonial period and is, in actuality, a modern incarnation of the tradition of the medieval jester (Blair 1960:116).

American humor was well represented on the platforms of the lyceum and Chautauqua assemblies. Many of the best humorists were important platform personalities. Along with Samuel L. Clemens ("Mark Twain"), other major platform humorists included Charles Farrar Browne ("Artemus Ward"), David Ross Locke ("Petroleum Vesuvius Nasby"), Edgar W. Nye ("Bill Nye"), Henry Wheeler Shaw ("Josh Billings"), Melville D. Landon ("Eli Perkins"), Robert J. Burdette ("Burlington Hawkeye Man"), and James M. Bailey ("Danbury News Man"). As authors, these humorists created comic characters whose names served as pseudonyms; eventually the public personalities of the humorists were subsumed into those of their characters and total identification with the fictive characters took place. Writing of Charles Farrar Browne and his fictive character Artemus Ward, Walter Blair stated: "The character of Artemus Ward . . . merged with that of his creator, and, in time, people used, the name Brown or Ward interchangeably, having no feeling that the comic writer differed from the comic figure he had created" (1960:114). This kind of identification of humorist with fictive character was quite common and, in fact, still occurs today. A contemporary equivalent is Paul Rubens's identification with his character Pee Wee Herman. So total is the Rubens-Herman identification that Rubens never appears publicly (e.g., for interviews) except in the character of Pee Wee. Significant in the process that brought the nineteenth-century humorists into identification with their characters was the act of public performance. "Important, perhaps," Blair points out, "in bringing about the identification of an author with his pen name were the appearance of many of the comic writers on the lecture platform" (1960:114).

The fictive characters created and assumed by the American humorists, although possessing individual personality traits,

Rowlandson engraving from *A Lecture on Heads by Geo. Alex. Stevens, With Additions, as delivered by Mr. Charles Lee Lewis, London, 1808.* Reprinted courtesy of the Hargrett Rare Book and Manuscript Library, University of Georgia Libraries.

MR. MATHEWS,
in his "AT HOME" of 1820.

Charles Mathews in his "At Home" of 1820. Reprinted courtesy of the Theatre Collection, Museum of the City of New York.

Mr. Charles Dickens's Last Reading, from the *Illustrated London News*, 14 March 1870. Collection of the author.

Edgar Allan Poe as drawn by William Oberhardt from a daguerreotype in possession of Poe's family. Reprinted courtesy of the Billy Rose Theatre Collection, New York Public Library at Lincoln Center, Astor, Lenox and Tilden Foundations.

Anna Cora Mowatt, engraving from a daguerreotype by Paine of Islington.
Reprinted courtesy of the Billy Rose Theatre Collection, New York City
Public Library at Lincoln Center, Astor, Lenox and Tilden Foundations.

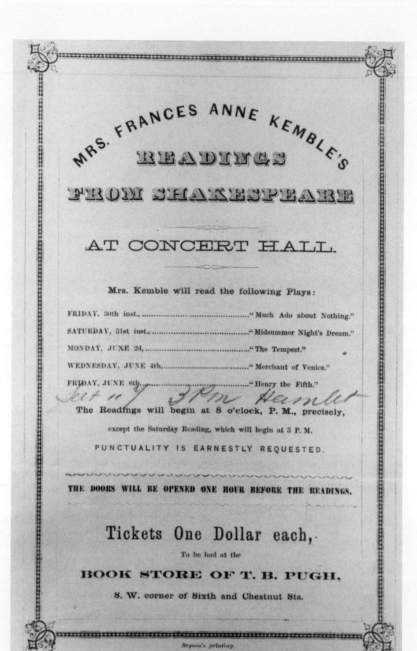

Announcement for Fanny Kemble's *Readings from Shakespeare* in Philadelphia. Reprinted courtesy of the Dartmouth College Library.

above: Sir Thomas Lawrence's drawing of Fanny Kemble as Juliet, lithographed by R. J. Lane. Reprinted courtesy of the Billy Rose Theatre Collection, New York Public Library at Lincoln Center, Astor, Lenox and Tilden Foundations. *below:* Fanny Kemble's *Readings from Shakespeare,* from the *Illustrated London News,* 10 August 1850. Collection of the author.

MORNING AND EVENING READINGS,

FROM SHAKSPEARE AND THE POETS.

Miss Charlotte Cushman

Will have the honor to give a series of Four Readings,

AT STEINWAY HALL,

IN THE FOLLOWING ORDER.

ON MONDAY EVENING, MARCH 17.

KING HENRY VIII.

ON WEDNESDAY MORNING, MARCH 19.

PART I.

SELECTIONS FROM ROMEO AND JULIET.

PART II.

MISCELLANEOUS.

BATTLE OF IVRY,	MACAULAY
DEATH OF THE OLD SQUIRE,	ANONYMOUS
BETSEY AND I ARE OUT,	CARLETON

ON FRIDAY EVENING, MARCH 21.

MACBETH.

ON SATURDAY MORNING, MARCH 22.

MISCELLANEOUS READINGS.

PART I.

THE YOUNG GREY HEAD,	MISS SOUTHEY
THE GRANDMOTHER.	TENNYSON

PART II.

THE SKELETON IN ARMOR,	LONGFELLOW
HIRVE RIEL,	BROWNING
THE CHARGE OF THE LIGHT BRIGADE,	TENNYSON
BETSEY AND I ARE OUT, (By request.)	CARLETON

THE EVENING READINGS,	THE MORNING READINGS,
At 8 o'clock precisely.	At 2 o'clock precisely

Admission to each Reading, - - One Dollar.

No extra charge for Reserved Seats,

TICKETS TO ANY OF THE READINGS, FOR SALE AT STEINWAY HALL, FROM 9 A. M. TO 4 P. M. DAILY.

Seer. Steam Printer. 10 West 4th Street, N. Y

Announcement for a series of readings by Charlotte Cushman at Steinway Hall, New York. Collection of the author.

Charlotte Cushman, engraving from a painting by Chappel. Reprinted courtesy of the Theatre Collection, Museum of the City of New York.

Mabelle Carolyn Church

READER

"EVERYMAN," the popular Sixteenth-century English Morality Play.

POPULAR PROGRAMS—readings from the most popular modern writers.

Next season MISS CHURCH will be one of the stars in an all-star company we are sending out.

MISS CHURCH will also be available for EVERYMAN, and other complete programs she has given so successfully this season.

MISS CHURCH has been on many of the largest and best courses and we have yet to hear a complaint. Her pleasing personality, her artistic readings, stir her audiences to enthusiasm.

MANAGEMENT, WINTER AND SUMMER

SLAYTON LYCEUM BUREAU
Steinway Hall   CHICAGO

Advertisement for Mabelle Carolyn Church, from the Slayton Lyceum Bureau, printed in *Talent*, March 1904. Reprinted courtesy of the Redpath Chautauqua Collection, University of Iowa Libraries.

Robert McLean Cumnock, from the cover of the October 1908
Lyceumite & Talent. Reprinted courtesy of the Redpath Chautauqua
Collection, University of Iowa Libraries.

MISS HELEN POTTER,

IN HER PERSONATIONS OF CELEBRITIES

Advertisement for Helen Potter's impersonations. Reprinted courtesy of the Billy Rose Theatre Collection, New York Public Library at Lincoln Center. Astor, Lenox and Tilden Foundations.

top left: Helen Potter as John B. Gough. *lower left:* Helen Potter as Susan B. Anthony. *right:* Helen Potter as Sarah Bernhardt in the role of Dona Sol. From *Helen Potter's Impersonations.*

LELAND POWERS

Leland Powers, from the cover of the January 1908 *Lyceumite & Talent*. Reprinted courtesy of the Redpath Chautauqua Collection, University of Iowa Libraries.

Mark Twain and George Cable. Reprinted courtesy of the New-York Historical Society, New York City.

MARK TWAIN'S TOUR

AROUND
THE WORLD,

Beginning in Cleveland, Ohio, July 15th, 1895

Closing in London, May, 1896.

ROUTE IN AMERICA.

JULY

Mon.	15.	Cleveland, Ohio	Stillman House
Tues.	16.	"	"
Wed.	17.	*Travel on Steamer.*	
Thur.	18.	Sault Ste., Mich	Hotel Iroquois
Fri.	19.	Mackinac	Grand Hotal
Sat.	20.	Petoskey, Mich	Arlington Hotel
SUN.	21.	Mackinac	Grand Hotel
Mon.	22.	Duluth, Minn	Spalding, Hotel
Tues.	23.	Minneapolis, Minn	Hotel West
Wed.	24.	St. Paul, Minn.	Hotel Ryan
Thur	25.	*Travel.*	
Fri.	26.	Winnipeg	The Manitoba
Sat.	27.	"	"
SUN.	28.	"	"
Mon.	29.	Crookston, Minn	Crookston Hotel
Tues.	30.	*Travel.*	
Wed.	31.	Great Falls, Mont.	Park Hotel

AUGUST

Thur.	1.	Butte, Montana	The Butte Hotel
Fri.	2.	Anaconda, Mont	The Montana
Sat.	3.	Helena, Mont	Hotel Helena
SUN.	4.	"	"
Mon.	5.	*Missoula mont*	
Tues.	6.	*Travel.*	
Wed.	7.	Spokane, Wash	The Spokane
Thur.	8.	*Travel.*	
Fri.	9.	Portland, Oregon	The Portland
Sat.	10.	Olympia, Wash	The Olympia
SUN.	11.	"	"
Mon.	12.	Tacoma, Wash	The Tacoma
Tues.	13.	Seattle, Wash	The Rainier-Grand
Wed.	14.	New Whatcom, Wash	*New Whatcom Hotel*
Thur.	15.	Vancouver, B.C.	Hotel Vancouver
Fri.	16.	*Sails from Vancouver for Australia.*	

Advertisement for Mark Twain's Tour Around the World, 1895–96.
Reprinted courtesy of the Henry W. and Albert A. Berg Collection, New
York Public Library, Astor, Lenox and Tilden Foundations.

shared important similarities. One similarity was the demeanor of the characters in performance. Typically, the character spoke in complete seriousness on a chosen topic and "unconsciously" exposed the absurd and the comic in life. The humorist-character thereby provoked the audience to laughter while supposedly remaining unaware that anything funny had been said. A more important similarity was the fictive characters' use of common language and speech. The characters were distinctly American: they spoke American vernacular, they were often representative of the rural lower-middle class (as opposed to the urban elite), and they offered homespun, native common sense. The humorists did not simply burlesque the stereotype of the American country bumpkin (which, of course, was part their appeal) but also argued implicitly in favor of the naive wisdom of country folk at the expense of the educated urban professionals. By using colloquial American English in their performances and published writings, the humorists improved the status of the vernacular. They proved it worthy of artistic expression and, therefore, paved the way for Mark Twain's masterpiece *The Adventures of Huckleberry Finn*.

Many of the American humorists achieved as platform entertainers a status enjoyed only by a privileged few. Among the most successful (to use their pseudonyms) were Artemus Ward, Josh Billings, Petroleum Vesuvius Nasby, and Bill Nye. Each of these men possessed comic genius. And yet, to later generations, much of their writings fall flat. Their brilliance as humorists was inextricable from their considerable talents as performers and was, ultimately, as ephemeral as each man's performance act itself.[19] Of Artemus Ward, the *Quarterly Review* wrote: "The humor of Artemus Ward hardly attains the dignity of literature. If Republicans kept their fools, we might class him with the court jester of old. He is a species of the practical joker who wears a cap and bells. To us it seems that the drollery would be spoken than written. It wants the appropriate facial and nasal expression to make it complete" (Massey 1876:225). The *Quarterly Review*'s comments may be attacked as a kind of snobbery for adhering to what Herbert J. Gans (1974) refers to as "the mass culture critique," in which high culture standards are forced upon mass culture products. Yet the fact remains that the *Quarterly Review* is correct in saying that the writings of Ward (or Billings, Nasby, Nye, or any of the others) do want performance, because that is the mode of expression for which they were intended. This applies not only to works of Artemus Ward but also to the writings of the platform humorists as a group. Only one—Mark Twain—achieved a level of artistry in his writing that transcended the ephemerality of performance. Twain remains the finest humorist that America has produced.

During the early years of his platform career, in January 1868, Twain attended one of Dickens's readings in New York's Steinway Hall. During the performance, he sat next to his future wife, Olivia Langdon. Whether Twain was more impressed with Miss Langdon or with Dickens's performance is debatable. But Fred W. Lorch, in his account of Twain's platform career, argues that "there is little reason to believe that she completely engrossed his attention that evening. It is evident that the readings by the celebrated English novelist also commanded his deep interest and that they suggested to him the possibilities of a platform artistry which he had never before imagined" (1968:70).

Dickens's readings may well have prompted Twain to include selections from his writings in his own appearances, but Twain was not among the enthusiastic many smitten with Dickens's talents as a performer. Twain wrote of Dickens in a letter that was printed in the *Alta California:*

He read *David Copperfield.* He is a bad reader, in one sense—because he does not enunciate his words sharply and distinctly—he does not cut the syllables cleanly, and therefore many and many of them fell dead before they reached our part of the house. (I say "our" because I am proud to observe that there was a beautiful young lady with me—a good deal disappointed in Mr. Dickens' reading—I will go further and say, a great deal disappointed.) The *Herald* and *Tribune* critics must have been carried away by their imaginations when they wrote their extravagant praises of it. Mr. Dickens' reading is rather monotonous, as a general thing; his voice is husky; his pathos is only the pathos of his language— there is no heart, no feeling in it—it is glittering frostwork; his rich humor cannot fail to tickle an audience into ecstasies save when he reads to himself (quoted in Meltzer 1960:111).

Years later, when Twain was writing his autobiography, he recounted his evening at Dickens's recital. His estimation of Dickens's talents as a performer had undergone a transformation in the intervening years, the reasons for which remain unknown:

Dickens's audience sat in a pleasant twilight, while he performed in the powerful light cast upon him from the concealed lamps. He read with great force and animation in the lively passages, and with stirring effect. It will be understood that he did not merely read but also acted. His reading of the storm scene in which Steerforth lost his life [was] so vivid and so full of energetic action that his house was carried off its feet, so to speak (Clemens 1959:175).

We can only speculate why Twain's appraisals of Dickens's performance are inconsistent. Perhaps Twain's own subsequent great fame as a writer allowed him to be more generous when speaking of the man who was considered to be the greatest novelist of his age. Perhaps Twain's own work as a platform reader in later years made him more sympathetic or sensitive to Dickens's platform artistry. In any event, what impressed Twain most about Dickens's public reading was not so much the execution as the concept.

Twain had already appeared on the platform as a humorous lecturer before Charles Dickens's American tour. His lectures were filled with anecdotes from personal experience and observation. His lecture on the Sandwich Islands remained in his repertoire for years. As Lorch points out, "[i]t has often been observed that the distinction between lecturing and reading from one's own compositions can be a difficult one to make" (1968:137). This is particularly true in Twain's case because many of his lecture anecdotes eventually appeared in written form in publication. Therefore, even in his early appearances "considerable portions . . . could be termed readings" (Lorch 1968:155).

Several years after seeing Dickens perform, Twain decided to present his first series of readings. He had avoided public appearances throughout the 1870s, but by 1884 he needed money for his new publishing house, which was about to release *Huckleberry Finn*. His readings would not only earn him significant sums in themselves but would also serve as a form of public relations and increase interest in his novel. In order to avoid the loneliness of being a soloist on the road, Twain invited the writer George W. Cable to share the platform for the tour of 1884–85. Despite an undercurrent of personality conflicts that developed over the course of the season, the two author-performers worked well as a double bill and the tour was a success. Cable's correspondence offers vivid descriptions of the excitement of their performances, such as this letter to his first wife, Louise Stewart Cable, written on the back of one of the programs during a performance:

> Philadelphia, Nov. 21, 1884.
> Mark is on the platform; there goes a roar of applause! We have a superb audience—both in numbers & quality————& we are beating ourselves. Mark says, as he passes me on the retiring room steps, "Old boy, you're doing nobly."
> Somehow I struck a new streak yesterday evening at Newburgh. We had a little audience & no end of fun. they kept calling us back—There goes another round of applause. The laughter is almost continual & even my milder humor is interrupted with laughter & applause. There they go again! The hall is a large one with two large balconies reaching twice around from stage to stage & full to the ceiling. Men standing thick in the back of the house. I thought you'd like to get just one letter from me from the lecture-hall, so here it is. There they go again! (Bikle 1967:133–34).

Although Twain previously enjoyed considerable success as a humorous lecturer, he did not master the art of oral reading easily. The tour of 1884–85, in fact, proved to be his education as platform reader. Naively supposing that Dickens's performances required no special talent or preparation, Twain tried early in the tour to simply read cold from his written texts:

I never tried reading as a trade and I wanted to try it. . . . It was ghastly! At least in the beginning. I had selected my readings well enough, but had not studied them. I supposed it would only be necessary to do like Dickens—get out on the platform and read from a book. I did that and made a botch of it. Written things are not for speech; their form is literary; they are stiff, inflexible, and will not lend themselves to happy and effective delivery with the tongue—where their purpose is to entertain, not instruct; they have to be limbered up, broken up, colloquialized, and turned into common forms of unpremediated talk—otherwise they will bore the house, not entertain it. After a week's experience with the book I laid it aside and never carried it to the platform again; but in the meantime I had memorized those pieces, and in delivering them from the platform they soon transformed themselves into flexible talk, with all their obstructing preciseness and formalities gone out of them for good (Clemens 1959:176).

Twain clearly did a disservice to assume that Dickens cavalierly walked out on stage and just "read from a book." Dickens, like Twain, had carefully selected his readings, edited the texts, and then painstakingly memorized each one. Although Dickens chose to hold a book on the platform (which held the edited performance texts,) he rarely looked down at the manuscript. In Dickens's performances, the physical text served an aesthetic purpose. Dickens did not, however, colloquialize his works as Twain eventually did, a difference noted by a reviewer of Twain's performances during the Tour Around the World of 1895–96:

Like Charles Dickens, he relies entirely on his old books for the pabulum of his discourses, but, unlike the author of "Pickwick," he does not read long extracts from these books. He takes some of his best stories—"The Jumping Frog," "Huck Finn," the difficulties of the German language, *par example*—and re-tells them, with many subtle additions of humor and some fresh observations, in the irresistibly amusing manner (R.C.B. 1896:286).

In short, whereas Dickens's method of reading tended to rely on full memorization and recitation of the exact content of his performance texts (albeit with occasional additional commentary), "Twain's method of reading might be described as memorization which was altered and changed into a kind of extempore speech" (Donner 1947:310). By the end of his world tour, Twain perfected his technique, expertly using what he referred to as "those studied fictions which seem to be the impulse of the moment and which are so effective" (Clemens 1959:181). The "studied fictions" were devices used in performance to foster the impression of spontaneity; Twain described them in his autobiography: "[F]ictitious hesitancies for the right word, fictitious unconscious pauses, fictitious unconscious side remarks, fictitious unconscious embarrassments, fictitious unconscious emphases placed on the wrong word with a deep intention back of it—these and all the other artful fictive shades which give to a recited tale the captivating naturalness of an impromptu narration" (Clemens 1959:181). Twain developed these devices over the course of his years as a platform lecturer and reader; he fully believed that such effects were impossible to achieve with the same degree of success by a "book reader" (i.e., a platform reader who actually used a book in performance).

A comparison of Charles Dickens and Mark Twain as performers would provide an interesting study.[20] Whereas Dickens appeared in formal evening clothes, stood erect behind a reading table, memorized his performance texts, and aimed towards a precise performance of well-rehearsed gestures, Twain cultivated a much more casual platform style. Although dressed "in regulation evening-clothes" (R.C.B. 1896:286), Twain's appearance and bearing conveyed a looseness or personal laziness: "He hung loosely around the [reading] desk or flirted around the corners of it, marching or counter-marching in the rear of it. He seldom stood still" (Lorch 1968:222). He often spoke with his hands in his pockets, filled his speech like the other platform humorists with quaint Americanisms, and disregarded the polished diction of most lecturers: "'It is not' is always 'twarn't' with Mark Twain. . . . He speaks slowly, lazily, and wearily, as a man dropping off to sleep, rarely raising his voice above a conversational tone; but it has that characteristic nasal sound which penetrates to the back of the largest building. His figure is rather slight, not above middle height, and the whole man suggests an utter lack of physical energy" (R.C.B. 1896:286).

Twain's casual platform manner was actually conscious artifice. Since his first reading tour of 1884–85, he had become a committed reader with high personal standards. Throughout his reading career, he strove to improve his performances. He did, however, remain determinedly self-taught. Twain never believed in formal elocutionary training. He detested the artificiality he associated with elocutionists and aimed instead toward a fully colloquial speech. When Cable studied with an instructor of elocution, Twain disparaged the results:

Cable has been scouting the country alone for three years with readings from his novels and he had been a good reader in the beginning, for he had been born with a natural talent for it, but unhappily he prepared himself for his public work by taking lessons from a teacher of elocution, and so by the time he was ready to begin his platform work he was so well and thoroughly educated that he was merely theatrical and artificial and not half as pleasing and entertaining to a house as he had been in the splendid days of his ignorance (Clemens 1959:176).

Twain's insistence that literature must be in the colloquial idiom for performance would have met with objection—most strongly by the very performers he disliked, elocutionists. Perhaps witnessing a performance by a superior elocutionist, such as Robert McLean Cumnock, could have convinced Twain that literature can be successfully performed while retaining all its literary qualities. We can only imagine what might have occurred had Cumnock and Twain met to discuss their performance philosophies. Twain would have had a major point in his favor: his own success on the platform. Yet his appeal as a performer lay in his personal charisma. We may suspect that had Twain been able to perform literary works with the same vivacity that he performed the colloquialized versions, his success would have been as great. In sight of the fact, however, that Twain was the original author of the literature he colloquialized, it may also be argued that there is an indistinct line between Twain as writer for publication and Twain as oral storyteller.

Twain's preference for colloquialized performance texts does pose an interesting question: can a qualitative judgment be made in comparing Twain's stories as written and his own retelling of them in performance? To read both silently would be a faulty method of evaluation: the performance text would then be judged as a printed text rather than as an oral phenomenon. Both are legitimate artistic creations by the same individual and each is intended to serve a different purpose. The issue becomes more complicated if the printed word is accepted as a substitute for the spoken act. If that premise is accepted, then Twain's stories in performance can be said to be superior to their printed versions.

Although Twain's reputation as a platform reader primarily rests on his achievements during his two major tours of 1884–85 and 1895–96, he did read periodically at other times for special occasions, such as his readings for charity in later life. For these special engagements he chose material he had used during his early lecture days (much of which eventually appeared in *Innocents Abroad* and *Roughing It*) and his tours. By the peak of his platform career, Twain's repertoire from his own works included selections from *The Adventures of Tom Sawyer, The Adventures of Huckleberry Finn, The Prince and the Pauper, Pudd'nhead Wilson,* and *Joan of Arc.* Along with these selections from his major works, he frequently performed segments of his autobiographical and minor writings. Much less often he performed the works of other writers, such as Browning, Shakespeare, Dickens, and Kipling; he usually reserved his readings from other writers for private gatherings of friends and family.

In the years following Dickens's great success on the platform, authors' readings by American writers became increasingly popular. Willingly or reluctantly, many American writers, including Thomas Bailey Aldrich, Thomas Nelson Page, Harriet Beecher Stowe, William Dean Howells, and Oliver Wendell Holmes, appeared publicly to read from their works. Twain occasionally performed at the authors' readings in a program of six or eight writers. A few of the American writer-performers were effective on the platform—such as George W. Cable and Harriet Beecher Stowe—but many others were simply unsuited for the work.[21] Twain remains arguably the best of the American writer-performers as well as the finest platform humorist of his age. His own high standards as a professional reader made him impatient with the amateurism of his colleagues.[22] He dreaded performing at an authors' reading, and it is fitting that our last words on Twain as a performer should be his own description of a particularly grim evening at a Longfellow Memorial Authors' Reading at the Boston Globe Theatre:

This reading was to begin at two o'clock in the afternoon. I was number three on the list of readers. The piece I was to read would ordinarily take twelve minutes to finish; but by art and hard work I reduced its length to ten and a half minutes before I carried it to Boston. My train was to leave Boston for New York at four o'clock. I vacated the stage of that theater the moment I had finished my brief stunt, and I had only barely time left in which to catch that train. When I left, third in the list, as I have said, that orgy had already endured two hours. Six other readers were still to be heard from, and not a man in the list experienced enough in the business to know that when a person has been reading twelve minutes the audience feel that he ought to be gagged, and that when he has been reading fifteen minutes they know he ought to be shot. I learned afterward—at least I was told by a person with an average reputation for trustworthiness, that at six o'clock half the audience had been carried out on stretchers, and that the rest were dead—with a lot of readers still to hear from (quoted in Fatout 1976:544).

CONCLUSION

The Victorian age was truly the golden age of platform performances. This performance phenomenon is related to a literary development that also deserves mention. Literary historians often associate the Victorian period with the highest development of the dramatic monologue as a poetic form. Historical studies have shown the evolution of the form and traced a tradition from such works as Chaucer's *Canterbury Tales,* Marlowe's lyric "The Passionate Shepherd to His Love," Michael Drayton's sonnet "Since There's No Help," and several poems by Andrew Marvell.[23] These early poems are often cited as forerunners of the Victorian dramatic monologue for their traces of the major components of the genre: a speaker distinct from the poet, a specified listener, and a dramatic situation. If the scholars then tended to qualify their classification of these works as dramatic monologues, it is on the grounds that the poems offer idealized speakers or speaker representative of a type rather than a distinct individual character. The movement toward a more fully characterized speaker in a dramatic monologue actually began in the late eighteenth century and throughout the nineteenth, both in England and on the Continent. The European tradition of the literary dramatic monologue included such works as Rousseau's *Pygmalion,* Goethe's *Prosperina,* Southey's *Sappho,* Matthew Lewis's *Captive,* Frank Sayer's *Pandora* and *Oswald,* Tennyson's "Maud," and Browning's "My Last Duchess." Critics agree that the dramatic monologue reached its highest level of sophistication in the writings of Tennyson and, especially, of Browning. Since Browning, the dramatic monologue form has been used less frequently, although examples appeared in the works of W. B. Yeats, Ezra Pound, and T. S. Eliot and later poets such as Robert Lowell, Ted Hughes, and Philip Larkin.

What relationship exists, if any, between the vogue of the Victorian literary dramatic monologue and the vogue of its performance counterpart? Our understanding deepens when the two genres are viewed as interrelated and belonging on a dynamic continuum rather than artificially polarized and separated as two distinct artistic phenomena. Lewis originally wrote his monodrama *The Captive* for performance; later he published it in a collection entitled *Poems* (1812). Tennyson's "Maud," called by the poet "a monodrama," was originally intended to be read as literature but gained considerable power and dimension according to various audience reports when performed by the poet.[24] Browning turned to the dramatic monologue after several disappointments in his attempts at playwrighting. In reference to Browning's example, Alan Sinfield wrote: "Hence we may conclude that it is a substitute for playwrighting for those who have little skill with plot; or, more generously, that it is a kind of drama especially suited to those whose main interest is in character" (1977:3). Browning's monologues were popular with nineteenth-century elocutionists and audiences and became staples in platform programs, effectively returning the literary monologues to orality. As A. Dwight Culler points out "it is no accident that the author of the first book on dramatic monologues, Samuel Silas Curry, was a Boston elocutionist" (1975:368). Curry's book, *Browning and the Dramatic Monologue*, includes a section dealing with the dramatic rendering of the monologue and a defense of the "Necessity of Oral Redition" (1965:133–47). The use of the dramatic monologue in elocutionary training rests on an educational tradition that stretched back as far as Quintilian; *On the Early Education of the Citizen-Orator* advised the use of *prosopopeia*, character speeches, for the oratorical training of young men.

We may conclude that any firm distinction between the literary and the performance monologue is arbitrary at best. Their history, and by extension the history of all written and spoken texts, confirms a continuous interchange between literature and performance, which may at times appear competitive but is more often productive. Once we accept the literary monologue and the performance monologue (i.e., the one-person show) as manifestations of the same impulse, we may then finally argue that the concurrent popularity of the two genre in the Victorian age was a result of the Romantic movement and its interest in the exploration of the individual. The desire of an audience to see a celebrity on the platform or to view a solo performance focused on an individual character (historical or fictional) appears itself to have been the product of the Romantic sensibility. The movement in solo performance toward an investigation of an individual psyche reaches its summit in the late twentieth-century biographical and autobiographical one-person shows, a concern for a later chapter.

By the time America entered the twentieth century, the number and variety of professional one-person shows presented throughout the country was truly prodigious. Hundreds of performers appeared in the directory *Who's Who in the Lyceum* under a multitude of titles, including: reader, dramatic reader, elocutionist, expressionist, entertainer, impersonator, characterist, character artist, interpretive reciter, storyteller, monologuist, and character impersonator. Apparently as creative artists, these performers had full freedom in choosing (or inventing) their professional titles. Although such freedom is the privilege of any artist, the titles are ambiguous and confuse anyone attempting to understand the subtle or nonexistent differences in the nature of the performance. Even at the time of relatively common usage, the nomenclature of solo performance caused great confusion. The June 1905 issue of *Talent* included a special symposium devoted to the question: "Is there a difference in meaning between the terms elocutionist, reader, reciter, characterist, impersonator, monologist?" Samuel Silas Curry of Boston's School of Expression, and other eminent academics in the field of elocution, offered their answers to the perplexing question of nomenclature. Curry said: "It must be borne in mind that a word is employed not only for the speaker, but for the world at large. It is may be invented by the whim or fancy of the speaker, but it is a mere local and odd use of the word unless adopted by the world" (1905:15).

Curry's words remind us that solo mode titles, like the field of elocution as a whole, were subject to popular fads.[25] And, indeed, some of the titles simply faded from use. Many of them, however, persist and continue to cause confusion in discussions of solo performance. The problem is intensified for those unable to see the performances in question; many of the more obscure titles belong to performers whose work is virtually undocumented. In such a case, the death of the performer has resulted in the loss of the only reliable source of definition. The rising number of platform performers throughout the closing years of the nineteenth century intensified this problem in nomenclature that still plagues twentieth-century theatre criticism. Herbert Mitgang addressed this problem in a 1980 article in the *New York Times:*

> Two matters frequently puzzle audiences and critics: What do you call it and is it really a play?
>
> I have seen one-man plays referred to as readings, lectures, recitals, adaptations, complications, monologues, monodramas, and vaguest and laziest of all, as "play" with quotation marks around the word (1980:6).

Indeed, the twentieth-century problem of classifying one-person shows was inherited from the nineteenth century, and as Mitgang's words witness, we are no closer to solving the problem than were our Victorian predecessors.

As the nineteenth century came to its close, the nation's authors, poets, actors, elocutionists, and humorists sought the artistic fulfillment, fame, and financial rewards accorded to successful platform performers. By the end of the century, Americans could see a one-person show in any city or town that subscribed to a lyceum or built a Chautauqua. The next century brought many startling changes. Among them was a phenomenon that would bring the one-person show form into America's heartland: in 1904 Keith Vawter and J. Roy Ellison opened the tent Chautauqua.

NOTES

1. For more information on eighteenth-century solo entertainments, see Fitzgerald (1910); Garrett (1979, 1983a, 1983b); Kahan (1977, 1984); and Bacon (1964).

2. For a defense of the use of *Victorian* as a descriptive term for nineteenth-century America, see the collection of essays edited by Daniel Walker Howe (1976), especially Howe's introductory essay. Several of these essays were originally published in a special issue of *American Quarterly* 27 (Dec. 1975), entitled "Victorian Culture in America."

3. Although greatly diminished from the Victorian age, the practice of reading aloud in American homes continues even in our media-sophisticated world, as witnessed by the popular success of Jim Trelease's *Read-Aloud Handbook* (1985).

4. I am indebted to Daniel J. Boorstin's triology of American history and culture. For his complete discussion of American attitudes towards

language, reading, speaking and literature, see 1958, parts 10, 11, and 12; 1965, parts 6 and 7; and 1973, part 8.

5. For a discussion of Smith's performances, see Merritt (1983).

6. For another discussion of Mathews's influence on Dickens as a performer, see Schlicke (1985:233–41).

7. See, for example, Fitzsimons (1970).

8. For a thorough defense of Dickens's public readings, see Paul Schlicke's fine discussion in chapter 7 of *Dickens and Popular Entertainment* (1985).

9. Philip Collins also commented on Dickens's practice of enacting scenes in front of a mirror while writing. "Indeed, in reading his works aloud," said Collins, "Dickens was re-enacting in public an important stage of his creative process, which took place before he set pen to paper" (1975:lix).

10. See "Mr. Dickens as a Reader" (1867:5) for a review that refutes every common opinion expressed by other critics of Dickens's performances. This reviewer felt that in dramatic characterization Dickens was a failure "more or less" and succeeded best in narrative passages.

11. The three lyceum periods have been adapted from Greef (1941). Greef refers to the last period simply as "the Chautauqua." Since the Chautauqua and the lyceum existed simultaneously, I have chosen to refer to that period as "the Chautauqua-lyceum."

12. See chapter 3, "The Development," in John H. Vincent's *Chautauqua Movement* (1886), for his account of Chautauqua's move to comprehensive programming.

13. Regarding Chautauqua's name change from "assembly" to "institution," the New York State Legislature granted a new charter in 1902, which is still in effect. This charter changed the name from Chautauqua Assembly to Chautauqua Institution. For a detailed history of the Chautauqua Institution in New York, see Irwin (1987).

14. "Restrained readings" is vague. A more precise term is "low-definitional performances," that is, performances that employ minimal physical cuing. For discussions of low and high definitional performances, see Hudson (1973) and Roloff (1983).

15. See Charlotte Chamberlain's advertisement in *The Lyceumite and Talent,* Oct. 1908:40, which is reproduced among the illustrations. My attack on Chamberlain's performances may be unwarranted. Eighteen years later, she was still actively performing on the Chautauqua circuits. By 1926 Chamberlain was appearing as a "lightning cartoonist" as well as continuing her work as a bird warbler (see her advertisement in *Lyceum,* April 1926:4). The longevity of her career indicates that she must have met with some success as an entertainer.

16. See Potter (1891). This book includes Potter's performance texts along with her suggestions to neophytes in platform art on such topics as "How to Prepare Impersonations," "Care of Voice, Health, etc.," and "The Artist's Make-up and Toilet."

17. The Chautauqua salute, mentioned by Vincent in the preceding

quotation, was a waving of white handkerchiefs by the Chautauquans after exceptional performances (see Irwin 1987:55).

18. Leland Powers was a ubiquitous presence in platform circles. He appeared in nearly every issue of the various lyceum and Chautauqua magazines during his active career. His photograph was printed on the covers of the February 1892 issue of *Talent* and of the January 1908 issue of *The Lyceumite and Talent*.

19. For a recent defense of the platform humorists, see McManus (1976, 1983). "The platform humorists," wrote MacManus, "have been unjustly criticized for their misspelling. . . . The phonetic transcriptions, of course, project the voice in writing. By ignoring the orality, critics have failed to realize the significance of the comedians: they were performers! The scripts record not only what was said, but *how* it was pronounced, another mark of their individuality" (1983:693).

20. Martha L. Brunson briefly compares the two performers in her essay "Novelists as Platform Readers: Dickens, Clemens, and Stowe" (1983). See also Donner (1946); Hipps (1975); Hobb (1945); Low (1956); Mello (1965); and Stephens (1942).

21. For more information on Cable as a reader, see Turner (1966). For accounts of Stowe's brief career as a reader, see Trautmann's two essays (1973 and 1974), and Brunson's essay (1983).

22. Twain usually requested the third position in an authors' readings program in order to make a timely departure if the evening proved to be a marathon.

23. For discussions of the dramatic monologue in literature, see Culler (1975); Curry (1965); MacCallum (1970); Martin (1985); Sinfield (1975); Fletcher (1908); Howard (1963); Sessions (1947); Hughes (1987); and Saradhi (1975).

24. See Ray (1968). The effectiveness of Tennyson's poem as a solo performance piece was recently demonstrated by Kenneth Branagh, who performed "Maud" (under its subtitle "The Madness") at London's Upstream Theatre in 1983. Although the general critical response was mixed, Branagh's performance of the poem did receive some excellent notices.

25. Curry went on to say: "When a man feels that he has something new and original—and who ever met an elocutionist or entertainer who did not feel that way?—he will endeavor to invent a new word for his original art" (1905:15).

2

The One-Person Show
in Early Twentieth-Century America:
Transition from "Platform Performance"
to "Solo Theatre"

The changes in American society and culture during the first fifty years of the twentieth century were profound. Advances in technology, in particular, so transformed the United States by midcentury that the nineteenth century appeared quaint in comparison. The one-person show as a public entertainment medium had to adapt to these societal and cultural changes. The first half of this century is arguably the most fascinating period in the history of the one-person show; during this period Americans saw the birth, expansion, and demise of the tent Chautauqua phenomenon, the reaction against Victorianism, and the rise of the one-person show as a legitimate form of theatre. Two important coinciding phenomena—the death of the tent Chautauqua and the rise of the one-person show form in Broadway theatre—transformed our critical point of view on the one-person show. Our perspective changed from one viewing the genre as a form of entertainment distinct from theatre to one accepting it as integral to theatre.

THE TENT CHAUTAUQUA CIRCUITS

By 1900 the American one-person show as an entertainment medium for Middle America was inextricably tied to the lyceum circuit and the Chautauqua assemblies. These institutions provided the market for professional solo performers, and therefore any changes in the fortunes of those institutions necessarily affected the one-person show as well. The year of 1904, because it marks a major development in the Chautauqua movement, stands as a significant date in the history of the one-person show in America. In *We Called It Culture,* an account of the tent Chautauqua particularly unsympathetic to its originators, the authors state: "The credit—or blame—for devising the Frankenstein mechanism which was both to exalt and to destroy Chautauqua, the tent circuit, must be given to two youths of similar temperament, imagination, and a common driving purpose. That purpose, bluntly, was to 'make a million'" (Case and Case 1948:51).

The ambitious youths who capitalized on Chautauqua's commercial potential were Keith Vawter and Roy J. Ellison. In 1904 the two young men first organized a touring variation of the permanent Chautauqua. This new Chautauqua, abandoning the leisurely study and vacation concept, brought instead a prepackaged week-long program of "uplifting" entertainment into the rural heartland of America. It was the touring Chautauqua, the tent or circuit Chautauqua, that spread wildly across America and popularized the one-person show to an extent far beyond the capabilities of the permanent Chautauqua assemblies or the more urban lyceum.

During his management of the by then venerable Redpath Lyceum Bureau, Vawter realized that his bureau could increase its profits by serving the permanent Chautauqua assemblies. To join him in this new project, Vawter invited his personal friend Ellison, who suggested that they not confine themselves to existing assemblies but persuade other communities to accept their program as well. Together the two men decided that instead of depending on towns that already had an existing assembly and pavilion, their touring Chautauquas would bring with them a circus tent that could house the Chautauqua anywhere. The Redpath Lyceum Bureau, besides handling the winter lyceum circuit, began to manage a summer Chautauqua circuit as well. Melvin H. Miller points out that the new tent Chautauqua was, in effect, a hybrid combining the concepts of the lyceum circuits and the Chautauqua assemblies: "This circuit Chautauqua was a lusty child whose father was the lyceum movement and whose mother was Lake Chautauqua in New York State. As with most children this one was a fascinating composite of good and bad, a child who grew up to have tremendous popularity for a few years and then died suddenly—while its less spectacular but hardier parents lived on" (1984:6). In addition to offering uniform programs of attractions sold to rural communities for consecutive dates in the summer months, the bureau also supplied the equipment and management of all transactions that entered into the building and delivery of such Chautauquas (Orchard 1923:113).

Although Vawter and Ellison were financially unsuccessful in their first attempts to commercialize Chautauqua via the tent circuit, within a few years they enjoyed a resounding triumph. Their stunning success by the summer of 1907 was due to their brilliant business sense: rather than allowing themselves to be dependent on ticket sales, as they originally had done, they contractually transferred the responsibility to the sponsoring community. They sold the tent Chautauqua to a local group "as a duty, a privilege, a consecration of local spirit. They would not talk about profits or financial values to the town but hold fast to uplift, inspiration, and culture" (Case and Case 1948:30). Under the new contracts, Vawter and Ellison still supplied the tents, the equipment, and the prepackaged program of attractions, but the local group fully sponsored the event in advance. The local group-sponsors were then responsible for selling tickets to recoup the expense. The difference between the winter lyceum and the summer tent Chautauqua was this: for the lyceum circuit, attractions were booked individually and no community group was required to underwrite the expense; for the Chautauqua circuit, a sponsoring local group had to guarantee the cost in advance and accept, without substitutions or individual choice, the program of attractions offered by the management. The new policy allowed Chautauqua to become big business; it also contained the reason for its own collapse. Because the communities were offered no choice in attractions, they had no protection from receiving inferior presentations. The policy ultimately worked against the Chautauqua managers: "[T]hey [the sponsors] must either take all or none; and when a sufficient number of communities concluded simultaneously to take none— as they did in the astounding year following the 'jubilee' year of 1924—Chautauqua [i.e., the tent Chautauqua] was through, finished, destroyed beyond possibility of salvage, since there was no intermediate ground upon which a modified structure could be built" (Case and Case 1948:31).

In 1907, however, the managers of the tent Chautauqua were enjoying the fruits of success. Vawter and Ellison quickly opened new circuits, and their subordinate personnel soon followed their lead and opened circuits of their own. Tent Chautauqua boomed across the nation, and Ellison, after separating from Vawter, launched circuits that went into Canada, Alaska, and New Zealand.

Competition between the new tent Chautauqua and the permanent assemblies was keen. By 1912 the blossoming tent Chautauqua so seriously threatened the permanent Chautauquas—those more faithful reproductions of the original, which had maintained the original premise of vacation and study—that only the New York Chautauqua and a few superior local assemblies were able to continue without capitulating and subscribing to the circuit's seven-day prepackaged slate of attractions. Today, less than twenty independent Chautauquas exist.[1] Frank W. Gunsaulus, a major lecturer at the beginning of the century, began his platform career appearing at the permanent Chautauquas. In 1908 he traveled a long distance to one of these assemblies only to find a small audience and the permanent Chautauqua near bankruptcy. Soon afterwards he met Vawter; the conversation between them is recorded in *We Called It Culture:* " 'You're ruining a splendid movement' Gunsaulus roared at Keith Vawter, whom he met at a railroad junction. 'You're cheapening Chautauqua, breaking it down, replacing it with something what [*sic*] will have neither dignity nor permanence'" (quoted in Case and Case 1948:73). The tent Chautauqua, however, was not to be stopped and even Gunsaulus joined the ranks of platformists appearing before the large crowds under the tents. Chautauqua had become big business—a commercial venture created for the financial profit of its multitude of managers.

While Chautauqua was becoming a major commercial venture, elocution was becoming a part of the American mass culture. Begun in England in the eighteenth century as an academic discipline, the study of elocution was transferred to the American colonies. The reaction against the epidemic of American vernacular speech catapulted elocution, perceived as a corrective to a cultural force. Professional platform readings by celebrities enhanced home reading circles and schoolroom elocutionary lessons by their prestige and glamour. Eventually, amateur readers—many of minimal talent and weak training—became common. The local "elocutionary lady" was a common malady in the small towns of America by the late nineteenth century. Tasteless elocutionary displays afflicted the platforms of the nation. With the demand for public readers increasing with the successive developments of the lyceum, the lyceum bureaus, and the Chautauqua assemblies, elocution became potentially lucrative as a profession. The desire for fame by amateur elocutionists coupled with the lure of monetary gain produced many deleterious results for the field of elocution: it attracted inferior performers to the public platform and spawned one-person entertainments that were little more than oddities; it resulted in the proliferation of quack teachers of elocution with slim background in the field of study; and it inspired the production of heavily illustrated "parlor books" of literature for elocution that were more decorative than substantially educational.[2]

The transformation of elocution into mass culture also resulted in the substitution of literary material by major writers with a plethora of sentimental and trite show pieces by hack writers. In the late 1890s, S. H. Clark, a professor of elocution at the University of Chicago, commented on the decline in the quality of literature used by public readers in the late nineteenth century:

[The elocutionists of the past] probably used a higher class of literature than the elocutionary world, as a whole, does to-day. The reason for this was that there was not the amount of poor literature in those days that we have now, and, consequently, the elocutionists dealt with a higher class of material. But we must remember that the average elocutionist had no real sympathy with good literature, and, consequently, sought out the cheaper and more catchy kind, until to-day the elocution world is flooded with cheap and meretricious productions that are turned out to supply the demand of so large a number of elocutionists. . . . Another reason why cheap literature is so prevalent on the elocutionary platform to-day is that it is easy for the reader to render, and for the audience to understand. It is palpable, tangible, and therefore meets with a certain amount of success with half-educated audiences. But the latter are

71

no judges of literature, and know still less of the recitational art (1898:77–78).

Clark's words remind us of those of Richard D. Altick, quoted in the preceding chapter, in his comment on the development during the latter half of the Victorian period of a mass-market literature "shrewdly attuned to the unsophisticated tastes and limited capacities" of the semiliterate populace (1973:241).

Elocution, by the turn of the century, had become a fad, a product (and victim) of the rising mass culture. Harry P. Harrison said of the elocutionary "plague" of the late Victorian age:

Elocution became a plague. No community was immune, but it was the small town that succumbed most quickly. Nightly in Odd Fellows' hall all over America the boy stood on the burning deck and women wept, unashamed, over the death of little Nell. Elocutionists wrecked the *Hesperus,* spared every gray hair on Barbara Frietchie's head, charged with the Light Brigade, rode with Paul Revere, came down like the wolf on the fold and glowered at the Turk, who in guarded tent dreamed darkly of the hour. *Thanatopsis* reached epidemic proportions (1958:191).

The popularization of elocution ultimately lead to its denigration as a serious academic discipline. Vawter and Ellison contributed to this outcome inadvertently by commercializing Chautauqua, the major market for elocutionists.

By 1910 the tent circuits were flourishing. The growing ranks of eager managers, displaying "our common American propensity for equating bigness with excellence" (Gould 1961:86), constantly strove to increase their territories in order to increase their profits. In doing so, they caused the demand to exceed the supply of available superior platform artists. Along with the increasing demand, the exhausting rigors of touring in the American hinterland and the low pay for platform readers finally drove away the best talent (Case and Case 1948:143). Yet to attribute the one-person show's fall from public favor simply to the inferior solo performers on the tent circuit would be simplistic. Although not among the nation's best, these performers were not uniformly devoid of talent. They were simply performers who had, as one scholar explained, "just emerged from the status of amateurs and not yet won their spurs on the professional stage" (Noffsinger

1926:117). It was a combination of forces within and without the field of solo performance that brought an end to the golden age of one-person shows. However, the negative side effects of the commercialization of elocution and the overexpansions of the tent Chautauqua were chief among these forces.

THE REACTION AGAINST VICTORIANISM

The breakdown of Victorianism in the United States during the early decades of the twentieth century was part of a major cultural upheaval appropriately termed by Henry F. May "the end of American innocence."

Everybody knows that at some point in the twentieth century America went through a cultural revolution. One has only to glance at the family photograph album, or to pick up a book or magazine dated, say, 1907, to find oneself in a completely vanished world. One side of some historical boundary lies the America of Theodore Roosevelt and William Jennings Bryan, of Chautauqua and Billy Sunday and municipal crusades, a world so foreign, so seemingly simple, that we sometimes tend, foolishly enough, to find it comical. On the other side of the barrier lies our own time, a time of fearful issues and drastic divisions, a time surely including the Jazz Age, the great depression, the New Deal, the atom bomb. Clearly on one side of this line lie Booth Tarkington and O. Henry and the American Winston Churchill, and also, we should not forget, Henry James. Clearly on our side lie Ernest Hemingway, Thomas Stearns Eliot, and also the writers of television advertising. At some point, if not an instantaneous upheaval, there must have been a notable quickening of the pace of change, a period when things began to move so fast that the past, from then on, looked static (May 1959: ix).

The 1920s are a time remembered for wild iconoclasm, speakeasies, rotgut, frantic college antics, cigarette smoking, sensual dancing, and the Lost Generation. Any montage of the decade must be scored with the hedonistic music that gave the decade its name—jazz, a music denying the traditions of classical and romantic European masters, a music that elders feared would seduce their young people into hopeless sensuality. The Roaring Twenties meant that anything Victorian was stodgey, dated, and ridiculously old-fashioned. The new women's fashions alone—the bobbed hairstyles, the short, waistless dresses, the bright makeup, the uncorseted torsos, the rolled-down stockings—were scandalous and showed a major break with the genteel past. If images alone could demonstrate the different sensibilities of two periods, we would need nothing more to contrast the pre–First World War and postwar periods than their respective ideals of feminine beauty, the Gibson Girl and the Flapper. The 1920s were clearly a time of great change. What had happened to Victorian America? The process of the disintegration of Victorian values is ably described by Stanley Coben:

Confidence in Victorianism eroded primarily as a result of continuous attacks on its conceptual foundations by academic and literary intellectuals—attacks which reached full force in the 1920's. This insidious criticism of the Victorian ethos diminished the conviction with which its formidable superstructure of institutions and behavior patterns had been defended, leaving them more vulnerable to onslaughts by minority groups (1976:161).

Although the 1920s marked the high tide of anti-Victorianism, the origins of the reaction may be traced back as far as the last quarter of the nineteenth century. By 1870 America as well as England had past the high noon of the Victorian age. What W. L. Burn called "The Age of Equipoise" in reference to Britain was over. "From the seventies [1870s] onward," writes Richard D. Altick, "a strong tide set in against the confident orthodoxies of the mid-Victorian period" (1973:300). The trend gained momentum in the 1890s—the Gay Nineties—which were marked by changing mores in correct social behavior among polite society. John Higham ably describes the loosening of Victorianism during the last decade of the nineteenth century:

It was everywhere a hunger to break out of the frustrations, the routine, and the sheer dullness of an urban-industrial culture. It was everywhere an urge to be young, masculine, and adventurous. In the 1890's the new, activist mood was only beginning to challenge the restraint and decorum of the "Gilded Age." . . . Yet the dynamism that characterized the whole political and social scene from the turn of the century through World War I emerged during the 1890's in large areas of popular culture . . . a boom in sports and recreation; a revitalized interest in untamed nature; a quickening of popular music; an unsettling of the condition of women (1965:79–80).

Attendance at vaudeville houses, as we have already seen, became an acceptable leisure activity of the respectable middle class during the last decade of the nineteenth century. The acceptance of vaudeville was symptomatic of the "growth of public nightlife starting in the 1890s [which] accompanied the decline of Victorianism" (Erenberg 1981:xii).

After the turn of the century, the whole atmosphere of the era was "electric with an exultant and slightly selfconscious sense of liberation—liberation, that is, from the stuffiness, the obscurantism, the false verities, the repressions and taboos now attributed, fairly or not, to the Victorian mind" (Altick 1973:301). This liberation manifested itself in many forms: the "new woman," the "new drama," the "new poetry," and the "new art." All of these forms of liberation chipped away at the Victorian culture long before the Archduke Franz Ferdinand of Austria-Hungary was shot in Sarajevo. Of America on the eve of the Great War, Henry F. May wrote: "[In] the few years just before the impact of the war on America ... [w]e can see the massive walls of nineteenth-century America still apparently intact, and then turn our spotlight on many different kinds of people cheerfully laying dynamite in the hidden cracks" (1959:xi). Stanley Coben in his analysis of the disintegration of Victorian values refines May's metaphor for the effort of anti-Victorian intellectuals. "Their accomplishment," said Coben, "resembled more closely the role of termites which irreversibly weaken a structure which then suffers irresistible pressure" (1976:161).

The World War of 1914–18 was a devastating experience for the American people bred on optimism, earnestness, and a belief in the established institutions. The idealism of going to war to make the world safe for democracy was disillusioned by the realities of modern warfare and the selfishness of the European victors over the spoils at the treaties of Paris. Speaking of the effect of the World War, Edward Robb Ellis wrote:

The war altered the consciousness of all mankind. Most people had assumed that the world was rational, but an entire world at war was obviously a world gone mad. Most had considered man reasonable, but the war demonstrated that passions are stronger than reason. Whatever their religion, most people had believed God to be a just deity, but the slaughter was so senseless that God Himself became a casualty of war. Progress was not inevitable, after all. Peace was not permanent. The perfectability of man was brought into question (1975:479).

The old order of Europe—everything representing permanence, tradition, and the highest achievement of Western civilization— was swept away. Disillusionment followed along with a bitter recognition of the folly, complacency, and myopia of the older generation—the Victorians—who were still in positions of power and, thus, held responsible for the catastrophe. During the last months of the war, Lytton Strachey's *Eminent Victorians* was published. The book, an iconoclastic biography of four representatives of Victorian culture (Cardinal Manning, Dr. Arnold, Florence Nightingale, and General Gordon), epitomized "this intensified feeling of betrayal [and] ushered in the most virulent phase of anti-Victorianism" (Altick 1973:302). As Altick explained, Strachey's mode of debunking biography became extremely popular, inspiring imitators in England and the United States, and "every time its subject was a Victorian eminence such as Tennyson, Matthew Arnold, and Disraeli the period's reputation sank still lower" (1973:303).

Literary tastes of the era rejected the Anglo-American nineteenth-century tradition of mellifluous verse. " 'Noble thoughts,' neat little uplift labels wrapped in the tinfoil of pretty verse," commented Amy Lowell, "have their place in the scheme of existence, no doubt, but to the modern poet it is anathema. . . . [F]or people who like to be drugged with fine, conventional sentiments there is no cure in heaven or earth, that I am aware of" (1918:125). The major poets of the period, Ezra Pound and T. S. Eliot, established a difficult and obscure poetry removed from the bourgeoisie. Esoteric and dense, the modern poetry was hardly suited for platform declamation for a general middle-class audience. Modern art likewise renounced conventional ideals of beauty and became unintelligible to the general public. The divisions between high culture and mass culture became firmly established.

The social scientists of the 1920s proved even more effective in undermining Victorian doctrines.[3] Throughout the decade, study after study by various scholars exposed as myths the beliefs upon which the Victorian W.A.S.P. society was based. "Probably the most significant achievement of the academic intellectuals," argues Stanley Coben, "was their crucial role in the nearly complete repudiation of every scientific rationale for racism" (1976:166). Victorianism, thus diminished by the intellectuals (as well as by the literati and the artists), was attacked by the minority groups—particularly blacks and women—who fought for equality within a reorganized system. Eventually such movements, supported by the recent influx of non–Anglo-Saxon immigrants, reduced British-Americans, the chief bearers of Victorian culture, to just another—albeit powerful—minority. In turn, the anti-Victorian activities resulted in reactionary movements by the supporters of the old system. Most violent was the resurgence of the Ku Klux Klan, whose motive was to protect the good, old-fashioned values against the dangerous and corrupting tides of liberalism. Any such reactionary movements—so counter to the new social realities of a culturally diverse American—was doomed to failure: "The Klan and its upper-class counterparts had attempted to protect the dominance of Victorian culture in America. Their efforts foundered primarily for two reasons: potent groups within U.S. society rebelled against basic Victorian culture patterns, and the defenders themselves, hounded by intellectuals and faced with empirical evidence of societal change, lost much of their own confidence in the validity of the Victorian ethos" (Coben 1976:180).

America's transformation in the early twentieth century from a strongly predominantly W.A.S.P. nation to one of ethnic diversity resulted in indelible changes in the culture of the country. Such changes were particularly felt in the areas of language and speech. The migration of blacks to the northern cities, the influx of non–Anglo-Saxon immigrants, and the resultant growing numbers and increasing diversity of high school and college populations demanded the "democratization," to use Daniel J. Boorstin's term, of American education. Increasingly, students came from homes neither using standard English nor supporting the values of a liberal education. Concurrent with these social changes, the new science of linguistics, which focused on the usage of spoken form, denigrated the traditional methods of teaching English by standard rules of grammar in favor of new methods of advancing the descriptive view of language as it was actually spoken. "This new attitude toward language," declared Boorstin, "carried contempt for the grammarians' knowledge, which was now labeled superstition" (1973:457). The full effects on the teaching of language in American public schools and colleges were not felt until midcentury, but the necessary groundwork for pedagogical changes was developing throughout the preceding decades.

More quickly felt in the classroom were the changes in the teaching of speech. Elocution, a study devoted to the standardization of American speech—and in effect devoted on a greater scale to the assimilation of variant speech patterns into the American W.A.S.P. mainstream—was as doomed as the Klan's efforts in suppressing social realities and cultural pluralism. "[T]he irrepressible heterogenity of American culture," wrote Mary Strine, "especially the diversity of growing minority populations, made standardized elocutionary expression appear stilted or artificial, or worse, aligned politically with restrictive middle-class cultural values" (1983:525). Elocution, faced with a modern literature unsuited to declamatory performances on one hand and a new diverse society on the other, ultimately subdivided into specialized fields now broadly classified under the umbrella term *communications*. The two descendents of elocution most closely involved with delivery skills—public address and oral interpretation—moved into distinct areas.

Public address no longer adhered to classic standards of eloquence and instead aimed "to help students learn to 'relax' before an audience, and tried to give them a better understanding of the audience's point of view" (Boorstin 1973:466). Boorstin commented on the new position of speech education: "The shift in focus was dramatic: from the models and standards of 'eloquence' and 'oratory' to the person and his problems, from 'elocution' and 'declamation' to self-improvement and personal success" (1973:467).

Oral interpretation (or simply "interpretation") was even more directly a descendent of elocution than was public address. Major elocution teachers of the late nineteenth century, embarrassed by the mechanical excesses of poorly trained elocutionary entertainers and intrigued by the new discoveries in the area of psychology, shifted the field's emphasis away from performer training towards the psychology of expression and text analysis. Among the most influential in the movement away from the Victorian elocution were Samuel Silas Curry, whose school of Expression in Boston and fourteen books helped shape the next generation of leaders in speech education, and Solomon Henry Clark.[4]

Clark, a talented and inspiring reader as well as teacher,[5] served on the faculty of the University of Chicago and as head of the New York Chautauqua Assembly's School of Expression (the term *elocution* was dropped, significantly, in 1894 when Clark assumed the post once filled by Robert McLean Cumnock). Influenced, perhaps, by the spirit of renewal and transformation that pervaded American culture in the 1890s and lead to the rhetoric of the "new art," the "new woman," the "new poetry," etc., S. H. Clark was an outspoken advocate for what he termed "The New Elocution." He delivered addresses by that title at the Chautauqua Assembly and at the National Association of Elocutionists in which he clarified the distinctions between the old-style elocution and the new. His words accurately predicted the direction the field of elocution would take: "What does the new elocution claim to be? First, not merely an accomplishment; second, it is truly educative. It aims to develop self-expression. It aims to make of its students ministers of literature, extempore speakers, public orators, and I repeat, lastly and only incidentally, does it aim to make entertainers of its students" (1895:2).[6] Twenty years later, when Clark published his text *Interpretation of the Printed Page*, he continued the shift in emphasis away from performance toward the study of literature: "To conclude then: expression is good, valuable, but it must be the natural, spontaneous response to an impression. *Elocution, or expression, or vocal interpretation, whatever it may be called, is not the goal of the reading lesson....* Beautiful as is the adequate vocal interpretation of literature, it is of infinitesimally less worth in a system of education than the ability to interpret silently" (1915:14).[7]

The shift away from performance as an end, as seen in Clark's writings, was characteristic of the field of elocution as a whole. The shift was reflected in the change in nomenclature that the field underwent during the first two decades of the twentieth century:

from "elocution" to "expression" to variations of "oral interpretation." Clark's philosophy was formed in reaction against the elocutionary excesses that "plagued" America in the later portion of the nineteenth century and the beginning of the twentieth century. In his memoir of his father, Barrett H. Clark explained Clark's disgust with extravagant elocutionary display:

From the earliest days of his teaching career up to the very end, the destructive part of his mission may be accurately described as the debunking of Elocution. Before his time, the art of reading was evidently a sort of combination of pantomime and acting. Elocution, recitation—whatever you choose to call it—was one of the more profitable forms of faking. Curly-headed young men and simpering ladies would take a few lessons in "voice" and gesture, memorize narrative "poems," join a Lyceum Bureau and with no brains and little personality become elocutionists. The type is of course not yet entirely extinct, but when my father began reading, it prevailed from coast to coast. Against the stupidity and insipidity of this class of entertainer my father set forth resolutely to do battle, first by his own example, and then as a teacher. . . .

A reader must first know what he is doing: appearance, voice, diction, and the rest, are mere details. My father always squirmed when anyone told him he had a good voice or an imposing platform manner (1928:11).

The significance of the movement from elocution to oral interpretation (and all the inherent attitudinal changes) for the professional one-person show was profound. The changes meant that would-be professional solo performers were no longer trained in a field devoted to solo performance. Their training as performers now had to come from theatre schools, which were primarily focused on the ensemble production of dramatic scripts. Since the 1920s the professional solo performer has usually been self-trained or has come from a background in acting in ensemble play productions.

ENTERTAINMENTS ON THE TENT CHAUTAUQUA CIRCUITS

The tent Chautauqua offered rural audiences programs of remarkable variety. One week's slate of events often included not only the lecturers, music concerts, and platform readers—all of which had been common at permanent assemblies—but also boasted such disparate entertainments as Swiss yodelers, jugglers, and bellringers. In their drive to contract patrons year after year, the Chautauqua managers often appealed to the audiences' desire for novelty and booked acts that cannot even by the most extreme measure be considered cultural or educational. The shift away from culture and education to amusement is typically noted with a tone of condescension by scholars in Chautauqua studies. Valid arguments have been made against such elitist attitudes towards popular entertainments.[8] However, value judgments are difficult to avoid as we watch the Chautauqua programs gradually move away from events of artistic and intellectual merit to those of simple diversion.

As the overall programs of the Chautauqua circuits changed during the first decades of the twentieth century, so did the platform readings. The movement towards theatricality in platform performances was slow in developing but eventually it left an indelible mark on Chautauqua.

Changes in the kind of solo readings presented on the Chautauqua platforms were already occurring before Vawter and Ellison were even out of childhood. As early as the 1880s Helen Potter appeared at the Chautauqua Assembly in her solo impersonations of Talmage, Gough, and Susan B. Anthony. In the next decade Leland Powers presented solo performances utilizing full characterization at Chautauqua. Along with Potter and Powers came other performers imitating their innovations in theatricality. Theatrical one-person shows proved to have a great impact on Chautauqua attitudes in the years ahead.

A popular follower of Leland Powers's style of performance was Montaville Flowers, whose "manner was sophisticated; his 'lightening changes' were of voice and facial expression, never of costume. He wore white tie and tails, whether he was impersonating the melancholy Hamlet or Barbara Frietchie" (Harrison 1958:193). Flowers appeared at the Chautauqua Assembly and was active on the lyceum and tent Chautauqua circuits. His performance masterpiece was a full evening of General Lew Wallace's *Ben Hur*, in which we are told Flowers "took all the parts, except the horses" (Harrison 1958:194). Platform performances that emphasized strong characterization could be traced back from Flowers to Powers and to Dickens and Charles Mathews. Therefore, highly defined characterizations in platform readings were hardly new when the tent circuits exploded across America. What was new was the growing number of performers who adopted this style of performance and the Chautauqua audiences' acceptance of it.

Why did Chautauqua performances move closer and closer toward theatricalization? The answer lies in the breakdown of the Victorian intolerance for the theatre and the theatrical. When the nontheatregoing Chautauqua audiences at the turn of the century saw before them a platform performance that approached the theatrical, their general reaction was one of fascination and delight rather than righteous indignation. The performances received a warm reception, the managers recognized a profitable commodity, and the performers were encouraged to pursue further theatricalization in their platform readings. Eventually two schools of thought on platform art developed, one composed primarily of academics such as S. H. Clark, who stressed restrained readings, and the other primarily composed of public entertainers who preferred the more theatrical performances. Gay MacLaren, a Chautauqua performer during the height of the tent circuits, described the conflicts between the two kinds of platform performers in *Morally We Roll Along:*

A warfare now sprang up between these two cults. The impersonators, as the erstwhile elocutionists were called, were frowned upon by the new "exponents of the spoken word." Schools "broke out" all over the country dedicated to the study of the new "platform art," and the classroom debated solemnly whether to act or not to act. The Speech Arts Convention met each year and gravely denounced these cheap shysters who "over-stepped the bounds of the profession by resorting to acting."

Simmered down to fundamentals, the controversy resolved itself into simply this: those who could act believed in acting; those who could not were "agin" it (1938:49–50).

William Sterling Battis, "another performer who helped it [Chautauqua] turn the corner from elocution to conventional play acting," clearly favored theatrical performances (Harrison 1958:197). Battis advertised himself as "The Dickens Man" and presented, in costume, monologue adaptations of Dickens's novels and stories. Harrison spoke of Battis's performances:

Battis brought out his Dickens props and bag of tricks and laid them on a table for all to see—a walking stick, a large white bonnet and a linen duster. He wore the shawl to give the illusion of costume changes, over his head for Little Nell, high around his ears for Bob Cratchit, tight over the shoulders for Fagin. In the role of Sydney Carton, he slipped into the duster, letting it hang loosely about his upright figure as he lifted his left foot to a small box, presumably to mount the guillotine, while his clear, trained voice declaimed the "far, far better thing" (Harrison 1958:197).

As well as his Dickens performances, Battis offered lectures on the lyceum and Chautauqua circuits, such as "Dickens as a Reformer," "Dickens as a Humorist," "Dickens' Schools," and "Dickens' Child Studies" (Wright 1906:64). Battis, however, first and foremost "*was* an actor and an English gentleman; not an elocutionist, not a reader, but an actor, body and soul" (Harrison 1958:197).

Even writers were not immune to the temptations of adding theatrical elements to their platform performances. Two successful writer-performers of the tent Chautauqua were Carl Sandburg and Lew Sarett, twentieth-century inheritors of "the poet-performer movement," a tradition of poets who were public performers and whose verse was decidedly an *oral* expression. Like the writings of the vernacular platform humorists, the majority of the verse of the poet-performers does not stand up to traditional literary criticism. Paul H. Gray cautions that the writings of the poet-performers must be judged as "literature in performance, rather than literature in print" (1984:9). Although Gray speaks specifically for one poet-performer, James Whitcomb Riley, his words apply to all the poets in the movement.[9] Traditional literary standards, writes Gray, "force Riley's poems into a genre for which they were never intended, relate them to an audience Riley had no interest in, and assume a purpose for them he never conceived" (1984:9).

The poets of the platform were gifted entertainers and their wide popularity as writers among common people (as opposed to the literati) during their lives was contingent on their ability as performers. "Success within the movement," continues Gray, "depended as much on the poet's ability to perform his work as to write it, and the poet's publishing career often *followed* his fame on the reading platform" (1984:1). Other poet-performers belonging to this tradition include Will Carleton, Vachel Lindsay, Eugene Field, and Edgar Guest. The verse produced by the poet-performers "was self-consciously and deliberately 'low-brow,' seeking a following among neither the readers nor writers of traditional poetry. Instead, it aimed unerringly at the *petite bourgeoisie*—farmers, merchants, salesman, and housewives—people who claimed they hated poetry but flocked by the thousands to hear these poets perform and then bought their books by the millions" (Gray 1984:1).

Sandburg and Sarett, both managed by the J. B. Pond Lyceum Bureau, often toured together in a joint program much like Mark Twain and George W. Cable had done. Advertisements for the Sandburg/Sarett program billed the two writers as "The Poet of the City" and "The Poet of the Wilderness," respectively, in "A Joint Lecture and Recital From Their Own Writings." [10] The Pond management joined the two poets together in one program for the first time in 1916 because both men were new to the Chautauqua circuits (Hansen 1923:267–68). The venture proved successful and was continued for several seasons afterward. The contrast in personalities and performance styles, as well as the complementary nature of their material, reportedly made for a dynamic program:

Dressed in woodsman costume Sarett sang the love songs of the Chippewas, bellowed the call of the moose and repeated the chants of the medicine men. Some survival of the primitive hates and loves and passions vibrated through the audience as they listened to this eloquent, fiery singer and his drum. Then came the more deliberate slow-spoken, deeptone Sandburg. Poems about men and women toiling in mean streets, of life in the by-ways of the city, displaced poems of the wilderness, of the natives, of the beasts and birds and good and evil spirits of the hills. That was a program to talk about, a rich study in contrasting moods (Hansen 1923:268).

Sarett was the more flamboyant performer of the two. Often appearing in full American Indian dress, he not only recited his poetry, but "held his audience from start to finish . . . with his wonderful tales of woodland lore and his interpretation of animal howls, bird calls, etc. was well nigh the real thing. He danced the Indian dances and impersonated them at their powpows. He told his own life story, and its touching incidents brought tears to the eyes of his listeners. He spoke from the heart and those who heard him felt well repaid for coming" (review of Sarett's performance, [Williston, ND] *Herald*, 1 Aug. 1918. In box 8, Lew Sarett Papers).

Sandburg's performances were subdued in comparison. Instead of the high energy and overt theatricality of Sarett, Sandburg cultivated an informal and relaxed stage presence. The apparent folksy carelessness of his performances, however, was actually deliberately calculated. One Sandburg devotee stood with the poet-performer just before going on stage at Bates College in Lewiston, Maine. "I noted that before going on the stage," remembered this particular observer, "Mr. Sandburg carefully disarranged his hair" (quoted in Sutton 1979:215).

After several years of performing on the Chautauqua circuits, Sandburg incorporated singing and guitar playing into his lecture-recitals. An account of Sandburg's debut as a folksinger in 1920 appears in Harry Golden's biography of the poet:

[A]fter a lecture at Cornell College, Iowa, Carl suddenly dug out a guitar from behind the lectern and said, "I will now sing a few folk songs that somehow tie into the folk quality I have tried to get into my verse. If you don't care for them and want to leave the hall it will be all right with me. I'll only be doing what I'd be doing if I were home, anyway." . . .
The audience stayed, liking the songs as well as the poems and since [that] day Carl's singing has been part of every program (1961:79).

The addition of folk songs and guitar playing theatricalized Sandburg's lecture-recitals and became a popular feature of his performances from 1920 onward.[11] Carl Sandburg continued to perform long after the demise of the tent circuits, delighting audiences at universities and colleges.

Many Chautauqua and lyceum performers of the 1900s and 1910s incorporated theatrical elements into their "readings."

Among the most popular were Benjamin Chapin, who was known for years for his dramatic monologue version of his play *Lincoln,* Sidney Landon, Jessie Rae Taylor, and Elias Day.[12] One Chautauqua performer, Mrs. M. C. Hutchinson, who presented full-length solo versions of *Rebecca of Sunnybrook Farm* and *The Importance of Being Earnest,* reportedly "astounded and delighted the audience by changing her voice, making love to herself, responding, breaking in as a great blustering villain, resuming as a mild shrinking maid, creating and maintaining the illusion to the last curtain—and finally taking her bow, alone, on behalf of 'the entire cast'" (Case and Case 1948:54). More and more Chautauqua-lyceum performers developed full-length programs comprised of solo adaptations of popular plays or dramatized novels. As early as 1902, a *Talent* editorial remarked that "the day of reading short selections has largely passed away."[13] The miscellaneous literary readings of the early days of the Chautauqua had become one-actor dramas. The term *readings,* in fact, no longer accurately described these performances events. Although the term is obscure, *monopolylogue* best defines the solo performances of the later Chautauqua era; they were entertainments in which a single performer sustained many characters. Although the form may initially strike us as strange, contemporary monopolylogues exist today and continue to delight audiences if only for the sheer technical virtuosity of the lone performer. *Charles Busch and His Cast of Thousands,* a contemporary performance, is in form a classic monopolylogue. As for Chautauqua, the development of the one-actor dramas—along with the use of costuming, make-up, and full characterization—moved the conservative and righteous audiences ever closer to a complete acceptance of the theatre.

The End of the Victorian Intolerance for the Theatre: Drama at Chautauqua

As Victorianism loosened its constraints on American culture, various leisure pursuits that had heretofore been considered inappropriate for the genteel classes became acceptable. Among the newly embraced activities was the attendance of the theatre. Theatrical one-person shows had become specialties of the Chautauqua and lyceum during the early years of the twentieth century. They were, wrote the Cases, "an astounding phenomenon to the audience and highly satisfactory to the manager, since these one-man prodigies saved the expense of a full troupe of a dozen or more" (1954:54). As the century progressed, audiences proved so responsive to theatrical one-person shows that the managers, in their ever-present desire to exploit popular taste, started offering full-play productions.

First came the impersonators and the dramatic readers. Who could object to them? Then came lecturers reading extracts from great plays in resounding, musical, frightening voices. This was still above reproach, but with each passing season the dramatic offering—always reflecting an increasing public demand—came closer to the crumbling walls of prejudice. Soon there were bits of opera and Shakespearean excerpts; and finally, without squirming, Chautauqua audiences were sitting through a real play in which up to a dozen actors appeared, and the curtain actually rose and fell between acts. The conscience of the most devout churchgoer was soothed by the fact that this was Chautauqua—the lofty principle, the well-sponsored—and by the further fact that the minister on the bench at the right, and the deacon's wife up front, who had also bought season tickets, were laughing as heartily as the unwashed flock. . . . First the impersonator, then the play reader, and finally the one-man or one-woman complete plays—these were the successive steps whereby the stage reached the corn belt (Case and Case 1948:52–55).

The professional performers, of course, went along with the tide of popular opinion and moved headlong into full-play productions. Many of the Chautauqua so-called readers and elocutionists were actually actors who had been billed under different titles to appear respectable to Middle America with its Victorian intolerance for the theatre. As suggested earlier, that Victorian sensibility was being slowly swept away in the early years of the new century. The process was actually aided by those very products of High Victorianism: the lyceum and Chautauqua. It was the one-person show, by experimenting with theatricality, that dissolved the middle-class prejudice against the theatre in rural America. In doing so, it committed a kind of professional suicide. It had destroyed the major reason for its being and, along with that, its public vogue.

While these changes were occurring across America on the lyceum and tent Chautauqua circuits, similar changes were seen at the original assembly. In 1907 George E. Vincent, son of the institution's cofounder, became its president. Unlike his father and the previous generation, young Vincent was never opposed to the theatre. In fact, while at Yale, George E. Vincent was attracted to the stage and wanted to participate in college productions. The differences in opinion between the father and son caused tension in their relationship. John Heyl Vincent wrote to his son, requesting that he refrain from pursuing his theatrical ambitions until after reaching his majority: "In everything about which there is no question I try to stand by you and give you opportunities for pleasure. And I should appreciate it very much if you would stand by me until you are twenty-one, even if you do not look at things as I do. When you are twenty-one you must decide for yourself and I shall have nothing further to say" (Vincent 1925:251). The future permitted young Vincent to fulfill his interest in the theatre. Years later, as the Chautauqua's president, George E. Vincent was instrumental in bringing the theatre to the Chautauqua Institution. He expressed his belief in the benefits of educational theatre in "University Extension Drama," an essay that appeared in *The Chautauquan* in 1913. Young Vincent's sensitivity to the Chautauquans' slow acceptance of theatre manifested itself in the essay's last paragraph; here Vincent seems to be calming the fears of those more conservative: "The whole history of the drama shows how important a part it has played in the development of civilization, and there is no reason to believe that it may not *under proper guidance and influences* continue to be a most important factor in the cultural development of the United States" (Vincent 1913:120, emphasis added).

As early as 1904, the New York Chautauqua presented Ben Jonson's masque *The Sad Shepherd;* by 1910 a visiting company was performing the plays of Shakespeare.[14] And by 1913 opera (Sullivan's *Golden Legend*) was being offered, along with Mrs. Maud Miner's solo performances of Beaumarchais's *Barber of Seville* and Moliere's *Miser*. Lectures that same summer included Prof. Richard Burton's "Plays, Pleasant and Unpleasant" and

"The Meaning of Plays" ("Program of the Fortieth Assembly" 1913).

The trend once begun gained momentum and further accelerated with the profound societal changes sped on by World War I. The Victorian intolerance for the stage, already weakened, fully dissolved after the Great War. Arthur William Row, a Chautauqua actor, wrote his personal account of Chautauqua's acceptance of theatre in the postwar years:

The actor in a Chautauqua program is a comparative novelty, in fact only a few years ago the idea was treated with utmost scorn by the powers that rule the 100 per cent American institution that is known as Chautauqua. Actors are born and trained to entertain, but for some inscrutable reason the combination of actors and Chautauqua was deemed impossible and something not to be considered. . . .

Lecturers, soloists, instrumentalists, conjurers—indeed, nearly all kinds of entertainers had long been current in Chautauqua, but when an actor of my acquaintance attempted to have real plays and actors in Chautauqua he was met by a refusal that lasted for years. Fragmentary bits of entertainment were all right, but a concerted, coherent attempt like a real play was for a long time, strange to say, taboo.

Then the miracle occurred and after endless correspondence and literally years of negotiations a play was interpolated into a Chautauqua program and placed on the circuit. It was an immediate success and the play gradually became what we call in vaudeville, "the feature attraction" and placed at the end of the week's offering, so if there was any doubt in the superintendent's mind if he really was to get his contract for next year—and there usually was—the play proved a veritable piece de resistance and so mesmerized the guarantors by its charm that they placed their august signature to the contract the following year.

Of all forms of entertainment a play is the most vivid and appealing and, what is more, convincing! Chautauqua audiences are the most virgin soil in all America (1925:229–30).

"The drama," acquiesced *The Lyceum Magazine*, "has evidently come to stay at Chautauquas" ("Chautauqua Drama Wanted" 1922:27). Indeed, of all the attractions, the plays—which were typically adaptations of Broadway successes—quickly became the circuits' most popular feature. The use of Broadway drama, however, seemed inappropriate to some Chautauquans. New York City represented the antithesis of Chautauqua ideals and published appeals were made to compose drama specifically for Chautauqua:

> The announcement that we are going to try to get plays written specially for the platform instead of plays written for Broadway is certainly cheering. . . . However good they may be, these plays were written for a different kind of audience. . . . The Broadway plays have few or no moral standards. The atmosphere of the hero must be luxury. Broadway cannot think of a hero that doesn't get rich. Let us have a chautauqua drama now and then with a hero that stays poor. . . . Surely America needs such heroes. Broadway heroes win too easily. There is not enough struggle ("Chautauqua Drama Wanted" 1922:27).

The saga of Chautauqua's slow acceptance of the theatre reached its climax in 1929. In that year, the Chautauqua Institution opened Norton Memorial Hall, a theatre "complete with stage equipment." From that date onward, "plays and operas became an established part of the Chautauqua scene" (Bestor 1934:13).[15]

THE COLLAPSE OF THE TENT CHAUTAUQUA AND LYCEUM CIRCUITS

The original Chautauqua Institution continued through the 1920s greatly changed but intact. Its dedication to quality, its ability to adapt to current public needs, and its nonprofit philosophy helped it weather many cultural changes. The decade of the 1920s, however, was a watershed for the tent Chautauqua and the lyceum circuits. Rot from within and pressures from without rapidly caused disintegration. Throughout the postwar years, various publications commented on the developing trouble signs for the once-thriving circuits. In *Correspondence Schools, Lyceums, Chautauquas* John S. Noffsinger described the "Modern Lyceum" and the "Modern Chautauqua." By the 1920s, both, according to Noffsinger, were wallowing in "hokum":

> In short, the popular Lyceum is as the popular magazine—it gives the public what the public wants or is conventionally supposed to want, that is, supposed by those who make a profit out of giving it just that. . . .
> The weakness of the modern Lyceum is that it is a purely commercial venture. Nothing is even attempted that is not sure to yield a profit,

which means that the old, old devices to win popularity are resorted to, the old, old change rung—that hokum, in theatrical slang, is the stable provender (1926:118).

In general, what was said of the Lyceum program applies equally to the traveling Chautauquas. . . . The Chautauqua gives the public what it thinks the public wants, and the public takes it, which makes money for the Chautauqua and thus spares the Chautauqua any need of conceiving and carrying out a program with more specific gravity. But it is also possible that the public would also be found to want—that is, be willing to pay for—something better. Nobody knows, and certainly the Chautauqua makes no effort to find out (1926:129–30).

The very titles of the articles published about Chautauqua during the 1920s indicate that the decline of the circuits was apparent and that the demise of the movement imminent: "What's Wrong with Chautauqua?" by Anne Suhm Etty (1924); "The Town That Doesn't Want Chautauqua," by Mary Austin (1926); "Other Towns That Do Not Want Chautauqua—and Why," by Edward T. Devine (1926); "After Lyceums and Chautauquas, What?" by Edward C. Lindeman (1927); "Is Chautauqua Worth While?" by Albert E. Wiggam (1927); and "Chautauqua Pro and Contra," by Harry Hibschman (1928).

The causes cited for the demise of the tent Chautauqua vary from article to article, as they do in the later retrospective studies of the movement. Victoria and Robert Case, as seen earlier, suggest (1948) that the reason for the circuits' collapse lies in the very policy set by Vawter and Ellison. Joseph E. Gould agrees with John Noffsinger, stating that, "the once vigorous Chautauqua movement was drowned in a flood of pap" (1961:96). Gould also notes that the Chautauqua managers, in their desire to please their audiences, initiated a control system whereby any topic that was not considered "safe" was avoided. Leonard P. Oliver recently elaborated on this censorship policy: "When the tent Chautauqua bureau managers began in the mid-1920s to avoid the 'great issues' of the day, when they no longer felt comfortable entertaining controversy on the circuit, and when they sought control over the lecturers' texts, they were signaling the end of Chautauqua's vitality as a 'free platform' for ideas. The tents disappeared a few years later" (1984:16). Ultimately the managers' censorship of controversial topics resulted in programs composed of "inspirational lectures" and productions of insipid plays that were, in Gould's words, "innocuous bits of sunshine" (1961:83). Gould concluded one chapter with a fitting statement for 1961, which is even more appropriate today as network television faces increasing competition from private video cassettes, public television, and subscriber television: "The policy-makers for circuit Chautauqua discovered too late, if at all, that attempts to please everyone end by pleasing no one; a discovery that the television networks of our own day have yet to make" (1961:96). A more recent study commented that "[i]n later years of the [Chautauqua] movement, value orientations expressed in the programming became increasingly conservative and in Marxian terminology might be viewed as an opiate that was comforting and reinforced the status quo" (Synder 1985:88).

The causes for the demise of the Chautauqua circuits were complex and varied. Robert A. McCown (1984) cites not only the decreasing quality of the programming as a major cause but also points to the economic difficulties in rural America in the 1920s, the Great Depression of the 1930s, and the changing a social values of the postwar era as significant. McCown explains: "America itself was changing. The small town, the little red schoolhouse, evangelistic Christianity, and William Jennings Bryan were losing their hold as the isolation of the middle border broke down before the onslaught of rural free delivery, mail-order catalogs, hard-surface roads, automobiles and trucks, rural electrification, the telephone, radio, talking motion pictures, golf courses, and summer vacation trips" (1984:39). The social and cultural changes surely reshaped the American use of leisure time and such changes brought their effect on Chautauqua. As Keith Vawter wrote in 1929: "I still insist that the radio did not materially effect lyceum and chautauquas, but rather the advent of Country Clubs and Dancing Mothers" (Keith Vawter, letter to C.A. Peffer et al., 17 Jan. 1929, Keith Vawter Papers).

As the nation changed, the small town, the sponsor and lifeblood of the Chautauqua circuits, was transformed. "As the social life of the American town," wrote David Mead, "became more complex and fragmented, the unity of purpose among its citizens was weakened" (1968:346). The decline of community spirit, a necessary motivating force for local sponsors of the Chautauquas, resulted: "[T]he kind of common effort and community fervor that supported the Chautauqua is rarely observed. Indeed the once-familiar phrase 'community patriotism' has all but lost its meaning in our language. It belonged to a less distracted age, when citizens had a strong sense of community identity rather than the impersonal bond linking them to modern society" (Mead 1968:346).

While the great circuits floundered and fell, Chautauquans realized that an era was coming to a close. The complex reasons for the decline of the circuits, fastidiously analyzed by successive generations of scholars, were succinctly acknowledged by the Chautauqua magazine *Platform World* in one of its last issues:

Chautauqua was a product of the horse and buggy age. It nobly served while there was a need for it. In the days when a person's travel radius was limited to the distance that could be made by horse and buggy Chautauqua was the Big Moment in the life of the community. It was the community cultural center. Under the Brown Tent gathered the good people from several towns. The program was talked about for months. Abuses crept into the system. Selling methods deteriorated. Amusement gradually usurped the place inspiration and education formerly held in many programs. In their eagerness for single admission some bureaus overlooked the fact that contracts were signed by the small cultural group of leaders in each town. These leaders were alienated. They no longer found the features of real and lasting value as in earlier days. They dropped out. Some became definitely antagonistic to the Chautauqua movement. This was especially true among the ministers and school men, who in the early days were Chautauqua's strongest supporters.

Then, to cap the climax, came almost universal good roads, and automobiles everywhere. These were the determining factors in Chautauqua's downfall. No longer were people dependent on their local communities for entertainment and amusement. The lure to the Big Town fifty or even 100 miles away—now easily accessible—was too much. Small town amusement suffered. Then along came the Bogy Man, "D. Pression." He finished the job (Harvey 1933:5).

In 1925, one year after the "jubilee" fiftieth anniversary celebration of the founding of the original assembly at Chautauqua Lake, the true decline of the tent circuits became apparent. Towns nationwide simultaneously failed to renew their Chautauqua contracts; circuits across the country failed; and Vawter and Ellison— with characteristic financial sense—sold what they could and left the business. The few remaining circuits limped on until the early

1930s, when Chautauqua as a tent circuit vanished forever. The lyceum circuit experienced a less startling demise. Instead of experiencing anything comparable to the 1925 collapse of tent Chautauqua, the lyceum continued into the next decades, gradually diminishing, while universities and colleges across the country assumed its function by sponsoring guest lecturers, writers, and performers.

The year 1925 could be considered the end of the golden age of platform performances in America. By the 1930s, the platform performers not only suffered from the competition of play productions and the dissipation of the once prevalent prejudice against the theatre, but had also lost two major nationwide markets. In 1933 came the death knell: *Platform World,* the promotional magazine for platform artists and managers, ceased publication.[16] If the one-person show was to survive as an art form and as a public entertainment medium, it had to adapt to vastly different expectations as a theatrical event than in the 1870s. It also had to seek new avenues of reaching the public. Even the Chautauqua Institution could no longer promise the one-person show high visibility; once the tent circuit closed, the original assembly lost its primary means of publicity and much of its national celebrity. In order to forge a new market and to obtain a widespread acceptance, the one-person show had to use the very modes of education and entertainment that had superseded the Chautauqua and lyceum: theatre, universities, and electronics. In the second quarter of the twentieth century the one-person show began to integrate into these modes and institutions. At the same time there was a change in our critical perspective on the genre of the one-person show, as it moved from "platform performance" to "solo theatre."

The Transition from "Platform Performance" to "Solo Theatre"

The second quarter of the twentieth century was a transition period for the one-person show in the United States. Designating the earlier period as a golden age and a later period as a renaissance risks reducing the intervening years to a dark age. Such an assumption is simply untrue. The years between 1925 and 1950 are not so much a dormant stage as a transitory phase between two flood tides. The Chautauqua and lyceum circuits dissolved during this period, and Broadway increasingly became the center of live theatre in America.

As long as Chautauqua adhered to its antitheatre bias and offered (as substitutes to theatre) one-person shows, it did not compete with Broadway. Broadway was synonymous with the theatre, and although major platformists did perform in New York, the one-person show as a performance genre was more welcome at Chautauqua. When the Chautauqua tent circuits exploded across the country, they initially modeled their offerings on those presented at the original assembly. But once the Chautauqua Institution and the tent circuits turned to play productions, Broadway became their model. The one-person show, in order to regain a nationwide visibility, had to succeed on Broadway. To do so, it had to compete with fully mounted play productions, something that had never been the case in the early days of Chautauqua or the lyceum. On Broadway, the one-person show had to play to a theatregoing audience and so had to face vastly different expectations as a performance event.

The "elocutionists" and "readers" of the late nineteenth century enjoyed the benefits of having a large audience who believed them to be more morally respectable than (and therefore superior to) actors. With such an audience, the one-person show thrived; for it to be considered distinct from theatre was advantageous. However, by the 1920s—the period that marked a violent backlash against anything Victorian—such an audience simply did not exist. The one-person show had, as stated earlier, helped dissolve the prejudice against theatre. In the 1920s an antitheatre attitude, like everything Victorian, was dated and old-fashioned. In the post–World War I era, solo performers were suddenly forced to prove themselves to be as worthy of an audience's time as were a full cast of actors. To be distinct from "real" theatre was now a disadvantage for the performer. To succeed as a professional solo performer in this period required a keen awareness of public taste. (Had Emlyn Williams attempted his solo impersonation of Dickens-on-the-platform during the 1920s and 1930s, it is doubtful that he would have met with great success.) The one-person show did not, however, completely vanish in the interim between its golden age and its renaissance. Solo performers of the period included Cecilia Loftus, Dorothy Sands, Charles Laughton, Ruth Draper, and Cornelia Otis Skinner. Two of these performers, Draper and Skinner, made major contributions to the art of solo performance both as writers and performers. They, perhaps more than any other performers, are responsible for initiating the change in our critical perspective from one that had viewed the one-person show as a "platform performance" to one that accepted it as "solo theatre."

SOLO PERFORMERS, 1920–50

Cecilia (Cissie) Loftus, Dorothy Sands, Ruth Draper, Charles Laughton, and Cornelia Otis Skinner were the major solo performers of the transition period that began after World War I and ended with the one-person show renaissance in the 1950s. Loftus, Sands, Draper, and Skinner each developed solo forms peculiar to their special talents. The combined successes of these four artists made the one-person show genre seem the privilege of women. Charles Laughton, a popular film and stage actor, also made important contributions to the field of solo performances. He may be credited for keeping alive the tradition of professional public readings in the era following the demise of the Chautauqua circuits.

CISSIE LOFTUS

Cissie Loftus began her solo appearance late in her career. Her impersonations of popular singers, comics, music hall and cabaret stars, and legitimate actresses had delighted vaudeville audiences for years and she frequently acted in legitimate plays since her American debut in 1895. Loftus's versatility was remarkable and she had little patience for skeptics who believed that a mimic could not also be a fine dramatic actress: "If it isn't acting, what is it?" Loftus said of her impersonations. "I lose my own identity completely in the impersonation, and what's the difference between impersonating a living person and a character made up by a playwright?" (quoted in Anderson 1938:115). Her impersonations included Yvette Guilbert, Fanny Brice, Beatrice Lillie, Ruth

Draper, Paul Robeson, Pauline Lord, Sarah Bernhardt, and Elean-ora Duse. Yet Loftus was reluctant to present a full-length solo recital of her impersonations. "I can't make an entire evening's entertainment of them [i.e., her impersonations]," declared Loftus, "Therefore they belong in vaudeville" ("Cecilia's Ambition," 12 Feb. 1905, found in Locke scrapbook NAFR v. 313, Billy Rose Theatre Collection). Constant persuasion by her friends, the de-cline of the vaudeville circuits, and dwindling offers from the legit-imate stage finally convinced her to expand her short variety im-personations into a showcase recital. In 1924 Loftus presented a program at the Henry Miller Theatre in New York with Beatrice Herford, a longtime friend and monologuist, who alternated her monologues with Loftus's impersonations. A favorite portion of the program was Loftus's impersonation of Herford.

It was not until 1932 in Chicago that Loftus presented her first one-person show. Despite excellent reviews, Loftus delayed bringing her show to New York. In March 1938 at the Little The-atre, *An Evening with Cecilia Loftus* finally opened in New York. The show included impersonations, folk tales, scenes from plays in which she had acted, an original sketch, and an adapted dia-logue. In October of the same year, Loftus offered New York au-diences *Impressions and Impersonations,* which maintained many of the impersonations of her previous show and substituted others with two monologues. "Miss Loftus has dwelt on the favorites of today and yesterday with impartiality," wrote the *New York Times,* "and to each she brings her amazing variation in voice and facial expression which make for the uncommon verisimilitude of her impersonations" (J.G. 1938:12). Cissie Loftus clearly pos-sessed the requisite talent and versatility demanded of a first-rate solo performer. Yet the brevity of her solo career due to her own reluctance unfortunately dwarfs her accomplishments when com-pared to her great contemporaries Ruth Draper and Cornelia Otis Skinner. Only five years after her New York solo debut, Loftus died on 12 July 1943.

DOROTHY SANDS

Dorothy Sands, like Cissie Loftus, was both mimic and legit-imate actress. Unlike Loftus, however, Sands developed one-person shows relatively early in her career and surpassed her predecessor in her contributions to the art of solo performances. After her graduation from Radcliffe College in 1915, Sands studied at the Curry School of Expression in Boston, which had been founded by the noted elocutionist Samuel Silas Curry; she later served briefly on the faculty. Thus through Sands we have a direct link in the modern era between the academic elocutionary movement and world of professional solo performance.

Sands left the faculty of the Curry School of Expression to pursue a professional career in the theatre. She made her professional debut in the national touring production of *Children of the Moon* in 1923 and her Broadway debut in *Catskill Dutch* in 1924. In December of that year, she joined the Neighborhood Playhouse Repertory, a resident company in New York, where she acted in several plays and on 18 June 1925 made her debut as an impersonator in *The Grand Street Follies*, an annual comedy revue of current Broadway plays. Her work as a mimic in *The Follies* over the next several years prepared Sands for her career as a solo performer.

Encouraged by the reception of her *Follies* impersonations, Sands decided to create a full-length solo program. "Having begun her theatrical profession in an academic setting," wrote Linda S. Long, "Sands took a particular interest in theatrical history, especially acting styles. Her one-woman shows resulted from the merger of these interests with her mimic talents" (1982:20). Whereas her work with *The Follies* always limited Sands to impersonations of contemporary actresses, her one-person shows offered her complete artistic freedom in choosing her subjects. Sands chose broadly and developed showcases, as Long points out, for both her scholarship in theatre history and her talent in impersonation.

Styles in Acting, Sands's first one-person show, was presented by James B. Pond at the Booth Theatre in New York on 3 April 1932. The program was a lecture-recital in which Sands explained the cultural context of period acting styles and demonstrated scenes from plays representative of different historical eras. Beginning with the Restoration, Sands moved from Millament in Congreve's *Way of the World* through the modern period of Shaw's *Candida* and O'Neill's *Anna Christie*, in which she recreated Pauline Lord's performance in the title role. The finale was a sure audience pleaser: Sands performed the sleepwalking scene in *Macbeth* as it might be portrayed by Haidee Wright, Ethel Barrymore, and "that sulphurous phenomenon" Mae West (Atkinson 1933:20). Of her debut as a solo performer, Brooks Atkinson wrote:

> To the select company of one-woman theatres now add the name of Dorothy Sands. . . . [Sands] is an extraordinary person. She has not only a student's knowledge of the whole course of the theatre, but also a vast enthusiasm for acting, and everything she does is inspired by humorous intelligence. To many of us her portfolio in "Styles in Acting" is the most vivid sort of theatre history in existence. Out of the theatre's mute memorabilia, Miss Sands, who is a modernist, has brought romantic history to life (1932:13).

Sands followed *Styles in Acting* with *Our Stage and Stars* in 1933, another lecture-recital similar in format to her first one-person show. For this second performance, Sands exclusively focused on American theatre history, moving from a 1787 comedy, *The Contrast*, through scenes representing the frontier theatre, the theatre of the gold rush and mining camps, the romantic theatre of the late 1800s, vaudeville, and realism. The show also concluded with a popular finale: a study in comparisons and contrasts of film character types: "Ingenues—Now and Then" (Helen Hayes and Mary Pickford), and "Vampires—Now and Then" (Greta Garbo and Theda Bara). To re-create the theatre stars and acting styles of previous generations, Sands moved beyond personal observation and had to rely on her research and descriptions by other people who had actually seen the stars of the past. With *Our Stage and Stars* Dorothy Sands confirmed her newly established position as one of America's foremost solo performers. In his review of Sands's second one-person show, Brooks Atkinson continued his admiration for her work in solo performance, which he recognized as "a formidable art": "The one-woman theatre is a formidable art. It places an actress pitilessly on view. In the current instance grants her some vigorous and handsome costumes, which abet acting with color and design, but it gives her no support. Miss Sands can meet that searching test. She is the mistress of technique; she has to a degree rare in the theatre the integrity

of an artist, and she has an enthusiasm for the work she is doing"
(1933:20). Yet for all his praise of Dorothy Sands's ability as a
performer, Atkinson found the script limiting as a proper showcase. "But still," wrote Atkinson, "the items in 'Our Stage and
Stars' give no more than a hint of her full quality. Beneath all the
amusing byplay of this program there is a fine actress whose powers have never been properly revealed on the dramatic stage"
(1933:20).

Sands developed three more one-person shows: *Stars of Today and Yesterday* (1935) and *Tricks of the Acting Trade* (1940),
both of which expanded her repertoire of impersonations of contemporary actresses, and *American Theatre Highlights* (1949). For
this last show, Sands returned to much of the material of *Our
Stage and Stars,* substituting new impersonations for the segment
on the contemporary period. In the same year in which her last
one-person show opened, Dorothy Sands received an honorary
A.A. degree from the Curry School of Expression.

After *American Theatre Highlights,* which she took to Ger-
many under the auspices of the state department as part of the
reorientation program,[17] Dorothy Sands devoted her talents to
acting in legitimate plays and teaching period acting styles. In
1959 she received an Antoinette Perry (Tony) Award for her teaching at the American Theatre Wing. Her work as a solo performer
was just one of her many contributions to American theatre, yet
her achievements in the specialized field of one-person shows
earned her a position of importance in the history of solo performance in America:

Miss Sands as a diseuse has proved herself an impersonator of the first
rank. Nothing could be keener than her unerring observation of the living persons she depicts. She catches them perfectly and with the lightest,
wittiest, or most jauntily humorous caricature, pins them forever in one's
memory. Her irony, one surmises, could be merciless, if she chose to use
it, but she doesn't except the most fleeting, subtle, tinge. She has lifted
impersonation to an art of brilliant perfection. In this field, her own, she
is unsurpassed (Eames 1935:360).

CHARLES LAUGHTON

Charles Laughton was the only major male solo performer
during the thirty-year period following the war when women

dominated the field. His readings from the classics and the Bible were successful across the country and lead one journalist to exclaim: "One might have thought the movies, radio, and television had never been invented, and that the golden years of the Chautauqua circuit were back again" ("The Happy Ham" 1952:62). Laughton's celebrity was, in fact, first earned from his work in one of the entertainment forms often credited for assisting in the demise of Chautauqua—the movies. Before ever turning to public readings, Laughton was recognized as a major film star for his acclaimed performances in such motion pictures as *The Private Life of Henry VIII* (for which he won an Academy Award), *Mutiny on the Bounty*, and *The Hunchback of Notre Dame*. With his reputation already established throughout the country, Laughton's readings immediately attracted the attention of both the critics and the public. Earlier public readers, like Charles Dickens, Fanny Kemble, and Charlotte Cushman, were established celebrities for their work as writers or stage actors; Laughton was the first celebrity whose reputation was made through films to become a platform reader.

During the years of World War II, after his film career was well established, Laughton found his time and creative energies little consumed by Hollywood. Remembering his own lonely hours spent in an army hospital after he had been gassed during World War I, Laughton decided to channel his energies and perform for the wounded servicemen at the Birmingham General Hospital in the San Fernando Valley. On the night of his performance, the men understandably assumed that Laughton would enact scenes from his famous film roles. They were immediately disappointed when Laughton announced that he would read to them. A biography reports one GI's reaction: " 'Hell, anybody can read,' he shouted, 'I thought actors acted' " (quoted in Singer 1954:209). Undaunted, Laughton read, offering limericks to warm up the audience and free them from the idea that the program would be too academic. Once the simple limericks achieved their purpose, Laughton moved to selections from the works of Thurber, Aesop, Dickens, Thomas Wolfe, Andrew Marvell, and Shakespeare. He closed with a stirring recitation of the Gettysburg Address. The skeptical audience was thoroughly won over and the program was a success. The following week Laughton returned to the hospital and read from the Bible. Word of mouth had increased the number of audience members and this time they were eager listeners. News of Laughton's performances quickly spread and he soon received requests from churches and synagogues to perform—as a reader. Writing of Laughton's wartime readings, his biographer wrote: "They were one-man shows, one-man theater and one man's great contribution to the morale and spirit of a nation at war" (Singer 1954:216). Indeed, Laughton's wartime readings are reminiscent of those of James Murdoch, the elocutionist who read to preserve the morale and patriotism of the Union troops during the Civil War.

Laughton's occasional readings eventually developed into a new career. Dissatisfaction with the mediocre film scripts offered to him by Hollywood caused Laughton to put more and more into his readings. His boundless energy became channeled toward a self-directed study of literature and the history of platform readings. "I then began to read," wrote Laughton, "about reading aloud. I read of two famous tours of Charles Dickens; of Fanny Kemble and of the Chautauqua circuit; and learned that I had invented nothing, but was carrying on an American tradition" (Laughton 1950:72). In fact, Laughton's study of Dickens's reading tours had a direct (if small) influence on his own performances. Laughton, wrote Charles Higham in his biography of the actor, "wanted a light to shine in his face if possible. He had obtained the idea from descriptions of Charles Dickens' famous British and American reading tours, in which the novelist had insisted on a light to illuminate his eyes" (1976:156). Ultimately word of Laughton's readings reached the entertainment industry and the actor was invited to read on Ed Sullivan's *Toast of the Town* television show. With great force Laughton read a segment of the Book of Daniel from the Bible. By a stroke of luck, the televised reading was seen in a Manhattan bistro by Paul Gregory, then head of the Concert Department of the Music Corporation of America. Gregory was deeply impressed by Laughton's performance: "Impassioned, marvelous, the reading fascinated him. He seized on the idea of promoting Charles in one-night stands across the country" (Higham 1976:155). He called Laughton after the performance and the two men met the next afternoon. "By the time [Gregory] left," wrote *Time*, "he had convinced Laughton that he should go on a cross-country tour and make people pay to hear his readings" ("The Happy Ham" 1952:67). With Gregory as his manager, Laughton began his distinguished career as a professional public reader. One biographer wrote: "In the Hollywood studios people were saying that Laughton had done the impossible. He had made himself independent. His *one-man theatre* was the greatest platform phenomenon in America since the days of Mark Twain. Here was one theatrical personality who had broken free from the commercial contingencies of Hollywood and Broadway" (Singer 1954:228).

An Evening with Charles Laughton, as his readings were called, proved to be a lasting success for Laughton and he periodically toured the country through the 1950s. As a professional reader he continued to offer selections from the Bible, Andersen's fairy tales, Thomas Wolfe, Dickens, and Thurber, as well as segments from his past films. Critics noted Laughton's mastery of the art of reading and in particular, his informal platform manner: "What impresses more than the content of the material is the portly actor's own personality, his apparent and contagious enjoyment of the particular scene or the passage he is reading, reciting, or emoting. But his informality has progressed through the years just about as far as it should go. One more bounce, ear scratch or slangy debunk might become coy" (Vene 1953:55). Typically, Laughton would first appear on stage neatly dressed in a suit and carrying an armful of books. Once into readings, the tremendous energy that he gave to his performances would be unleashed. The following review gives an indication of the vitality and force of Laughton's readings:

Laughton starts the evening spick and span in his dark blue suit and his contrasting light blue shirt, looking as uncomfortable as a small boy dressed for a party.

As soon as the words start to roll forth, though, the ends of his shirt collar get caught up in the excitement and they curl to meet his chin.

Next his hair, at first plastered to his head, rises in revolt from its forced order. The neatly arranged white handkerchief in his breast pocket wilts from the thunderous heavings of the man's chest. The double-brested jacket, so recently draped with Bond St. pride, now climbs around the actor's middle and becomes a budging sack.

Laughton is lost in a world of words. Petty words like neatness and tidiness and order have been stampeded by the soaring words that pour out of the mountain (Rice 1953:52).

The teaming of Laughton and Paul Gregory proved one of the most fruitful collaborations in theatre history. As well as Laughton's solo reading tours, in the 1950s they developed landmark group performances of literature that used experimental presentational staging techniques, including *Don Juan in Hell* and *John Brown's Body*. Despite his continued work in the theatre and in Hollywood, Laughton maintained a schedule of frequent readings including his regular Christmas season readings of Dickens's *Christmas Carol*. Laughton remained dedicated to the value of classic literature and the art of reading aloud. "I plead for more reading aloud," Laughton is quoted as saying, "It makes us participants rather than spectators. Instead of sitting by to let the professionals amuse or enlighten us, *we* can get into the act, make contact with new ideas, exercise our imaginations" (quoted in Singer 1954:239). When Elsa Lanchester wrote of Laughton's readings in her autobiography, she said of her husband: "Charles believed that in America people never stopped wanting to learn. That was one of the things that attracted Charles to reading in America in the first place—the eternal student point of view, the tendency of people of all ages to continue studying" (Lanchester 1983:203).

Today Laughton's readings may still be enjoyed through the recordings issued during his career. They remain a lasting contribution by the Hollywood star turned platform reader who once said: "That is what I want to be—a storyteller. I would like to be the man who knows all the stories, who has on his back a bag full of stories as bottomless as Santa Claus's bag of toys" (Laughton 1950:72).

RUTH DRAPER

Ruth Draper dominated the field of professional solo performance during the second quarter of the twentieth century. As an international celebrity, Draper had performed with great success throughout the United States and Europe. Her following in Great Britain rivaled, and perhaps even surpassed, that in her native America. She had made her debut as a professional solo performer in London, which probably accounts for the strong affectional ties between Draper and the British. John Gielgud wrote of her that "I have always felt that Ruth Draper was (with Martha Graham) the greatest individual performer that America has ever given us" (Gielgud 1979:xi).

Since childhood Draper had a penchant for recitation and composing original character sketches. Her failure in her one attempt at ensemble acting (in a small role in *A Lady's Name* with Marie Tempest in 1916) pointed her in the direction of solo performance as a professional. Two inspirations helped Draper in her decision: the solo performances of Beatrice Herford, a comic actress, and an early presentational ensemble production. "I saw Beatrice Herford perform her monologues and realized what could be done," Draper said, "And I saw a Chinese play, *The Yellow Jacket* without scenery—small steps that went up and down, so when one wanted to enact climbing a mountain—and I understood the extraordinary illusion that can be created with nothing." [18] At thirty-five years of age, after years of private and charity solo appearances, Ruth Draper booked the Aeolian Hall in London for a matinee on 29 January 1920. From that date onward, indeed right up to her death in 1956, Draper devoted her professional life to solo performance (Warren 1979:15).

Draper's one-person shows differed in kind from those of the majority of the early lyceum and Chautauqua solo performers in that she performed original character sketches (or "monologues") rather than selections of published literature. Early in her life, she discovered that she was unable to perform material other than her own compositions. Henry James had written a monologue specifically for Draper in 1913; upon reading James's manuscript, Draper (who was a devotee of James's novels) was "Faced with a style so totally at odds with the easy fluency and realism she gave her own characters [that she] found the monologue wholly impracticable. 'I think he was disappointed,' she said later, 'but I never learned it or tried it on anyone'" (Zabel 1960:52).[19] Her monologues were composed orally and specifically intended for performance. John Gielgud recounts that she had once told him "that she never wrote them down until quite late in her career, and that she could shorten or lengthen them while she was playing as she felt the reactions of her audience demanded" (Gielgud

1979:ix). Although not obvious at first glance, many parallels exist between Draper and Charles Dickens as creative writers and as solo performers. Although Dickens wrote for publication, he composed his texts by performing in front of a mirror (Dickens n.d.: 48). Both Dickens and Draper performed their own material; both had memorized the texts. Dickens, in the minds of many, was foremost a writer, yet his talents as a performer are undeniable. Draper, in the minds of many, was foremost a performer, yet her talents as a writer (or more accurately, as oral composer) were recognized by Thornton Wilder, Robert Emmet Sherwood, Alexander Woollcott, and Brooks Atkinson. In 1954 Wilder and Sherwood proposed her for membership in the American Institute of Arts and Letters—as a playwright. The proposal was turned down: "To their [Wilder's and Sherwood's] dismay, the Institute's definition of a playwright was too rigid to permit her election" (Warren 1979:xvii).

The decision made by the American Institute of Arts and Letters reflects the difficulty in categorizing Draper's art. Had she published her work she might have been easily recognized as a writer-performer, as was Charles Dickens. But because her texts were oral compositions, she was even more difficult to classify than most solo performers. Of herself Draper said: "Diseuse, recitalist, monologuist—I am not any of these, I am a character actress" (Warren 1979:xv). She regarded her monologues as character dramas and avoided the terminology associated with the platform. "Miss Draper dodges the word recital," observed Alexander Woollcott, "possibly as a chilling and dismaying word, and uses in her announcements and programs merely descriptions 'Ruth Draper in Original Character Sketches'" (1921:16). Draper was determined to perform on a stage; she disliked performing on a platform, whether in a college or a hotel ballroom, "and possibly felt her theatrical image to be diminished if she regularly, even for a season, accepted less than a theatre. As far as the actual performance went, she would work anywhere, but whatever the psychological effect may have been—on audience or on performer—the *theatre's stage* was where she felt herself to belong" (Warren 1979: xv). Draper's intolerance for the platform is indicative of the anti-Victorian feeling of her era. The negative connotations that are associated with terms like *recitation, platform, elocution, elocu-*

tionist, declamation, reader, and *readings* all seem bound in a re-action against things associated with the Victorian age.

The Chautauqua and lyceum people were well aware of the implications of Ruth Draper's preferred rhetoric. Quite likely they interpreted her choice of nomenclature as a disdain for their world. Draper's outstanding success in New York, London, and other major cities was also noted with skepticism by Chautau-quans. The Chautauqua perspective on Draper can be summed up as such: Here is a woman of obvious talent, doing what scores of Chautauqua-lyceum performers have been doing for years, being hailed as a genius by the very people (the urban elite) who have disparaged everything associated with the Chautauqua movement. In 1930 *Platform World* commented: " 'What's in a name?' Every-thing. Ruth Draper calls herself a 'diseuse,' and as no one knows what that is, she packed 'em into the Cleveland Playhouse Dec. 4th. Ruth is a high class performer, but if she called herself an impersonator, which is what she is, would society folk claw each other out of the way to reach her box office? Would they? Well, Ruth is a wise woman and she's 'une diseuse' " (Editorial, Jan. 1930:18).[20]

Draper's brilliant success as a solo performer in her era re-mains remarkable. In *The Art of Ruth Draper,* Morton Dauwen Zabel recognized that solo performance had fallen into doubtful repute when she began her career. Zabel's commentary, which traces Draper's heritage as a solo performer back to Dickens, re-flects S. H. Clark's beliefs that elocution had become debased by the turn of the century:

It took his [Dickens's] particular combination of popular literary texts, comic genius, histrionic eloquence, and lurid or sentimental appeal to make the dramatic "reading" a huge success in his age; and in America Mark Twain and his fellow-humorists soon rivalled him on their own ground. But what these vogues of humor and melodrama descended to in the vaudeville, lyceum, or Chautauqua circuits of a later day easily accounts for the disrepute into which the solo reading or recitation fell by the time the twentieth century opened. It had become either an elo-cutionary stunt or a form of humorous exhibitionism. It continued to have its talented exponents on the popular stage, but they survived either as singing performers like Marie and Alice Lloyd or Alfred Chevalier, or

as satirists and yarners of the day's news of public events and foibles—
Grossmith, Grain, Roberts, Will Rogers (1960:107–8).

Zabel then points out that Draper did not entirely repudiate the
Victorian ancestry of her art by drawing parallels between various
Draper monologues and Victorian literature. Draper's "Miner's
Wife," Zabel states, "is in the Dickensian tradition, and so are
some of her satires of society and 'culture'" (1960:108). Yet there
are distinctions between Dickens's and Draper's material, as Zabel
indicates:

But most of her sketches are explicit in their repudiation of exaggerated
caricature and melodrama; she found the knack of applying irony or
understatement to the elements in which she dealt. . . . [S]he was fortunate enough to arrive on the scene when certain performers had prepared
the way for the refinements she was to cultivate. Beatrice Herford had
done something to span the gap between Victorian extravagance and
modern irony. So had a mimic like Cissie Loftus, with her brilliant caricatures of stage types, and so on an even higher level of dramatic and
vocal impersonation had Yvette Guilbert, with the rich tradition of the
Parisian *café-concert* and sardonic revue to support her genius in realism
and comedy. These can be counted as Ruth Draper's immediate predecessors; and at times, in her folk *patiches,* Balkan parodies, or broader
caricatures, her derivation from them is clear (1960:108).

In performing her monologues, Draper portrayed a single
character while evoking imaginary on-stage listeners. Although a
few of Draper's sketches (such as "In a Church in Italy" and "At
an English House Party") consisted of linked monologues, she did
not move between enacting speaker and listener nor did she enact
the interactions of multiple characters in quick succession. Here,
then, lies the distinction between a monologue and a "monopolylogue" and, consequently, the distinction between a monologuist
and a monopolyloguist (or "polyphonist"). In a monologue a
single character speaks to a silent listener (or *unheard* listener—
except in an imaginary sense) for the duration of a piece; in a
monopolylogue (which more resembles a drama) multiple characters speak although all are performed by one actor. Hybrid
forms, such as Draper's linked monologues discussed below, blur
distinctions and render the terms useless.

Descriptions of Draper's performances quickly become convoluted. In lieu of a general survey, these three summaries provided a solid indication of Draper's monologues and their range in style and subject matter:

"The Actress" (19 minutes)
1st performed: before 1920.
Characters: portrayed, 1; evoked, 11

Speaks in English, French, and a simulated mid-European language, possibly Polish. . . . Into the Drawing Room of her apartment in a Paris hotel strides a middle-aged actress, famous, consciously theatrical in manner, gesture, and temperament. Although fatigued, she welcomes with feigned delight a succession of visitors: a rich, fat, elderly American visitor, who leaves her his car and chauffeur; a young poet at her feet, who writes for her an unsatisfactory play; her manager; her leading man (on the telephone); at the end a group of twenty. She speaks to five of these individually.

"In a Church in Italy" (30 minutes)
1st performed: 1925.
Characters: portrayed, 6; evoked 20.

A church in Italy. The characters enter and exit left and right.
1. An English woman in hat and smock sits painting. She chats with a fellow artist.
2. A bent old Italian crone, shawl over her head, begs of various tourists, pleading age, poverty, "cinque bambini." "Tante grazie"—is refused: "che brutta gente!"
3. An American tourist—long grey coat, flat hat, umbrella, and a red Baedeker from which she reads aloud, compelling her friends to listen.
4. A lovely young Italian girl eagerly rushes into the church, seeking her young man. With a black shawl over her shoulders and a lace scarf over her head, she carries a red rose with which she plays alluringly. She whispers of her love, of the difficulties of meeting, and arranges a rendezvous for the evening, crosses herself before the Madonna—the gesture ending in a blown kiss—and lightly runs off.
5. A German tourist—tall, gaunt, with metal-framed spectacles, green loden cape, and Bavarian felt hat, cane, and many bundles on strings—guides her party to look at the Madonna. "Einmal was der Kaiser hier—und Goethe auch." They exit in search of Munchener Bier, protesting, "Macaroni, macaroni, macaroni!"
6. A mature Italian peasant woman with a long black shawl over her

head enters quietly, gazes sorrowfully at the Madonna, crosses herself, and sinks to her knees in an agony of prayer, eyes closed. Gradually her expression changes to one of peace and as she opens her hands the curtain slowly descends.

"Three Breakfasts" (30 minutes)
1st performed: before 1920.
Characters: portrayed, 1 at 3 ages; evoked, 7 (1 at 3 ages)

1. Eager young bride in a suburb—her first breakfast with her husband in their first home.
2. Fifteen years later they breakfast in a city house; she is bored; cool—both are annoyed and ill-tempered. He is being laughed at for taking a young girl out dancing, and she has her own romance.
3. Forty years later they breakfast in their farmhouse with six grandchildren at the table. The atmosphere is mellow and warm as they remember the events of a long and happy marriage—completing the events of the two earlier scenes. (All three breakfasts are served by "Mary.") (Quoted in Warren 1979:350–57.)[21]

Although these three monologues are somewhat longer than many of Draper's pieces (the average length being about fifteen minutes), they do indicate many typical elements: Draper's use of dialects and foreign languages (including her simulated Slavic language), her blends of humor and pathos, her presentation of a central female character, her characters' wide range of social, economic, and professional status, and her creative use of suggestive costuming. In only one monologue, "At the Court of Philip IV," did Draper wear full representational costuming.[22] Otherwise, according to one account, she used "[a] few hats, mostly rather battered, a dressing gown, a raincoat, and a collection of shawls. These last were her only indispensable accessories: draped in a hundred different ways, they turned her into an old Irishwoman, a young Italian girl in a church, a Dalmatian peasant, a great Spanish lady" (Origo 1958:57). The stage requirements for her monologues were minimal, usually calling for a single chair or table that served as a transformational object, as indicated in this description of her performances:

To see Miss Draper is an experience. She achieves her astonishing effects by the simplest of means. She plays always against a background of cur-

tains with practically nothing to create illusion, no music, no trick lighting, no set. The bare stage suffices, with perhaps a table or a chair. It is
really wonderful to see how a plain ordinary chair, by some alchemy of
hers, becomes, in turn, a three-legged stool in a peasant's cottage, prie-
dieu in a foreign cathedral, a bench in a child's school or a luxurious
chaise-lounge in a society woman's boudoir (Eames 1935:342).

Draper's one-person shows were an appeal to the audience's
active use of imagination. Her talents as a performer link her to
all the great solo performers of the past in their ability to help their
audiences create, without the trappings of realistic stage accoutrements, an entire world. *The New York Times* said of Draper:

Listening to her, and watching her, one soon forgets that he is in a theatre
in the presence of a monologist. There is illusion, the complete illusion
of a telephone operator, say, an operator at a public switchboard with a
brother dying at home; or of an earnest, debutante who knows, just
knows, that there, there must be, more to life than "just this, you
know"—"absolutely"—or of a distracted mother chaperoning four children who will go in different directions at once and trying to gossip with
her neighbors and flatter their children at the same time. It's all real
("Ruth Draper Warmly Greeted" 1923:15).

CORNELIA OTIS SKINNER

Cornelis Otis Skinner began her career as a solo performer
following closely in Draper's path; she was both to benefit and to
suffer from the success of her great contemporary. When Draper
began her solo career in the early 1920s, she was faced with the
task of revitalizing a dying performance art form. Skinner, who
first appeared as a solo performer in the late 1920s, rode the new
crest of public enthusiasm for solo performance initiated by Draper's trailblazing work. The negative effect for Skinner of Draper's
success lay in the inevitable comparisons and in the difficulty she
faced in trying to achieve individual success under the shadow of
another artist whose very name had become synonymous with the
best in solo performance. Ultimately, Skinner moved beyond
Draper to create one-person shows distinct in structure and scope
from those of her fellow monologuist.

At the outset of her solo performance career, Skinner appeared, like Draper, in short, disconnected monologues of her own composition. Soon dissatisfied with the limitations of the form, she developed scripts of a more elaborate, complex, and dramatically unified nature. In a comprehensive study of her work, G. Bruce Loganbill (1961) calls Skinner's scripts "monologue-dramas." They were, in effect, extensions of the "linked monologues" that Draper had previously developed on a more limited scale. But Skinner's monologue-dramas differed from Draper's monologues in subject matter as well as in structure. Draper had based only one of her sketches ("At the Court of Philip IV") on an historic incident.[23] Skinner, conversely, made her unique contribution to the American one-person show by creating and performing in full-length monologue-dramas based on the lives of historical figures.

After opening in Great Britain, Skinner performed her first historic monologue-drama, *The Wives of Henry VIII,* in New York in 1931. The performance ran for forty-three minutes and was, as one critic said, "the *pièce de resistance*" of a program that included other short monologues (J.B. 1931:22). For the monologue-dramas, Skinner used minimal set pieces but wore full realistic costuming. (Whereas Draper's performances consistently favored presentational staging techniques, Skinner's performances moved toward the more representational.) The script of *The Wives of Henry VIII* was comprised of six monologues; in each monologue Skinner portrayed one of the Tudor queens while evoking other on-stage characters. Like Draper, Skinner did not move back and forth between characters in rapid succession, nor did she portray both speaker and listener. She, too, remained in one character for the duration of a monologue. *The Wives of Henry VIII,* although presented in a program with other Skinner monologues, marked a movement toward the creation of a full-length original script created for solo performance.

The success of *The Wives of Henry VIII* prompted two subsequent Skinner historical monologue-dramas: *The Empress Eugenie* (in 1932) and *The Loves of Charles II* (in 1934). In *The Empress Eugenie,* Skinner portrayed the French monarch at three different ages; in *The Loves of Charles II* she played six important women in the life of the English king. Skinner followed these two one-person shows with two based on fiction rather than history.

above: A tent Chautauqua, circa 1910. *below:* A Chautauqua in Iowa. Reprinted courtesy of the Redpath Chautauqua Collection, University of Iowa Libraries.

TENTS!   TENTS!

Chautauqua Managers! Let us make you an attractive proposition in regard to your 1909 assembly.

Our Tents are stylish and reliable
Service top notch and terms reasonable

We have served the biggest and best assemblies that have ever gathered and we want to serve you next year.

Correspondence solicited, and promptly answered. Get our illustrated catalogue.

Baker & Lockwood Mfg. Co.
KANSAS CITY, MO.

above: Advertisement for tent rentals from the October 1908 *Lyceumite & Talent.* Reprinted courtesy of the Redpath Chautauqua Collection, University of Iowa Libraries.

facing page: Advertisements appearing in the October 1908 *Lyceumite & Talent.* Reprinted courtesy of the Redpath Chautauqua Collection, University of Iowa Libraries.

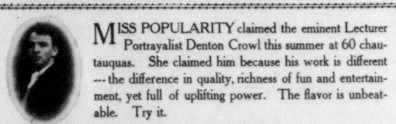

"Dobbin's tail must grow backward."

LAUNCELOT.

The Merchant of Venice.

"By the drunken son of Semele! What is it to be Jew?"

MESSALA.

Ben-Hur.

Montaville Flowers as Launcelot in *The Merchant of Venice (above)* and as Messala in *Ben-Hur (below)*. Reprinted courtesy of the Redpath Chautauqua Collection, University of Iowa Libraries.

"Hath a dog money?"

SHYLOCK.

The Merchant of Venice.

"Well done, boys and girls; well done!"

FEZZIWIG.

A Christmas Carol.

Montaville Flowers as Shylock in *The Merchant of Venice (above)* and as Mr. Fezziwig in *A Christmas Carol (below)*. Reprinted courtesy of the Redpath Chautauqua Collection, University of Iowa Libraries.

William Sterling Battis as Sam Weller from *The Pickwick Papers* (*above*) and an advertisement for Battis as "The Dickens Man" from the *Lyceumite & Talent,* October 1907. Reprinted courtesy of the Redpath Chautauqua Collection, University of Iowa Libraries.

The J. B. Pond Lyceum Bureau

Presents

Carl Sandburg

"The Poet of the City"

Author of

"CHICAGO POEMS"
"CORNHUSKERS"
Etc.

and

Lew Sarett

LONE CARIBOU

"The Poet of the Wilderness"

Author of

"MANY, MANY MOONS," Etc.

in

A JOINT LECTURE AND RECITAL

From Their Own Writings

—

*Americans All in an
All American Program*

—

Managed by

J. B. POND LYCEUM BUREAU

50 East 42nd Street - - New York
Fine Arts Building - - Chicago

Announcement for joint lectures and recitals by Carl Sandburg and Lew
Sarett. Collection of the author.

Cissie Loftus as Sarah Bernhardt (photograph by W. & D. Downey). Originally published in the *Pall Mall Budget*, 16 August 1894. Reprinted courtesy of the Billy Rose Theatre Collection, New York Public Library at Lincoln Center, Astor, Lenox and Tilden Foundations.

"THE LONDON FLOWER GIRL"

CECILIA LOFTUS

in her World Famous Program

"IMPRESSIONS AND IMPERSONATIONS"

"Her sketches are infallible — I took
astonished delight in her performances!"
—ALEXANDER WOOLLCOTT.
The New York Times

Management:
O'DONNELL & SHAW, 334 East 53rd Street, New York, N. Y.

Announcement for Cissie Loftus in "Impressions and Impersonations."
Reprinted courtesy of the Billy Rose Theatre Collection, New York Public
Library at Lincoln Center, Astor, Lenox and Tilden Foundations.

Charles Laughton

Cover for the promotional brochure for *An Evening with Charles Laughton*, showing his typical entrance with an armload of books. Reprinted courtesy of the Billy Rose Theatre Collection, New York Public Library at Lincoln Center, Astor, Lenox and Tilden Foundations.

Ruth Draper in a composite photograph of her characters. Reprinted courtesy of the Theatre Collection, Museum of the City of New York.

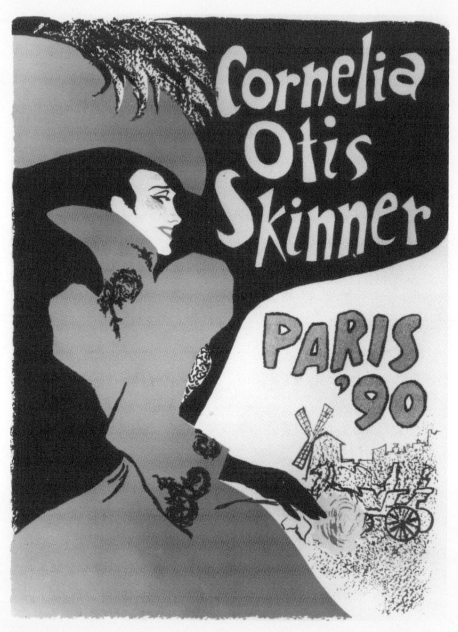

Cover of the original souvenir booklet for Cornelia Otis Skinner in *Paris '90*.
Reprinted courtesy of the Theatre Collection, Museum of the City of New
York.

Mansion on the Hudson (1935) was an original Skinner monologue-drama in which she portrayed a succession of mistresses of a great country house. In 1937 she appeared in her only monologue-drama not composed of original material, a solo adaptation of Margaret Ayer Barnes's novel *Edna His Wife*.

Skinner presented her most ambitious effort, *Paris '90*, in 1952. The full-length original monologue-drama consisted of fifteen thematically linked monologues, each presenting either historical or fictitious women of Paris in 1890:

The solo-drama is designed in three acts. The first act is set on the Champs Elysees where five characters are seen successively: the Nou-Nou, a Fashionable Parisienne, La Duchess de Vertpres, La Belle Conchita, and the New Woman. The second act, introduced by a monologue of an Angel from her niche in a portal of Notre Dame, presents the women of the Left Bank. They are a Laundress, a Boston School Teacher, a Woman of Virtue, and a Professor's Wife. The third act portrays the women of Montmartre, friends of Toulouse-Lautrec including La Goulue, a Lion Tamer of the Medrano Circus, Berthe La Sourde, and Yvette Guilbert (Loganbill 1961:123).

With *Paris '90* Skinner's work moved closer still into the realm of realistic representational drama. The production was fully mounted with elaborate sets, lighting, costumes, make-up, and original music. The playing time for the production was two and one-half hours. After touring eight weeks, *Paris '90* opened in New York on 4 March 1952 at the Booth Theatre. The show earned highly favorable reviews, such as John Chapman's, which appeared in the *Daily News:* "Miss Skinner has set herself a really formidable task, but she breezes through it beautifully, changing voice, character and accent without seeming effort. . . . 'Paris '90' is, to me, a charming theatrical novelty" (1952b: 49).

Draper and Skinner deserve a special place in the history of solo performance for their success in winning respect for the one-person show when it could no longer claim a wide, select audience. The platform, along with the Chautauqua and lyceum, had fallen in public esteem and the violent backlash against Victorianism had swept away respect for anything smacking of elocutionary declamation. Against these tides of prejudice, Draper and Skinner were able to win acclaim and a public following from a theatre community whose main interest lay in play productions. They helped earn for the one-person show an integral place in the American theatre; their great achievements in developing the monologue form did not go unnoticed: "They have already enriched the monologue, making it a new, delightful, and creative force. They have taken something time worn and frayed and endowed it with a fresh vigor and fascination. Thanks to these gifted artists the monologue is no longer the Cinderella, but the Proud Princess of the American theatre" (Eames 1935:360).

CONCLUSION

All five of the major artists of the transition years between 1920 and 1950—Loftus, Sands, Laughton, Draper, and Skinner—remain significant for their respective contributions in revitalizing solo performance as a mode of public entertainment in the United States. At the beginning of the period, solo performances suffered from their association with the worst excesses of the dying elocutionary movement. By the end of the period, the one-person form was about to enjoy a remarkable renaissance both artistically and commercially.

Interestingly, each of these five important artists revitalized the one-person show mode by a kind of return to the roots of solo performance. Cissie Loftus and Dorothy Sands, with their expert impersonations of contemporary celebrities, returned to a basic element of theatre: mimesis. Charles Laughton, with his readings of literature by major writers, moved away from the trite and sentimental elocutionary hack pieces of the late-Chautauqua era and returned to literature of true merit. Ruth Draper and Cornelia Otis Skinner, the two most important solo artists of the period, composed their own material and, in effect, restored the bardic tradition to solo performance by becoming their generation's storytellers and oral poets. Skinner once wrote of her aspirations for the future of solo performance:

I see no reason why this form of dramatic presentation [the one-person show] should not in its collateral way develop in proportionate measure with the modern theatre. There is no reason that a "one-man" or "one-woman" show should continue in the fusty tradition of the dramatic recitation. The character sketch or monologue has for so long been regarded as so polite a form of entertainment that it seems lamentably remote from drama and theatre. Instinctively one associates it with the gifted amateur. The idea recalls an army of artistically inclined ladies calling themselves "readers" (a word as incomprehensible as it is distressing) who present on the stage of their local parish house a program of school-of-expression recitations. . . . [M]y argument is that the monologue should approach more and more to theatre until it is recognized as the legitimate offspring and not a left branch of the concert stage (Skinner 1931:4).

The years since 1950 have proved Skinner's words prophetic.

NOTES

1. For more information on the existing independent Chautauqua assemblies, see Snyder's two essays (1985, 1983). Also see the special Chautauqua issues of the *Michigan Connection* (Winter/Spring 1984) and the *Henry Ford Museum and Greenfield Village Herald* 13.2 (1984).

2. A good example of a parlor book is *The International Speaker and Popular Elocutionist* (1895). The book, as its front page boasts, is "illustrated by original photo-engravings" of young elocutionists (usually young girls dressed in white, flouncy costumes) executing standard Delsarte poses with captions such as "Adoration" (p. 81) or "Horror" (p. 55). Selections cover a wide range of literature, including Shakespeare's "Marc Antony's Address" and "Othello's Apology" and such elocutionary pieces as L. M. Hadley's "Babies and Kittens" and the anonymous "Mama's Kisses." For further comment on the parlor book phenomenon, see Rickert (1978).

3. This paragraph is largely based on Stanley Coben's cogent and highly recommended essay "The Assault on Victorianism in the Twentieth Century" (1976).

4. For discussions on the influence of S. S. Curry and S. H. Clark on the field of elocution, see Robb (1954, 1968:163–83); Gray (1954, 1966); Current (1938); Quick (1942); and Edwards (1983). A condensed history of oral interpretation may be found in Bahn and Bahn (1970) and specialized essays on the subject in Thompson (1983b). The field of oral interpretation is currently experiencing changes as significant as those that occurred during the careers of Curry and Clark. It is moving beyond Clark's vision described in this chapter toward a broader study of the nature and function of various texts and performances. One of the results of the changes within the field is a renewed interest in the one-

person show genre as a vehicle for popular entertainment, as witnessed by the numerous reviews of solo performances in the field's major journal, *Literature in Performance*. Recent developments are reflected in the latest name change; for discussions on the transformation of *oral interpretation* into *performance studies*, see Gentile (1983b); Pelias and VanOosting (1987); and Bacon (1987).

5. See Alford (1896:351–53): "Mr. Clark can do much with his voice. His is a magnificent organ. Perhaps no reader in America has a finer voice" (p. 351).

6. Clark delivered this address on 9 July 1895 in the Hall of Philosophy at the New York Chautauqua Assembly. On 30 June 1897 Clark delivered another address of the same title at the National Association of Elocutionists; this second address was cited earlier.

7. The lasting impact of Clark's text is indicated by the appearance of a revised reprint twenty-five years later (see S. H. Clark and Maud May Babcock, *Interpretation of the Printed Page*, rev. ed. [New York: Prentice, 1940]).

8. See, for example, Herbert J. Gans's discussion of "The Critique of Mass Culture" (1974:17–64).

9. Also see Gray (1985).

10. For more information on Lew Sarett, see Rein (1978).

11. For a photograph of Sandburg performing, see "The Years of Carl Sandburg" (1967:50).

12. For a fuller discussion of these performers, see Reynolds (1960, 1961).

13. For two view points on the controversy of the decline of the miscellaneous readings, see Williams (1902).

14. See "*The Sad Shepherd:* Ben Jonson's Pastoral Comedy Presented Tonight" (1904); "Nicholson Sylvan Players Will Present Shakespearian Comedy Tonight," (1910); and Mumford (1902).

15. A final note regarding Chautauqua's acceptance of theatre: in 1982 *The Chautauquan* announced the opening of a new theatre school. Robert R. Hesse, then president of the Chautauqua Institution, stated "[t]heatre always has been an integral part of the comprehensive Chautauqua experience" ("Acting Company Plans to Return" 1982:1). We can only wonder what John H. Vincent and the early Chautauquans would have said about such a statement. For more information on the Chautauqua movement, see Horner (1954); Jameson (1979); Morrison (1974); Richmond (1943); Scott (1939); Slout (1972); Ellwood (1925); Farma (1946); Graham (1953); Hedges (1976); Jenson (1970); Smoot (1954); Tapia (1978); and Tozier (1932).

16. The platform periodicals began in 1890 with *Talent*, which served the independent Chautauquas and the lyceum. *Talent* merged with another platform periodical, *The Lyceumite*, in June 1907 and assumed the name *The Lyceumite and Talent*, which served the independent Chautauquas, the lyceum, and the newly formed tent circuits. In June 1913 the periodical changed its name to *The Lyceum Magazine* and

maintained this title until a new publisher changed it to *Platform World* in April 1929. *Platform World* ceased publication in October 1933.

17. Dorothy Sands toured *American Theatre Highlights* in Heidelberg, Berlin, Comburg, Frankfurt, and Munich, 2–13 July 1949.

18. From "The Interview [with Ruth Draper]" (1954:23). Herford's monologues are available in *Beatrice Herford's Monologues* (1940). For more information on Herford, Loftus, and Sands, see Long (1982).

19. Henry James's monologue appears in *The Complete Plays of Henry James* (1949).

20. Draper, as noted above, did not use the term *diseuse* but preferred *character actress*.

21. Neilla Warren includes summaries of thirty-six Draper monologues in *The Letters of Ruth Draper, 1920–1956* (1979). Zabel's book (1960) includes thirty-five Draper monologues. Late in her career, Draper recorded several of her monologues for Spoken Arts Records; the recordings are still available.

22. For Draper's comment regarding her costume for the monologue "At The Court of Philip IV," see her letter to Hariett Marple, 22 May 1922, in Warren (1979:40–41).

23. Draper's "Vive la France!—1916" and "Vive la France!—1940" were monologues based on fictional events placed in an historic frame.

3

The Renaissance of
the One-Person Show in America:
1950 to the Present

"The one-man play," wrote Herbert Mitgang, "has proliferated on and off Broadway, and especially on the national touring circuit, in recent times" (1980:6). During the nearly forty-year period following 1950, the one-person show has enjoyed a popularity reminiscent of the popularity of platform readings during the Victorian age. Two major productions stand at the vanguard of the current soloist movement: *Emlyn Williams as Charles Dickens* and Hal Holbrook's *Mark Twain Tonight!* Their influence pervades the contemporary resurgence of solo performance in this country.

Emlyn Williams as Charles Dickens

In 1950 Emlyn Williams was asked to appear as part of a special benefit performance. The producers requested that he perform in a scene from his play *Night Must Fall*. His answer to that request was: "Well, I said if I were too old to play it professionally, I was too old to play it for charity!" [1] Williams happened to be reading at the time a biography of Charles Dickens that discussed Dickens's reading tours and his success as a platform performer. Williams decided that he would fulfill his commitment to appear at the benefit by re-creating Dickens-on-the-platform performing a ten-minute selection from *Bleak House*. The performance was a success and Williams decided to expand it into a full evening's entertainment: "I sat down . . . for a year trying to work out that evening. . . . It was a nerve-racking idea for me. Not since school had I ever appeared alone on stage, and I knew this was to be a rather more demanding audience" (Gerst 1981:D3).

In *Emlyn Williams as Charles Dickens*, Williams again re-created Dickens as he appeared on the platform, complete with Victorian formal evening clothes, Dickens's red boutonnier, and a replica of the novelist's reading desk. Although Williams studiously replicated many elements of Dickens's performances, he did not offer a duplicate of the author's readings. Williams's understanding of contemporary audiences led him to make important concessions. Whereas Dickens performed programs comprised of two lengthy segments from two works, Williams, in deference to contemporary audiences' shorter attention spans, devised programs containing short (approximately ten minute) selections from a variety of Dickens's works.[2] Typically, Williams chose selections from texts that are not generally well known. For example, he avoided the perennial *A Christmas Carol*, fearing that the audience was too familiar with either the book itself or stage and film adaptations of the old favorite. Williams's programs included: "Moving in Society" from *Our Mutual Friend*, "A Call upon a Strange Man" from *The Black Veil*, "Mr. Bob Sawyer Gives a Bachelor Party" from *The Pickwick Papers*, "Paul" from *Dombey and Son*, "Mr. Chops" from *The Tale of a Little Person*, "Once Upon a Time" from *The Battle of Life*, "Moving Higher in Society" from *Little Dorrit*, "The Fancy Ball" from *A Tale of Two Cities*, and "A Bedtime Story for a Good Child" from *The Uncommercial Traveller*. During his own career as a platform reader, Dickens could correctly assume that his audiences were generally familiar with his works and could, therefore, readily understand isolated excepts. Williams, on the other hand, knew that he had no such common ground. To compensate, Williams's selections were thoughtfully edited for contemporary audiences; his program included this statement: "In adapting carefully, but freely, the actor has thought it only fair to assume (as he would were he writing a play based on a novel) that his audience knows nothing of the book in question: his aim being to make each item complete and totally comprehensible in the theatre" (Program notes for *Emlyn Williams as Charles Dickens*, *North Light Magazine* [North Light Theatre, Evanston, IL.], Sept./Oct. 1981:20). Both in performance and in silent reading, it is evident that Williams's recital was not a simple anthology. The program of selections was a performance text that stood as a unified dramatic whole carefully orchestrated in mood and tempo to maintain audience interest and to achieve maximum theatrical effect.

After opening at Cambridge's Arts Theatre on 25 July 1951, Williams went on a tour of English cities. His tour of England culminated in a highly successful run at London's Criterion and Duchess theatres; after his London closing, Williams immediately left on a world tour. Williams's first international tour as a solo performer took him to America, where he (like Dickens nearly a century before) first stopped in Boston. After appearing in Boston, *Emlyn Williams as Charles Dickens* opened at the John Golden Theatre in New York on 4 February 1952; the reviews were enthusiastic:

Make no mistake about it: the show that Mr. Williams is providing is not a literary affectation for the benefit of the famous novelist's cult. It is authentic theatre, and drama of a high order and almost universal appeal. It is not even correct to call it a "reading," any more than the successful recent presentation of "Don Juan in Hell" was a "reading." The visiting star does have books in front of him, and he does make a pretense of turning the pages from time to time. But he never once has to refer to them, and he acts out every character and every accent with the varied brilliance of the superb player he is (Watts 1952:25).

The review sounds remarkably like those notices of Dickens's own readings in which the critics struggled with language to find a proper description of the event: the term *reading* seems insufficient to describe the performance of either Dickens or Williams. The struggle is a result of the persistent problem of genre classification of solo performance. In spite of the critic's difficulty in finding a suitable terminology, he fully accepts Williams's performances as "authentic theatre." His review stands as an affirmation of the acceptance of the one-person show as a form of entertainment integral to theatre proper. As seen in the following review by William Hawkins, theatre critics, despite their own lack of experience in evaluating solo performances, found the form intriguing: "The star wisely begins in a low gear, and you may wonder for the first few minutes how on earth he is going to hold an audience all evening. Shortly, the existence of actor and method are forgotten. The spell takes hold to continue a fabulous fabric of inventive color" (Hawkins 1952:12). When confronted with an exceptional solo performance, such as *Emlyn Williams as Charles Dickens,* the critics of the mid-twentieth century have seemed taken by surprise. The fact that a solo performer provides a fully satisfying evening of entertainment surpasses critical expectations. The lingering negative side effects of the elocutionary movement, however, continue to surface, as seen in John Chapman's review of Williams's recital:

> An extraordinary professional audience—managers, directors and good actors at liberty, like Lunt and Fontanne—went to the John Golden Theatre last evening for a lesson in show business. This audience took the lesson, liked it and cheered for more.
>
> The teacher was Emlyn Williams, who got himself up in whiskers and costume to look like Charles Dickens, stood behind a curious-looking red plush covered desk and recited bits and pieces of Dickens. That's all he did—recite; and this was enough to make a heart-warming evening.
>
> Elocution, they used to call this kind of thing when I was a grammar-school urchin with a passionate loathing for all the elocution teachers in all the public schools of Denver. I not only hated the teachers; I hated anybody who was silly ass enough to get up and elocute (Chapman 1952a:12).

Although *Emlyn Williams as Charles Dickens* received a generally enthusiastic reception from the New York critics, there were those who reacted negatively: their reaction was not aimed, however, at Williams's talents but at the form of solo performance itself. The following review, entitled "Readings, Talents, Don't Justify Price," voices a lingering resistance against accepting a solo performance as legitimate theatre:

> Emlyn Williams, a Welshman of inestimable talents as an actor and writer, has finally evolved the absolute all-time money-makingest idea in show business. He comes out all alone at the John Golden Theatre and for more than two hours "reads" from Dickens. For this the customer pays $4.80 per seat.
>
> Last night, at his opening on Broadway, I was making a private tally of his overhead. He is made up to look like Dickens and he works from a desk that is supposed to be similar to the one used by the great Victo-

rian author when he engaged in a similar and equally lucrative endeavor in the 1860s.

He is thus laying out about $200 for costumes, $20 for beard, $100 for desk, and he uses a couple of books which he might easily have borrowed from the Public Library. I suppose the union laws are such that he is paying for some unnecessary scene-shifters, but the fact remains that this kid stands to make a load of loot.

No Cast, No Sets

There is no supporting cast and no sets. What if the show only brings in a miserable $20,000 a week? Our boy is still doing all right.

On a critical basis I would say you have to accept two things. First, you have to be a big Dickens fan and, second, you must want to have it read to you—especially by Emlyn Williams.

This provokes a further point: will he read the things you want read? Will he also read it that much better than you might read it at home, yourself, with the light switch handy when you have had enough?

In my meager opinion neither the writings of Dickens nor the performance of Williams justifies the journey to the John Golden Theatre.

I am the first to applaud anybody who discovers a new dodge to uncover a quick dollar, but come, come, chums, why don't we put a long playing phonograph on the stage and engage the clients with a series of Shakespearean records for the evening?

This is meant neither as a blast at the author or the actor, however it sounds. I would welcome a proper production of "Tale of Two Cities" with Emlyn Williams in the cast, but I felt let down at the proceedings last night.

Is this THEATRE? I wonder (McClain 1952:12).

The review raises perplexing questions regarding the reasons behind the critic's negative reaction. Was this critic simply unable to evaluate a solo performance of prose fiction? Apparently McClain's problem was one of genre classification. Unable to place Williams's solo performance into its proper frame of reference, he instead persisted in his demands that the performance meet his set expectations of what he felt constituted "theatre" (i.e., standard dramatizations). Professional critics, however, should be artistically sensitive enough to know when their expectations are out of place. E. D. Hirsch discusses the importance of genre expectations in *Validity in Interpretation*. Although Hirsch refers to literary genres, his statements apply to our discussion of performance genres: "[A]n interpreter's preliminary generic conception of a text [Hirsch, of course, means literary text; we may substitute "performance"] is constitutive of everything that he subsequently understands, and that this remains the case unless and until that generic conception is altered" (1967:74). Paul Hernadi develops Hirsch's examination of genre classifications in *Beyond Genre*. According to Hernadi, the responsible critic would not allow his or her set expectations to distort a reaction to a work of art: "Instead of permitting preconceived generic expectations to distort his response to the work, he will stay ready to revise his idea of a genre in the light of new experience. Such flexibility in deciding what 'kind' of work we are considering is indeed essential" (1972:3). Judging from his review of Emlyn Williams's recital, I suggest that John McClain on a very basic level did not understand solo performance nor possess an elementary appreciation of the aesthetics of the genre. His comparison of Williams's solo performance to a fully mounted drama implies that McClain simply was mistaken in his initial generic conception of the performance and never revised his expectations as the performance experience continued. "[O]ur ability to comprehend a text [or performance]," writes Thomas L. Kent, "is related directly to our generic perception of it" (1986:1). McClain, mistaken in his generic perception of *Emlyn Williams as Charles Dickens* and unable to adjust his expectations, was incapable of evaluating Williams's work on its own merits. Instead, the critic rejected the performance within its first few moments and spent the rest of the evening tallying production costs. Had McClain been flexible in his generic expectations, he would have grown into an understanding of the differences between the aesthetics of realistic drama and those of the solo performance of prose fiction.

The success of his *Dickens* recital encouraged Williams to develop other solo vehicles. The first of these subsequent performances had Williams again return in the guise of Charles Dickens but this time, instead of a mixed bill of selections, Williams-as-Dickens performed a highly condensed adaptation of one novel. Williams's full-length solo performance based on Dickens's *Bleak House* premiered in Britain in 1952; he toured the United States the following year and opened in New York at the Bijou Theatre on 20 April 1953. Williams's *Bleak House* drew positive reviews but did not achieve the same popular success as his mixed-bill *Dickens* recital. Perhaps the concentrated focus on one novel, and a darkly satiric one at that, proved too much for a general public audience.

In 1955 Williams developed a third one-person show, choosing as his focus the prose writings of Dylan Thomas. Williams avoided Thomas's poetry, fearing that Thomas was an incomparable verse reader and that the poems themselves were too difficult for a theatre audience. A press release quoted Williams on the subject: "I am an actor, not a reader."[3] Originally titled *A Boy Growing Up*, the show was later retitled *Dylan Thomas Growing Up*, with its selections linked by the theme of maturation from childhood to early adolescence. The prose selections included scenes from "Quite Early One Morning," "Portrait of the Artist as a Young Dog," "A Prospect of the Sea," and "Adventures in the Skin Trade." The only poems in the program were "The Hand" and "And Death Shall Have No Dominion."

For his *Thomas* solo performance, Williams moved further away from impersonation to focus the performance on his interpretation of the author's writings. It is important to note that Williams did not feel that impersonation played an important part in his work. In reference to his *Dickens* recital, Williams explained his thoughts in a personal interview: "I do not do impersonations. How can anyone impersonate Dickens? We don't know what he was really like, his mannerisms, his voice. Each report is different. I wear his clothes and pretend to be Dickens. I do not impersonate Dickens. Dickens had what is called phlebitis in his leg. If I were to imitate him everyone would think I had something wrong with *my* leg!" (interview, 30 Dec. 1982). Williams considered his "impersonation" of Dickens secondary to his interpretations of the novelist's writings. In preparing his solo performance, Williams's energy was directed toward polishing his own personal interpretations of Dickens's prose, after which he simply added costume and beard. Williams did not, despite similarities in performance styles, attempt to imitate either Dickens as a performer or Dickens as a man. In *Dylan Thomas Growing Up*, Williams linked his selections from Thomas's stories by addressing the audience as if he were Thomas; he made no effort, however, to look like Thomas. We saw Emlyn Williams speaking as if he were Thomas: he referred to his (Thomas's) curly brown locks, but we saw his (Williams's) own gray hair.

After premiering his *Thomas* one-person show in Britain, Williams toured with it throughout South Africa before opening at New York's Longacre Theatre on 7 October 1957. Again Williams received excellent reviews. Throughout the next two decades and into the 1980s, Williams continued to perform his *Dickens* and *Thomas* one-person shows with outstanding success. In 1977 Williams developed a fourth solo performance, *The Playboy of the Weekend World*, based on the writings of H. H. Munro (Saki). When *The Playboy of the Weekend World* opened in New York in 1978, its reviews, while generally positive, tended to favor Williams's earlier *Dickens* and *Thomas* programs. The critics' choice had less to do with Williams's own performance—the actor was unanimously praised as a consummate performer—than with the writings of Saki. "After the strong, bracing coffee of Williams' evenings of Dickens and Dylan Thomas," wrote one reviewer, "Saki, I'm afraid, is rather like Postum" (Kissel 1978:24). Another claimed that the Saki evening lacked "the robust flair of Williams' famous impersonation of Charles Dickens or the lyricism of his Dylan Thomas" (Wilson 1978:72). Other critics were even less kind in their estimation of Saki's stories as literature in performance: "Delicate and skillful as he is, Mr. Williams has chosen an author who simply can't survive the focus of attention that speaking him on a stage provides. I doubt that Saki would do even for reading aloud at a bedside" (Eder 1978:C3). The negative reactions to the Saki recital in spite of Williams's own commendable performance reminds us of the centrality of language and text in a solo performance. Although a good script is usually thought to be requisite for the success of a play, words are simply more featured in a one-person show than in most play productions, where elements of spectacle and performer interaction may more readily mask a weak script. Despite reservations about the merits of Saki's writings, the critics acknowledged Williams as the "long proven master of the art" (Beaufort 1978a:20) of solo performance. "Emlyn Williams," wrote Clive Barnes, "that centaur of a man, half-playwright, half-actor and even then half-entrepreneur—has made an art form out of the one-man show. His Charles Dickens recital began, for good or ill, a theatrical movement, full of pomp, prestige and potential profit" (1978:31). Williams was undoubtably the premiere solo performer of our time. His *Dickens* performance in the early 1950s began a trend and the following thirty years saw his one-person shows continue to grow in reputation. In 1975 Sheridan Morley wrote in *Punch Magazine*:

[W]hen, at the Lyric Hammersmith in 1951, Emlyn Williams first drew off those white gloves at the lectern and announced that he was Charles Dickens, he can scarcely realized what he was starting. The success of that solo evening . . . led him to take it around the world—something that with remarkable resilience he has been doing more or less ever since—and led other actors to start rifling through the library shelves in search of other authors who might stand up to an entire evening's reading (1975:465).

Hal Holbrook's *Mark Twain Tonight!*

Nearly coinciding with that fateful 1950 offer for Emlyn Williams to appear in a benefit, an offer across the Atlantic Ocean proved to be the beginning of another landmark performance in the history of the one-person show in America. In 1947 two Denison University theatre students were presented by the head of their department with an offer to tour in a two-person show. The show was to be comprised of scenes depicting the lives of famous historical personalities, such as Robert and Elizabeth Browning, John Alden and Priscilla, Queen Victoria and Prince Albert, and Mark Twain. The two young theatre students were a newly married couple; their names were Hal and Ruby Holbrook.

The years of touring with his wife in their two-person show ultimately led to Holbrook's solo in which he re-creates Mark Twain's platform performances. The Twain piece began as a short duo scene entitled "Mark Twain and the Interviewer," in which Ruby Holbrook played the interviewer. After several years and the birth of their daughter, Holbrook began seriously considering the possibility of developing an extended solo performance centered on Twain. It is one of the coincidences in the history of the one-person show that while Holbrook was just beginning to develop his Twain one-person show, he met James B. Pond, the son of Mark Twain's own lecture manager. "Bim" Pond (as he was known) had inherited the lecture business from his father and continued to develop it, to quote Holbrook, "to a point of preeminence in the field" (Holbrook 1959:27). Pond proved instrumental in launching Holbrook's one-person show.

The first performance of *Mark Twain Tonight!* was at the State Teachers College in Lockhaven, Pennsylvania, on 19 March 1954. Years would pass before Holbrook played Twain in a New York theatre. In the interim, audiences saw "Twain" on the platform in a variety of places. A suggestion by Lovey Powell, a friend of Holbrook's, finally led to a booking of *Mark Twain Tonight!* at the Purple Onion, a Manhattan nightclub. Holbrook writes of his nightclub performances:

At first it seemed a ridiculous suggestion, but I thought it over and decided it would be an interesting experience. She [Lovey Powell] got me an audition at a place called the Purple Onion, housed in a cellar beneath a bar on the corner of Fifty-first Street and Sixth Avenue in New York. They put me on the bill. I stayed there for three weeks and "Mark Twain" as a night-club performer seemed to go pretty well. I worked up three fifteen-minute routines and varied them during the two or three shows I did every night (1959:61–62).

Throughout the mid-1950s, Holbrook continued to play Twain in nightclubs, while hoping to perform eventually in a legitimate theatre. He wanted, as he has said, to establish the fact that his solo performance was "a three-act evening of theatre, not just a lecture" (1959:74). Holbrook's wish was granted on 6 April 1959, when *Mark Twain Tonight!* opened at the off-Broadway Forty-first Street Theatre.

Emlyn Williams as Charles Dickens and *Mark Twain Tonight!* stand as landmarks in the history of the one-person show in America. Over the three decades following their premieres, both performances have grown in acclaim and reputation. On the surface they seem to be related images of each other. Williams re-created Dickens on the platform; Holbrook re-creates Twain. There exist, however, important differences between the two men's performances. Whereas Emlyn Williams presented a series of readings of distinctly separate works, Hal Holbrook offers a continuous program that moves easily between informal lecture and scenes from literary texts. The central conceptual difference between the two shows concerns the actors' characterizations of the personae and the importance of impersonation in their respective shows. Williams's main focus in his *Dickens* recital was on his own interpretations of the Victorian author's novels and stories. His impersonation of Dickens as a man was secondary; Williams had said, "I wear his clothes and pretend to be Dickens. I do not impersonate Dickens." Holbrook, on the other hand, is interested in bringing Twain *the man* to the stage and simply uses readings from the author's works as a part of his re-creation. For Holbrook, the interpretation of Twain's writings is secondary. Holbrook has said:

> One of my biggest problems from the very beginning was to establish the character of Mark Twain firmly and then work out a technique of portraying other characters [in Twain's writings], such as the Guide, for instance, through the character of Mark Twain—a sort of double impersonation.
>
> The technique I settled upon is this: I first create the "character" to be played in the episode—such as the Guide, or Huck, or Jim. Once I feel I have conceived one of these characters properly I do him again and *think* Mark Twain. The voice quality immediately changes when I do that and the physical movements acquire a different pace and quality.
>
> It took a good deal of practice but in time I was able to come up with the illusion that I was Mark Twain doing these people, not Hal Holbrook. It is like straining soup through a sieve: all the vitamins and minerals get through, but the egg noodles remain (Holbrook 1959:37).

Through careful research, Holbrook has worked fastidiously to impersonate Mark Twain precisely. The program from the 1959 run of *Mark Twain Tonight!* at the Forty-first Street Theatre explained: "Twelve years of research have made Mr. Holbrook well acquainted with Mark Twain. In his quest for authenticity he has acquired a copy of the rare Edison film of Twain, a recording of his voice, studied reviews of his lectures, and talked with people who knew the Missourian personally or saw him on the platform. The authentic material which Mr. Holbrook uses has been adapted by himself and he created the make-up, which requires three hours to apply" (found in *Mark Twain Tonight!* file, Billy Rose Theatre Collection).

The New York performance of *Mark Twain Tonight!* proved to be the major turning point in Holbrook's career. The critics uniformly praised the performance, including John McClain of the *New York Journal-American,* who had earlier reacted so negatively to Williams's *Dickens* recital. Of the Holbrook performance McClain wrote:

> For lovers of homespun Americana, there is an enchanting evening offered in the underground 41st Street Theatre at 125 W. 41st St. A young man named Hal Holbrook gives readings entitled "Mark Twain Tonight!", excerpts from the author's books and speeches which are utterly delightful. It opened last night.
>
> Carefully made up in the flowing gray mustache and tousled white hair of a seventy-year-old Samuel Clemens, he totters about the stage set only with a chair, a table holding a collection of his books and a lectern which he rarely uses. He wears the white linen suit associated with his most frequent photographs because, as he explains it, it beats going around naked.
>
> This 34-year-old actor gives an incredible impression of the novelist who, late in life, captured the affections of the country as a platform humorist. It is a monstrous chore to stay alive on a small stage for a conventional theatre evening but he succeeds in skillfully toying with a cigar, using his young hands in the faltering gestures of the aged, and employing the calculated pause which was reputedly one of Mark Twain's greatest tricks. . . .
>
> These one-man readings . . . can be a booming bore. But this one is not. Mr. Holbrook has a splendid feeling for the temper of his audience, his timing is exact, and he steps easily in and out of the character of the author and the various fictional persons he portrays (1959:16).

During the seven years between his reviews of Williams's *Dickens* recital and *Mark Twain Tonight!* McClain probably had the opportunity to see other solo performances. His comment that "These one-man readings . . . can be a booming bore," certainly suggests a continued, albeit unfelicitous experience with the genre. McClain, however, still displays a disturbing lack of sensitivity when discussing the performance event. Reducing Twain's writing to "homespun Americana" is the first indication of a lack of an appreciation of language and the subtleties of Twain's humor. Even more reductive is his estimation of Holbrook's careful use of the cigar as prop and the actor's masterful "double imper-sonation." Whereas McClain simply reports Holbrook stepped "easily in and out of the character of the author and the various fictional persons he portrays," Holbrook, in actuality, maintains the persona of Twain and it is *through* this persona that he then performs the literary characters.[4]

Holbrook's 1959 off-Broadway performance of *Mark Twain Tonight!* established him as an important young talent. After his run at the Forty-first Street Theatre, Holbrook went on to other work in the theatre and soon earned the reputation as a fine dra-matic actor and as a solo performer. Over the years, Holbrook has periodically returned to *Mark Twain Tonight!* His Twain resume now includes two successful Broadway runs (in 1966 and 1977), international tours, two long-playing albums, a published script, and a CBS television special (aired in 1967). Holbrook received the theatre's highest accolade in 1966 for his performance in *Mark Twain Tonight!*—he won the Antoinette Perry Award for the year's outstanding performance by an actor.

THE BIOGRAPHICAL ONE-PERSON SHOW GENRE

The combined successes of Williams and Holbrook initiated a the-atrical movement of solo performances that may best be called "biographical" one-person shows.[5] Playwright Tom Topor helps define this genre of solo performances: "Shows of this sort are attempts at living biographies. The performer impersonates the historical figure (sometimes very closely, sometimes just impres-sionistically) and, using letters, and documents and other histori-cal (or quasi-historical) material, offers the audience a slice of the figure's life" (1980:31). There exists a tremendous variation within this genre, but the essential distinguishing characteristic is the solo performer's impersonation of a single historical figure.

Emlyn Williams as Charles Dickens and *Mark Twain Tonight!* proved that a single performer's impersonation of a single charac-ter could be accepted and acclaimed as a full evening's entertain-ment in a legitimate theatre. When Cornelia Otis Skinner was per-forming, a journalist said that her performances demonstrated that a solo performer must portray various characters to hold an audience: "she could not hold the stage for an entire performance portraying just one character. No one could" (Eames 1935:342). It took *Emlyn Williams as Charles Dickens* and *Mark Twain Tonight!* to prove resoundingly that such a statement was erroneous. Once Williams and Holbrook set a precedent, other performers realized the potential of the biographical one-person show as a vehicle and showcase. Among the first biographical one-person shows to follow the Williams/Holbrook lead was Michael Mac-Liammoir's *Importance of Being Oscar,* a solo centered on another nineteenth-century writer, Oscar Wilde, which opened in New York in 1961. MacLiammoir openly acknowledged his personal debt to Emlyn Williams in his published account of the making of his Wilde recital (1968). Williams, explains MacLiammoir, not only served as an inspiration but as a personal instructor of solo performance as well. Faced with the difficult task of editing his script, he called upon the experienced Williams for advice: "Emlyn, the hero and villain of many plays by himself; Emlyn, the interpreter of Charles Dickens, of Dylan Thomas, and of Emlyn George Williams, himself; Emlyn the Wizard of the Welsh West End. And there he performed a miracle of stage-surgery" (1968:78). The notion of solo performance at first daunted MacLiammoir. The brilliant successes of Draper and Williams seemed to have set standards against which it was impossible to compete. MacLiammoir wrote of his misgivings:

The idea of doing a one-man show . . . had never seriously entered my head. I think it had never entered my head at all, seriously or otherwise. One-man shows on the stage had always seemed to me the exclusive prerogative of the female sex, of one of its most breath-taking members in particular. Ruth Draper, whom I believe to have been a woman of genius, had done it and still was doing it. Watching her, as I did at every possible opportunity, it was plain to me that no male person could ever foster a hope of doing what she, with the aid of a hat or a shawl or a lace veil could do with no apparent effort and keep it going for a whole evening's entertainment (1968:40).

When Peter Ashmore, a personal friend of MacLiammoir, continually pressed him to try creating a Wilde one-person show, MacLiammoir resisted. MacLiammoir has said:

Suddenly I thought again of Ruth Draper. So I said: "Emlyn has done it already, you see."

What?"

"Emlyn. Emlyn Williams. With Dickens. Incomparable. He's the only man who could dare to compete with Her. All alone on the stage. My God."

"Who's Her?"

"Ruth Draper, of course. Once one man has challenged her seriously, no other man can. Or should" (1968:46).

Finally persuaded, MacLiammoir consented and *The Importance of Being Oscar* opened on 14 March 1961 at the Lyceum Theatre in New York to highly favorable reviews.[6] By 1971 the *New York Times* was referring to *The Importance of Being Oscar* as "a classic" one-person show. The article continued its belief that Mac-Liammoir's recital set a standard and that "No one-man show since has succeeded in being so total in its rich accomplishment, and it is doubtful if any ever will" (Rushe 1971:52). Mac-Liammoir's success lead him to develop a second solo performance, *I Must Be Talking to My Friends,* a recital in which he traced the development of Irish literature. He has since toured worldwide in both one-person shows and has enjoyed, as the *New York Times* indicates, critical acclaim as a solo performer.

The apparent major impetus in the movement of biographical one-person shows came in 1966, with Hal Holbrook's first Broadway run of *Mark Twain Tonight!* and his triumphant win of the American Theatre Wing's Tony award. Thereafter the biographical one-person show movement accelerated. The 1967 New York season included the premieres of Roy Dotrice in *Brief Lives* (in which he portrayed the seventeenth-century diarist John Aubrey) and Max Adrian in *By George* (Bernard Shaw). Just as platform performances had reached an apogee in the last quarter of the nineteenth century, biographical one-person shows have reached an apogee in the last quarter of the twentieth century. During the 1970s the biographical one-person show movement continued to gain in momentum and prestige; the 1980s have seen no abatement but rather an increasing proliferation. New York's theatre seasons and the international touring circuit of the 1970s and

1980s have included a prodigious number of memorable biographical one-person shows. A partial listing includes:

Title of Show	Character	Performer
Affectionately Yours, Fanny Kemble	Fanny Kemble	Eugenia Rawls
The Belle of Amherst	Emily Dickinson	Julie Harris
Blake	William Blake	Douglas Campbell
Blasts and Bravos	H. L. Mencken	Paul Shyre
Brendan	Brendan Behan	Shay Duffin
Bully!	Theodore Roosevelt	James Whitmore
Cast of Characters	Ruth Draper	Patricia Norcia
Charlotte	Charlotte von Stein	Uta Hagen
Churchill	Winston Churchill	Roy Dotrice
Clarence Darrow	Clarence Darrow	Henry Fonda
Confessions of a Nightingale	Tennessee Williams	Ray Stricklyn
Diversions and Delights	Oscar Wilde	Vincent Price
Dylan Thomas	Dylan Thomas	Jack Aranson
Edmund Kean	Edmund Kean	Ben Kingsley
Eleanor	Eleanor Roosevelt	Eileen Heckart
An Evening with W. S. Gilbert	W. S. Gilbert	Lloyd Harris
F. D. R.	Franklin D. Roosevelt	Robert Vaughn
From Sholom Aleichem with Love	Sholom Aleichem	Elliott Levine
Gertrude Stein Gertrude Stein Gertrude Stein	Gertrude Stein	Pat Carroll
Give 'Em Hell, Harry!	Harry Truman	James Whitmore
Goodnight, Mr. Poe	Edgar Allan Poe	Scott Keely
His Satanic Majesty	Lord Byron	William J. Norris
The Hitler Masque	Adolph Hitler	William J. Norris
Hizzoner—The Mayor!	Fiorello LaGuardia	Tony Lo Bianco
I Am His Wife	Helene Schweitzer	Lily Lessing
Longfellow Returns	Henry Wadsworth Longfellow	Humphrey Davis
Kipling	Rudyard Kipling	Alec McCowen
Lillian	Lillian Hellman	Zoe Caldwell

Lincoln	Abraham Lincoln	Fritz Weaver
A Lovely Light	Edna St. Vincent Millay	Dorothy Stickney
Macready!	William Charles Macready	Frank Barrie
Mister Lincoln	Abraham Lincoln	Roy Dotrice
My Astonishing Self	Bernard Shaw	Donal Donnelly
My Gene	Carlotta Monterey (O'Neill)	Colleen Dewhurst
Oh, Mr. Faulkner Do You Write?	William Faulkner	John Maxwell
Oscar Remembered	Lord Alfred Douglas	Mazin Mazumdar
Papa	Ernest Hemingway	George Peppard
Paris Was Yesterday	Janet Flanner	Celeste Holm
Paul Robeson	Paul Robeson	James Earl Jones
Poe in Person	Edgar Allan Poe	Conrad Pomerleau
Rab the Rhymer	Robert Burns	John Forrest Ferguson
Robert Frost: Fire and Ice	Robert Frost	Arthur Peterson
Samuel Pepys	Samuel Pepys	William Karlblom
Tallulah, A Memory	Tallulah Bankhead	Eugenia Rawls
An Unpleasant Evening with H. L. Mencken	H. L. Mencken	David Wayne
Vincent	Theo Van Gogh	Leonard Nimoy
A Visitation from John Keats	John Keats	Mark Stevenson
Vivien Leigh	Vivien Leigh	Jan Merrow
Whistler	James McNeill Whistler	John Cullum
Will Rogers' U.S.A.	Will Rogers	James Whitmore
Woody Guthrie	Woody Guthrie	Tom Taylor
The World of Ruth Draper	Ruth Draper	Ruth Brinkman
Yr. Loving Mama, V. R.	Queen Victoria	Anna Welsh
Zelda	Zelda Fitzgerald	Olga Bellin

These titles indicate that the historical figures selected for biographical one-person shows tend to be "larger than life" and have left an important legacy. George Spota, producer of *Will Rogers' U.S.A.* and *Bully!*, commented that "the type of figure who provides the most powerful theatrical personality is one with 'a universal quality, whose words live beyond his or her time' " (quoted in Carrol 1977:1). Preferably the figure is also well known by the general public, for simple economic reasons: often the character's name recognition will help boost the ticket sales as much as can that of the star performer. The historical figure's celebrity is even more important for a show whose performer is relatively unknown. In such cases, the figure's name is the single strongest selling point.

Several of these solo productions are notable. Among the most acclaimed are *Brief Lives, Clarence Darrow, Give 'Em Hell, Harry!, The Belle of Amherst,* and *Gertrude Stein Gertrude Stein Gertrude Stein.* Henry Fonda and Julie Harris both won Antoinette Perry Awards for their performances in *Clarence Darrow* and *The Belle of Amherst,* respectively. Pat Carroll won a Drama Desk Award and an Outer Critics' Circle Award for her performance in *Gertrude Stein . . . ,* the script also won an Outer Circle Critics Award as Best Play. James Whitmore's *Give 'Em Hell, Harry!,* Harris's *Belle of Amherst,* and Carroll's *Gertrude Stein . . .* won the National Academy of Recording Arts and Sciences' Grammy Awards for Best Spoken Words or Drama Recording in 1975, 1977, and 1979, respectively. Many biographical one-person shows have been taped and telecast on network, public, or cable television, and James Whitmore's *Give 'Em Hell, Harry!* was filmed and released as a motion picture in 1975. His performance earned him a nomination by the National Academy of Motion Picture Arts and Sciences for an Oscar award in the prestigious Best Actor category. Whitmore is the only solo performer to have received such a nomination. *Brief Lives* remains a landmark production in the history of the one-person show in America on the strength of its durability; *The Guinness Book of World Records* lists Dotrice in *Brief Lives* as holding the world record for number of performances by a single performer in a one-person show— 1,700, including 400 straight performances at London's Mayfair Theatre.

These shows indicate a movement away from the platform re-creations of Williams's *Dickens* and Holbrook's *Twain* toward intimate portraits of the private lives of the central characters. They maintain, however, the presentational mode with the central figure addressing the audience. Very few one-person shows—whether biographical or not—close off the audience behind the fourth wall of stage realism; those that do work on the basis of some conceit. Eugene O'Neill's one-act play *Before Breakfast* uses the conceit that its single character, Mrs. Rowland, speaks to her perpetually off-stage husband. Jean Cocteau's *Human Voice* has one character who speaks either to her lover over the telephone or to herself in soliloquy. In Samuel Beckett's *Krapp's Last Tape*, Krapp speaks to himself and to an audiotape of himself he made years before. Meade Roberts's *Vivien Leigh: A Portrait* combines several conceits by having Leigh speak into a tape recorder, make telephone calls, and talk to herself in asides. The fact that there are so few one-person shows that do not use some form of audience address and participation attests to the importance of the presentational mode for the genre. Sometimes this involvement requires of the audience a collaborative imagining to fill in suggested scenes and evoked characters. This kind of participation was a typical feature of Ruth Draper's performances.

Other shows require that the audience actually take on a role. The audience-performer relationship in one-person shows hinges on the device of "casting" the audience. Critics of the genre sometimes question its position as drama because, to their eyes, one-person shows lack drama's most essential requirement: the interaction and conflict between characters. Yet any survey of one-person shows quickly reveals that there *is* another "character" present, and that character is the audience. The most overt use of casting the audience occurs in Brazilian playwright Roberto Athayde's *Miss Margarida's Way*, which has a fictional rather than historical main character. The audience is cast as a class of schoolchildren who must respond to the tyrannical ravings of their teacher, Miss Margarida. Athayde's one-character play is an extreme example of a one-person show's casting of the audience. Other performances are more subtle but still depend on the device. Robert S. Wilson, in his introduction to Marty Martin's *Gertrude Stein Gertrude Stein Gertrude Stein*, explicitly discusses its importance:

At first, it [*Gertrude Stein* . . .] appears to be a one-character play—but do not be fooled. It is most definitely a two-character play. And by this I do not mean to refer to the off-stage presence of Alice B. Tolkas. . . . It is, rather, the audience that becomes, must become, the other character. Sometimes it takes the audience a little while to realize that it must do more than merely sit back and be amused. We *are* amused, of course, but to get the full enjoyment of the play we must participate—we must play back to Stein (1980:xi-xii).

The role in which the audience is cast varies from production to production. In *Emlyn Williams as Charles Dickens* and *Mark Twain Tonight!* the audience transcends time to assume the role of a Victorian audience. The effect of casting the audience in these two platform recreations was examined by one reviewer; although specifically addressing Williams's *Dickens* recital, these words apply to Holbrook's *Twain* as well:

It suggests that the whole thing is offered as a sort of period piece and therefore an audience which might consider itself too sophisticated to attend a "reading" and, for that matter, too sophisticated to be either amused or touched by Dickens' old-fashioned humor and old-fashioned pathos may permit itself to enjoy the whole thing if it is allowed to regard it as quaint. But having thus saved its face, this same audience settles down to enjoy precisely what its grandfathers enjoyed somewhat more directly (Krutch 1952:189–90).

Emlyn Williams as Charles Dickens and *Mark Twain Tonight!* present the audience with the relatively simple task of assuming the role of an historical audience witnessing the public performances of platform showmen. But what of the shows that move into the private world of the central character? How can an audience accept its presence in the private home of an historical figure?

Brief Lives, the highly successful one-person show based on the writings of the seventeenth-century diarist John Aubrey, places the central character not in a public situation but in his private chambers. In a fully mounted naturalistic set, the elderly Aubrey lives out a day. Initially, the audience is simply an observer watching Aubrey mumbling to himself much as we would watch characters in a realistic drama. Gradually, however, the convention of the invisible fourth wall breaks down and the audience realizes that Aubrey is neither speaking to himself nor to another character on stage; Aubrey speaks to us, the audience, and we assume the role of guest in his home.

The roles of performer-as-host and audience-as-guest function similarly in William Luce's *The Belle of Amherst,* in which the character of Emily Dickinson appears in her home in Amherst, Massachusetts. Unlike *Brief Lives,* which only gradually establishes the host/guest relationship, *The Belle of Amherst* casts the audience immediately as Dickinson enters her parlor with a teapot. Upon finding us in her home, Dickinson shyly welcomes us to tea, offers us cake, and proceeds to speak of her life. The nature of the discourse becomes more intimate as Dickinson warms to her visitors. We become not only house guests but also a collective ideal listener and confidant. The suspension of disbelief required of the audience necessary to accept the device of being cast as confidant proved too taxing for some critics of the play. The intense privacy of the true Dickinson seemed violated by the convention of the script: "We wonder a little at a recluse chatting away so readily about her private thoughts and when she starts telling us about the affair her brother is supposed to be having with someone's wife, we are sure she's an imposter—the Dickinsons wouldn't even have talked about this among themselves" (Sullivan 1976:32). As this review points out, once we fail to accept a show's basic premise, the whole performance is rendered ludicrous. Our acceptance of the convention of casting the audience is crucial to our acceptance of the entire production. Frank Galati, professor of performance studies at Northwestern University, spoke about the potential problem of casting the audience in one-person shows. Galati, who frequently performs his solo adaptation of Vladimir Nabokov's *Pale Fire,* addressed the problem concerning the central character's motivation to speak:

The hardest thing to establish is the conventional agreement between the audience and the performer about the nature of the experience they are about to share. The question that all solo performers must consider is "Why is this person speaking in this situation in front of this group or ignoring this group? Why should the audience listen to one person talk for an hour? What does this person have to say?" For my performance [in *Pale Fire*] I just ask them to accept that I am an expert who is giving a lecture. The audience realizes from the very beginning that it is a parody of a professor giving a lecture about poetry. The difference between that rather simple agreement and seeing Emily Dickinson [in *The Belle of Amherst*] drift around her private little Amherst cottage, musing privately about her life and then erupting into poetry periodically—I mean, what is that? Where is she? Why is she wandering around talking to herself? In the Twain piece [*Mark Twain Tonight!*] the situation is vastly different. Twain appears in a public situation. The critical aesthetic difference, in answering the question of "why are they speaking?" is whether or not the character is in a public situation with an audience—the real audience or the presumed audience that Twain might have had years ago when he was doing this sort of thing—or in a private world that the audience overhears and observes (interview, 17 Oct. 1982).

Galati's thoughts are appropriate not only for *The Belle of Amherst* but for all one-person shows that place the central characters in a private situation. Such important solo productions as *Clarence Darrow, Give 'Em Hell, Harry!* and *Gertrude Stein Gertrude Stein Gertrude Stein* all move into the private words of the selected figure and depend on the audience's willingness to accept the role as confidant. Indeed, no sooner are we tacitly asked to suspend our disbelief to become a confidant than we become privy to the central characters' interaction with imaginary characters on stage. This device, referred to as "double focus,"[7] permits the central character to break off direct address to the audience and to shift focus to imaginary re-created scenes of dialogue from memory. Galati's question "Why is this character speaking?" becomes all the more insistent at such points in the scripts. For those unable to accept the convention, the character merely seems deranged. The evocation of imaginary characters by the solo performer has proven to be a cumbersome and annoying affectation for some critics of the one-person show form: "I object . . . to the whole idea of watching an actor spend an evening conducting imaginary conversations. . . . If he still cannot bring himself to talk to us, then let him by all means talk to himself—but not, please, to invisible interlocutors in whom neither he nor we can believe" (Cushman 1979:16).

Yet if we can accept the convention, the evoked dramatic scenes from the central character's past can enrich the performance immeasurably. As Eunice Ruth Eifert describes in her detailed study of the performer-audience relationship, the shift from the narrative to the dramatic mode provides variety and rhythm to the performance: instead of simply *telling* us about past scenes from their lives, the characters are allowed to *show* us directly. The imagined dramatic scenes also possess an immediacy of emotion not appropriate in the narrative mode. In "doubling" our focus, to use Eifert's terminology, we not only see and hear the central character but through him/her we are able to see and hear the imagined other characters. The device, therefore, requires from the audience an active participation in the dialogue segments: since we only hear one side of the conversation, we must imagine the words and actions of the other characters. For those accepting the convention, the evoked dramatic scenes may actually prove the most engaging moments in a solo performance. Speaking of major biographical one-person shows, another critic praised the device: "[T]heatrically, these dramas advanced the one-person-on-stage form because they created other characters in their presence who almost became visible, and the actors transported their audiences back in time. The aim is for the audience to see the unseen, to let its imagination soar beyond time and the lighted place at the stage end of the theatre" (Mitgang 1980:12).

PERFORMANCE GENRES RELATED TO THE BIOGRAPHICAL ONE-PERSON SHOW

The biographical one-person show genre grows out of a tradition whose roots may be traced back to the very first time one person mimicked another. Undeniably crude and informal, such everyday imitative role-playing, as Aristotle tells us in *Poetics*, "is one instinct of our nature" (1971:50). So fundamental is the instinct for *mimesis* that Aristotle believed that it represented nothing less than a significant difference distinguishing humanity from the beasts. "The instinct of imitation is implanted in man from childhood, one difference between him and other animals being that he is the most imitative of living creatures, and through imitation he learns his earliest lessons; and no less universal is the pleasure felt in things imitated" (1971:50). To appreciate fully the range of imitative modes of solo performance, and their relationships to each other, the concept of a continuum is helpful. We begin with the simple mimicry of everyday role-playing placed at one end. As we move along the continuum, the next genre represents the work of professional performers, select individuals whose position in society affords them a special status not accorded to the common person. Among the ranks of professional performers, some achieve such a level of artistry or breadth of popular following as to lift them to star status. Such a star necessarily brings to his or her performances a heightened ethos that augments the performance experience.

The first professional genre, then, on the continuum of imitative solo performances represents an advance in sophistication from the everyday mimicry of ordinary people. These are the performances of nightclub humorists and impressionists. Contemporary examples immediately come to mind: Rich Little, Marilyn Michaels, Frank Gorshen, and the scores of comic actors on the popular television series *Saturday Night Live*. In *Performer Magazine* Bob Bronaugh writes: "The common denominator which these comedians share is humor; the goal of their impressions is to provoke laughter from the audience. They never attempt to actually portray the individual whom they're impersonating for any length of time. Rather their impressions are quick one-liners with a punch line and they change character at the bat of an eye-lash" (1971/72:1). The contemporary nightclub impressionist is an inheritor of a rich comic tradition that may be traced back to the performers of vaudeville and the music halls, and even to the jesters of the medieval courts.

Moving to the next genre on our imagined continuum, we find the work of the more "serious" impersonators. With this group of performers, we move further away from superficial mimicry, beyond exaggerated burlesques, to impersonations of depth and precision. Examples of this kind of impersonator already discussed in this study include Helen Potter, Cecilia Loftus, and Dorothy Sands. Although each of these women presented impersonations of depth, their performances nonetheless remained *limited* impersonations. That is, in a single performance these women presented a series of impersonations rather than one extended performance on a single historical figure. Cornelia Otis Skinner also offered her own kind of limited impersonations in her monologue-dramas. Her use of biographical material in composing her scripts prepared the way for the biographical one-person shows to come later in the century.

Moving to the end of the continuum, we finally reach extended imitative solo performances, or biographical one-person shows, as exemplified in figure 1. Because the difference between

FIGURE 1

DEPTH OF CHARACTERIZATION

Everyday life mimicry	Comic impressions	Limited impersonations	Extended impersonations (biographical one-person shows)

the work of a solo performer in a biographical one-person show and that of a comic impressionist is one of degree, not kind, theatre critics frequently dismiss one-person shows as "stunts," as if the genre were unable to shed the taint of its nightclub relative. This is unfortunate. Biographical one-person shows at their very best do not offer superficial caricature but, instead, present characterizations of depth. In his book *Seeming, Being, and Becoming,* Robert L. Benedetti speaks of impersonation and relates the topic directly to biographical one-person shows:

> Impersonation . . . must be understood in a broader, more useful sense than merely as the replication of another's appearance. For example, the last decade featured a number of one-man shows in which an actor impersonated a famous figure: Hal Holbrook as Mark Twain, Max Adrian as Bernard Shaw, Emlyn Williams, as Charles Dickens or Dylan Thomas. In none of these performances did the actor merely "look like" his subject in the literal sense; the actor's genius was expressed by going beyond (and beneath) literal appearance to create an experience which captured the *spirit* of the subject and, moreover, *captured it in a way that revealed some more universal human truth.* It is never enough for the actor merely to put on a convincing mask, to merely *seem* to be someone else; he must wear the mask of his character in such a way that he creates a new meaningful reality with its own deep truth in the process (1976:23–24).

Benedetti's words are particularly appropriate for this discussion because the act of impersonation is so absolutely central to the biographical one-person show genre. The successful one-person show hinges on the performance of the actor because the solo form itself mandates an emphasis on characterization. Of Aristotle's six dramatic elements discussed in *Poetics*, three are emphasized in one-person shows: character, theme or thought, and language, with character being the most important. Simply to avoid distracting the audience from the lone performer, the solo form minimizes the other three elements—plot, spectacle, and music. Benedetti justifiably states that the actor's impersonations move beyond the "literal appearances to create an experience which captured the *spirit* of the subject."

These words are supported by a study of various successful one-person shows. Research indicates that successful biographical one-person shows do not necessarily present a literal facsimile of the central persona. While it is true that for some solo shows part of the magic of the performance is the physical re-creation, such as Hal Holbrook's *Mark Twain Tonight!*, many of the most acclaimed one-person shows do not even attempt physical verisimilitude. Their success is due to the actor's ability to convey the essence or, to use Benedetti's word, the spirit of the impersonated figure.

PROBLEMS OF THE GENRE: THE USE OF BIOGRAPHY IN SOLO PERFORMANCE

When speaking of his work in *Will Rogers' U.S.A.*, James Whitmore said, "I've never attempted a photographic reproduction of the person. . . . My goal is simply to capture the essence of the man" (Carroll 1977:1). Over the years since his *Rogers* solo, Whitmore has developed into a master of the technique of suggestion in his impersonations. His work, not only as Will Rogers but also as Harry Truman in *Give 'Em Hell, Harry!* and as Theodore Roosevelt in *Bully!*, demonstrates the potency of suggestion as a technique to convey the spirit of the central character. Using no makeup, Whitmore has given the impression of Truman's physical self through the characteristic grin, glasses, and rapid speech pattern. In *Bully!* Whitmore simply has relied on glasses, facial expressions, and a mustache. When contrasting Holbrook's Twain to Whitmore's Rogers, *Time* commented: "Unlike Hal Holbrook in his *Mark Twain Tonight!*, Whitmore does not attempt to achieve a flesh-tinted, born-perfect reproduction of Rogers, nor does he even speak with Rogers' causal, careless Oklahoma drawl.

What he tries for, and succeeds in evoking, is a psychic affinity with the wit of the western corral" (MacNeil 1970:76). Similarly, Emlyn Williams used suggestion in his successful *Dylan Thomas Growing Up;* the *New York Times* wrote: "Mr. Williams never met Thomas and makes no attempt to portray him onstage. Yet, to a remarkable extent, he catches the poet's essence" (Barnes 1976:124). Other important solo productions rely on the performer's ability to suggest the presence of the central character. Both Julie Harris in *The Belle of Amherst* and Pat Carroll in *Gertrude Stein Gertrude Stein Gertrude Stein* suggested their characters' physical selves through a general resemblance in stature and size not through anything approximating a "photographic reproduction." The intent to suggest, as opposed to duplicate, often extends to the script as well. Instead of trying to deliver a factual record of biographic details, these shows aim to understand the character's subjective experience. Julie Harris said of *The Belle of Amherst,* "This is not a literal life of the poet. We tried to capture her mystique" (Wahls 1976:4).

Just as the successful biographical one-person shows owe their acclaim to the characterization of the central figure, most of the shows that fail do so because of the weakness of the actor's impersonation or the inability of the script to capture the persona's elusive essence. Sometimes failure in this area dooms the show to obscurity, as was the case with Elizabeth Garry's *One Perfect Rose,* based on the life of Rose Kennedy. Of the show, the *Chicago Reader* wrote: "[W]e see a limited picture. Rose Kennedy emerges as a devoted mother, ardent Catholic, and slightly ditzy public figure. . . . But doesn't this woman ever get angry? Isn't she hurt or shocked? Did she ever shed a tear for her children? . . . We are deprived of any sense of the private woman in moments of triumph or tragedy" (Abarbanel 1984:51). Even more scathing was the *New York Times* review of *Whistler* with John Cullum: "As vaguely written by Laurence and Maggie Williams and clownishly acted by Mr. Cullum, this play might just as well be the story of Al Capp. The authors have composed a monologue that tells us nothing about their subject's artistic sensibility and next to nothing of value about his life" (Rich 1981:C17). *One Perfect Rose* and *Whistler* are extreme examples of failures in characterization in biographical one-person shows. Occasionally, a solo production may actually receive a generally favorable critical response while still considered flawed fundamentally in the rendering of the central figure. Examples of such performances include *Paris Was Yesterday* with Celeste Holm as Janet Flanner, *Edmund Kean* with Ben Kingsley, *Kipling* with Alec McCowen, *Blasts and Bravos* with Paul Shyre as H. L. Mencken, and *Lillian* with Zoe Caldwell as Lillian Hellman.

Of *Paris Was Yesterday,* one critic wrote that "the most bothersome aspect of the production is that most of the time Holm seems to be *acting* Flanner rather than *being* Flanner" (Nelsen 1979:111). Paul Shyre, who adapted the script from Flanner's book and directed the production, agreed that Holm was miscast and did not convey the essence of the subject: "I think the problem with that [show] was the casting. They wanted a name actress; we couldn't find anyone and then we finally asked Celeste Holm to do it. It just didn't work with Celeste in the role. Janet was down to earth, whereas Celeste is ethereal, and it never quite worked" (quoted in Poschman 1982:32).

Shows with major stars, despite the drawing power of the star's own ethos, may still succumb to problems in characterization—as the many reviews of Ben Kingsley's *Edmund Kean* indicate. Critics argued that the *Kean* show "provided no sights into the real man" (Watt 1983:177). McCowen's *Kipling* suffered from the central paradox of thrusting Rudyard Kipling, an intensely private man, into a public performance. William Luce succeeded in developing the Emily Dickinson persona in *The Belle of Amherst* by moving into her private world, a liberty some purists argued ultimately violated the character. But Brian Clark, *Kipling*'s playwright, failed to develop a dramatic script by maintaining a fidelity to the history of his reclusive subject. At the beginning of the performance, Kipling "confides right off that he has no intention of telling us anything about his private life" wrote the *New York Times,* "His life, he explains, can only be found in his books" (Rich 1984a:22). While maintaining Kipling's reticence, Clark's *Kipling* remained responsible to history, but denied the audience the very thing we now expect from a biographical one-person show—an intimate examination of the life and persona of the central figure. Historical accuracy, as demonstrated by *Kipling*, is not a guarantee for success in the genre.

Conversely, distorting the history of the central figure in order to make the character more amiable for the sake of the performance can also result in a kind of failure. Two examples are *Blasts and Bravos* and *Lillian*. One critic wrote of Paul Shyre's characterization of H. L. Mencken in *Blasts and Bravos:*

As Shyre presents him, Mencken was all homespun wisdom and cracker barrel humor—sort of an urban Will Rogers. But the real Mencken was far from this. . . . Shyre, who adapted the play himself, is content to present us a man who was obsessed merely with attacking propriety and Fundamentalist Christianity. . . . Lines such as "America's the greatest show on earth" don't begin to convey the man's depth. And unfortunately, this quality is the thing "Blasts and Bravos" fails to capture (McKenna 1975:32).

Lillian suffered flaws similar to Shyre's Mencken show. Blessed with the talents of actress Zoe Caldwell and playwright William Luce, whose past monodrama credits include *The Belle of Amherst* and *Zelda,* the production received mostly positive reviews. Caldwell's physical impersonation of Hellman earned special recognition: "There are few, if any, more startling sights in a New York theatre right now than the one that opens *Lillian*. . . . As the curtain rises, we are confronted with an eerie reincarnation of the writer Lillian Hellman" (Rich 1986a:C3). The uncanny physical re-creation, however, was not enough to compensate for the script's timidity in exploring the essence of Hellman. The same critic went on to discuss the script's sweetening of Hellman's character. He concluded: "It's hard to reconcile the rather sugary, only slightly crumudgeonly figure presented here with the vinegary rebel who stirred up tempest for almost five decades on the public stage. In 'Lillian,' the unfinished woman who was Lillian Hellman has been given the polished finish that obscures as much as it glows" (Rich 1986a:C3). Both *Lillian* and *Blasts and Bravos* remain flawed by attempts to soften the abrasive central character in each. The playwrights, by opting to increase their subject's likeability, have actually bowdlerized the characters of Hellman and Mencken.

This discussion may very well have been subtitled "the *misuse* of biography in solo performance" because of our focus on the potential problems inherent in the biographical one-person show form. The major areas of concern—including the playwright's characterization of the central figure in the script, the casting of the central figure, the performance's responsibility to historical accuracy, and the need to fulfill the audience's expectations for the form—all directly impinge on the paramount aim of the genre: capturing the essence of the historical figure.

Biographical one-person shows are currently enjoying a popularity shared with other fact-based performance modes. Their appeal is similar to television docudramas. "Much of the interest in televised history," wrote Eric Foner, a critic of the docudrama form, "is simply voyeurism, a video expose of the secret lives of historical celebrities" (Foner 1979:724). This statement readily applies to the biographical one-person show genre, just as Foner's comment regarding the producers of docudramas also applies to the creators of biographical solo performances: "They want the creative freedom of the artist but also the imprimatur of the historian, an air of authenticity without the full responsibility that goes along with it" (1979:724). Ultimately, the real problem may be simply the act of biography itself. Virginia Woolf's comments in her essay "The Art of Biography" prefigure Foner's words on docudrama: "[T]he trouble lives with biography itself. It imposes conditions, and those conditions are that it must be based upon fact. And by fact in biography we mean facts that can be verified by other people besides the artist. If he invents facts as an artist invents them—facts that no one else can verify—and tries to combine them with facts of the other sort, they destroy each other" (1967:225).

FROM BIOGRAPHY TO AUTOBIOGRAPHY

Questions remain concerning the possible reasons for the biographical one-person show's popularity. One critic referred to the biographical one-person show as a "necrophilic genre" (Adler 1982:42), and although the label lacks delicacy, there does appear to be some truth to its implications. We are simply denied the honor of seeing Dickens on the platform or Emily Dickenson at home. The biographical one-person show re-creates an experience that we are denied by death and by the passage of time. Our fascination with great figures of the past is gratified in a manner of performance more intimate than allowed by standard dramatization. Beyond this, biographical one-person shows capitalize on the current vogue of printed biographies and autobiographies as Americans become increasingly enamored with nonfiction as reading material.[8] Biographic literature has surged in popularity on the reading market over the past few decades and the performing arts have reflected the current reading trends.

Scores of docudramas and fictionalized biographies have appeared on television in recent seasons. Two such television dramas based on the courtship of Prince Charles and Lady Diana Spenser were televised within a year of their marriage. The royal weddings were performance events themselves of epic proportions watched by millions of viewers around the world. Docudramas have even cast actual individuals as themselves, such as in *Sophia* and *Out on a Limb* in which Sophia Loren and Shirley MacLaine respectively played themselves. Television actress Deidre Hall (*Days of Our Lives* and *Our House*) created her own video autobiography, "Deidre Hall: A Video Biography," which showed her (ostensibly) going about her private life. The line between reality and performance blur to the point of nondistinction.

The ultimate examples of the biographical one-person show genre are the "autoperformances" by such performers as Jack Smith, Stuart Sherman, Jeff Weiss, Leeny Sack, Linda Montano, Bob Carroll, Theodora Skipitares, and Spalding Gray. Richard Schechner describes the difference between autoperformance and the usual one-person show: "I don't mean monologues in the traditional sense of a one-person show, but in the more radical sense of using the one person who is performing as the source of the material being performed. Compressed into a single presence is author-director-performer" (1982:44). At first glance, the work of these performers does not seem to belong in the category of biographical one-person shows. The performers do not appear as historical figures. They do not offer biography but *auto*biography.

SPALDING GRAY

Spalding Gray is probably the most widely known autoperformer. He began performing his first autobiographical monologue, *Sex and Death to the Age 14*, in 1979; his success led him to develop a series of monologues that he eventually performed in repertory under the title *Spalding Gray Retrospective.*[9] In his monologues, Gray appears as himself and speaks intimately of his own life. His role as autobiographer is of primary importance to Gray. "I am not just a solo performer," Gray has said, "I am also an autobiographer that happens to use solo performance as my mode of expression" (letter to the author, 27 Feb. 1983). Gray's performances are staged simply: the performer sits at a table with some note cards, a glass of water, and a spiral notebook, and speaks directly to the audience. The simple staging is significant, as Schechner points out: "Gray's own work, because of its Spartan avoidance of technical means, and his own insistence on simple language, comes across clear: Gray's path toward self-transcendence is through a thicket of ever more complicated self-remembering—complicated psychologically, even metaphysically, but not theatrically; his theatrical progress is toward minimalism" (1982:48).

In 1986 Gray performed two new monologues, *Swimming to Cambodia* and *Terrors of Pleasure,* at the Mitzi E. Newhouse Theatre at Lincoln Center, effectively moving into the theatrical mainstream. Gray's movement from avant-garde to mainstream is an indication of the contemporary wider acceptance of various solo modes as legitimate forms of theatre. His new monologues, one of which is a two-part narrative on his experience of filming *The Killing Fields,* the other of which is a comic tale covering the hazards of his attempts at home ownership, proved successful with the theatre critics: "Through a look or a comment, he offers intelligent analysis. Though the narrative is entirely centered around Mr. Gray himself, it never suffers from self-pity or self-indulgence. He remains the antihero in his own fascinating life story, the never ending tale of EverySpalding" (Gussow 1986:C19). Gray's monologues move beyond the actor's own particular life story to address themes of social and historical significance. In an insightful introduction to the published text of *Swimming to Cambodia,* James Leverett said:

[I]t would be false to consider these pieces to be the narcissistic exercises of an actor's overgrown ego, unconcerned with such irrelevant externals as politics history and society. *Sex and Death* [one of Gray's earlier monologues dealing with his youth] begins and ends with two cataclysmic punctuations: the A-bomb dropped at Hiroshima, the H-bomb at Enewetak. What Gray conveys in between, albeit in the subtlest and most indirect way, is the coming of age in this country after World War II. All of the monologues have had such an added, often hidden, dimension. If you stare at any one of them long enough, you find that what has happened to Gray reflects in a startlingly illuminating way what has happened to the world, or at least a significant section of it, you and I certainly included (1985:xi).

The complex weaving of social and personal history typical of Gray's monologues results from what he refers to as "poetic journalism." Instead of recording verifiable facts, Gray presents impressionistic memories: "So I like to think of myself as a kind of 'poetic reporter,' more like an impressionist painter than a photographer. Most reporters get the facts out as quickly as possible—fresh news is the best news. I do just the opposite. I give the facts a chance to settle down until at last they blend, bubble and mix in the swamp of dream, memory and reflection" (Gray 1985:xvi). The autobiographical texts created out of "dream, memory, and reflection" then evolve further in oral performance. Through live performances with audiences, Gray shapes and edits the stories into theatrical pieces. In 1987 *Swimming to Cambodia* was released as a motion picture. The critical success of the film version, which the *New York Times* referred to as "a breakthrough" (Canby 1987:19), moves Spalding Gray even more into the mainstream of American culture and may well encourage more soloists to appear on the big screen.

The impulse to tell his life story motivates Gray's monologues. "[T]he monologues come out of a compulsion," Gray has said in an interview, "an obsessive need to tell a story. And experiences keep coming up that need to be told" (quoted in Shewey 1986:8). This impulse toward storytelling links Gray to the entire solo tradition that is rooted in the art of storytelling and the basic human need to hear and to tell stories. Also tying Gray to the solo tradition is his use of solo performance as a means to invent his public persona.

Gray's performances and the theatrical phenomenon of the biographical one-person show as a whole are part of national movement that Richard Sennett refers to as "the fall of public man" (1978). Sennett discusses the gradual national devaluation of the public facade and the resultant emergence of private persona in the public realm. Gray's intimate monologues, the rise of autoperformances and biographical one-person shows, and the national preference for nonfiction as reading material all offer support for Sennett's thesis. Spalding Gray's work remains of special interest. Whereas much of our interest in nonfictional literature and biographical one-person shows exists because of our curiosity to find out more about an established persona/celebrity, Spalding Gray creates his persona through his monologues. Sophia Loren and Shirley MacLaine in their respective television dramas stepped into established public personae, their images as public/private individuals already set in the national consciousness. Gray, particularly at the very beginning of his solo career, had no public image. Through the process of exposing his private self in performance, Gray actually created a public self as a role to assume with an audience. His creation of an identity through the performance act has intrigued critics and audiences alike; Frank Rich of the *New York Times* wrote:

What you see is what you get in *Swimming to Cambodia*—or is it? What makes Spalding Gray so theatrical in his seemingly nontheatrical way is not only his talent as a storyteller and social observer but also his ability to deepen the mystery of the demarcation line between performer and role. His disciplined, scripted recital leaves us uncertain where Spalding Gray leaves off and "Spalding Gray," if that fictive character exists at all, begins. While that riddle may be beyond an audience's power to resolve, it's riveting to contemplate. Spalding Gray is the kind of actor who can send a theatergoer searching hungrily for clues at the stage door (1986c:25).[10]

The impulse to create a persona is of vital importance, not only for Spalding Gray's autobiographical monologues but also for the one-person show as a whole. As we have already seen, many of the major figures in this history have used solo performance as a means to invent or reinvent their public persona. Charles Dickens established himself through his readings not only as the favorite author of the period but also as the foremost overall (theatrical and literary) entertainer as well. Fanny Kemble, after her disasterous marriage, used solo performance as a way to reestablish her celebrity and her position within the Kemble family tradition of Shakespeare specialists. When her illness threatened her position as America's greatest actress, Charlotte Cushman recreated herself as a prominent platform reader. Although Spalding Gray's use of solo performance as a means to create a persona remains startling, we can see that such a phenomenon has been an integral part of the one-person form throughout its history.

An Evening with Quentin Crisp

Before leaving the autobiographical monologue for other solo genres, another show deserves special mention, for the creation of a public persona is not only its covert function as in Spalding Gray's monologues but is its explicit theme. *An Evening with Quentin Crisp* established Crisp's persona in performance and directly addresses the issue of image making with its audience. Crisp's solo is clearly autobiographical; like Gray, he appears as himself on stage. His text is a series of anecdotes, most of which deal with the development of personal style. As Crisp says, we do not need beauty, money, or talent to create our style. To those who despair of ever achieving it, he offers comfort: "Embrace defeat. . . . If first you don't succeed, failure may be your style" (quoted in Crouch 1986b:6C).

Although his show includes segments that appear in his books *The Naked Civil Servant, How to Become a Virgin,* and *Manners from Heaven,* it was never scripted in any formal sense. "There was no writing," Crisp explained to me in an interview, "No writing, no direction, no rehearsal, no anything." [11] The show's genesis bears witness to a remarkable lack of any preparation: Crisp was invited in 1975 to appear in a London public house during the lunch time hours and he simply went up on stage without any rehearsal save a mental collection of topics to talk about. The show met with no particular success until the airing of the television adaptation of *The Naked Civil Servant* brought Crisp an instant fame. Thereafter, the audiences grew and Crisp received invitations to tour his show, which he has done off and on ever since. Purely from repetition and his growing experience with working with live audiences, Crisp's show developed from its spontaneous composition into a more set oral text. The show as he now performs it consists of two parts. The first is an autobiographical monologue, which is more like a series of anecdotes than like the continuous personal narratives of Spalding Gray. The second part is devoted to a question and answer format.

The show is actually the culmination of Crisp's lifelong process of building an identity. Now in his eighties, Crisp invented his public persona during the course of his life as a social outcast. His blatant femininity and homosexuality made him an object of ridicule. But instead of forcing him to conform to a more traditional masculine image, the painful social ostracism only encouraged him to pursue more extravagant forms of effeminacy. By the time he received that first offer to appear on stage, much of Crisp's persona was already intact. The performance merely took a private persona and effectively made it a public one. Crisp, in fact, sees no distinction between his private and public selves: "I try to make as little difference as possible. I try to be exactly like myself. One critic tried to make distinction between me and my image, using the word generally, as image as someone who appears on television. But I really don't see any difference. I don't act." For Crisp, his public persona *is* his private persona. Having created an identity in the real world for its peculiar dramatic effect, Crisp simply brought it up on stage. He sees little distinction for him personally between appearing on stage and appearing anywhere else in public: "I've always been the one among the many. I've always been an object of speculation in a way that other people haven't. Other people can at least go into a restaurant or a shop and not think 'I must brace myself to do this because I am going to stand out.' . . . I would say that I am someone who had been forced by life to be self-conscious and has now tried to make that self-consciousness into a way of life." *An Evening with Quentin Crisp* represents yet another example of solo performance serving the individual's impulse to create a public persona. For Quentin Crisp, all the world is truly a stage.

Contemporary Shakespeare and Bible Recitals

Biographical one-person shows have dominated the field of solo performance for the past forty years, but they have not completely eclipsed other solo genres. Character sketches by monologuists and readings by poets and fiction writers have also been enjoying a renewed popularity. Among the nonbiographical forms of solo performance, Shakespeare and Bible recitals have achieved a true level of distinction during the current period.

The death of Charlotte Cushman in 1876 removed from the American platform its last great Shakespearean reader of international status. It is true that many other notable actors read from Shakespeare after Cushman's death, but their performances were occasional events that remained peripheral to their true careers in the theatre. Their Shakespeare readings were not important centers of their artistic life. It is also true that scores of elocutionists read selections from Shakespeare on the lyceum and Chautauqua platforms. Yet even the best of these readers, such as Robert McLean Cumnock and S. H. Clark, achieved only a limited celebrity within the lyceum-Chautauqua community. Certainly neither Cumnock nor Clark, however talented as readers and educators, could claim the renown of Fanny Kemble or of Charlotte Cushman. So although Shakespeare continued to be a favorite on the reading platform and eventually even found a place in the more refined vaudeville houses, no great figure comparable to Kemble or Cushman appeared from the last quarter of the nineteenth century through the first half of the twentieth century. Charles Laughton had the celebrity and talent requisite to become a major Shakespearean reader but chose instead to present primarily miscellaneous programs based on the works of a variety of authors. Shakespeare was typically just one among many literary selections presented by Laughton in a given performance. Perhaps Laughton's general failure as a Shakespearean actor made him hesitate from performing an all-Shakespeare recital. Dylan Thomas also proved capable of being a Shakespearean reader of considerable power but, like Laughton, preferred to present miscellaneous programs. Finally, in 1958 John Gielgud brought his *Ages of Man* recital to the United States. His work clearly placed him within the Anglo-American tradition of Kemble and Cushman and established him as a Shakespearean reader of the first order.

JOHN GIELGUD'S *Ages of Man*

An invitation to Gielgud by the British Arts Council to present a poetry reading was the beginning of the celebrated *Ages of Man*. Once the council accepted the actor's counteroffer to present a full recital of Shakespeare, Gielgud with the assistance of George Rylands (who directed Gielgud in *Hamlet* and *The Duchess of Malfi*) devised the first version of his program. For the British Arts Council, Gielgud appeared with a lutanist, whom he dropped before taking the recital to The Hague, Amsterdam, Zurich, Berlin, Milan, Paris, and eventually New York. *Ages of Man* opened at the Forty-sixth Street Theatre on 28 December 1958. The agreed tenor of the show's critical reception was that of Brooks Atkinson's review in the *New York Times*. "[O]ne thing is clear," wrote Atkinson, "the program is a masterpiece. It is a Shakespeare event of first importance" (1958:C21).

Gielgud appeared in *Ages of Man* with the full dignity appropriate to his position as "the most brilliant Shakespearean actor of our time" (Lewis 1959:16). Stressing simplicity and elegance, Gielgud wore formal black-tie evening clothes and stood on a stage devoid of props except a book and a lectern, both of which served aesthetic functions: they reminded audiences of the authorial presence and assisted in establishing the formality of the performance. Gielgud, moving freely around the stage, was not tied to either book or lectern. The sophisticated tone of the program was noted by the critics. Norman Nadel, when reviewing Gielgud's 1963 New York return engagement in the recital, contrasted Gielgud's platform presence with that of Charles Laughton. While refraining from specifically naming Laughton, who had then just recently died, Nadel's point of comparison was unquestionably clear: "Last night, Sir John was standing on the Lyceum stage when the curtain rose. . . . No need for gimmicks, such as the usual armload of prop books. No need to stride on stage, and stop, stunned, to discover an audience waiting. No such waste and distraction for this man" (Nadel 1963:13). While avoiding the loose informality of Laughton's platform manner, Gielgud also eschewed any flamboyancy in his performance. He shunned "fancy elocution and rhetoric" (Lewis 1959:16) and "histrionic glitter" (Nadel 1963:13). Gielgud's restrained but powerful performance was indicative of his own personal emphasis on good taste. He explained his goals regarding his style of oral interpretation in an interview:

The objective was to indicate the character with the voice, depending on the part. I always try to avoid too much gesture; there is practically no motion. This is a good thing, because the tendency in doing Shakespeare has too often been to substitute activity and restlessness for the musical and athletic power of the verse, which drives it along if you speak it correctly and are still. . . . What I've been trying to demonstrate is that the words are so wonderful that if you serve them properly, they will carry you (quoted in Millstein 1959:5).

Clearly Gielgud succeeded; *Ages of Man* was praised as "the most explosive theatre fare in New York" (Lewis 1959:16).

By the time of Gielgud's New York opening in 1958, the production concept of the program, which was based on George Rylands's anthology, was firmly realized. The program was divided into three major parts, each one devoted to a stage in the human-life cycle—the ages of man. Gielgud's selections from Shakespeare's plays and sonnets appropriately illustrated the main divisions: lyrical passages for Youth; scenes of decision, adult reverie, and action for Maturity; and reflective moments of wisdom and endings of careers of Old Age (Atkinson 1958:C21). Gielgud revealed that his rationale of text selection not only served the stated production concept but also permitted his return to roles in which he had succeeded on the stage earlier in his acting career: "I felt here was an opportunity to show myself to the present generation in parts in which I'd been a success, things I'd played and loved when I was young. And then I added some of the sonnets and poems, to give the whole thing a leavening, a leavening to the dramatic passages, that rested and soothed the audience between them" (quoted in Millstein 1959:5). We can, therefore, discern at least four major factors influencing Gielgud's choice of selection: (1) Rylands's anthology; (2) the production concept divisions of youth, maturity, and old age; (3) Gielgud's desire to showcase his past stage successes; and (4) his perceived need to include nondramatic pieces to assist the program's variety of tone. Among the plays represented in *Ages of Man* were *The Winter's Tale*, *The Merchant of Venice*, *Richard II*, *Julius Caesar*, *King Lear*, *Macbeth*, *Hamlet*, *As You Like it*, *Romeo and Juliet*, and *Othello*. Gielgud's decision to include scenes from his early stage successes proved felicitous. The high point of the program, according to many reviewers, was Gielgud's performance of the climax of his greatest stage triumph, *Richard II*. "Gielgud cuts through [Richard II's] self pity," said one critic, "with the white-hot knife of his own passionate intelligence. If ever a great role and a great actor were made for each other, it is Richard II and the mature Gielgud" (Hewes 1959:74).

Gielgud toured in *Ages of Man* for many years. When he wrote his autobiography, he spoke only briefly of his experience: "I toured *Ages of Man* for so many years that I feared I would be out of practice when it came to acting again with other people. Also, eight performances a week all by myself, and sitting alone in a dressing-room between the acts, was a very lonely and some-times depressing business" (1980:212–13). The drawbacks Giel-gud indicates are felt by many actors who have turned solo per-formers.

Ages of Man was an enduring triumph for John Gielgud, so much so that the genre of the Shakespeare recital became identi-fied with his particular program. When Ian McKellen decided to develop his own recital in the mid-1970s, he had to confront the Gielgud legacy. His response, ultimately, was to create a solo vastly different in tone from that of his distinguished predecessor.

Ian McKellen Acting Shakespeare

Ian McKellen's Shakespeare recital also began with an invi-tation. While working with the Royal Shakespeare Company in 1976, McKellen was invited to present a one-person show at the Edinburgh Festival. His theatrical background induced him to chose Shakespeare as his focus, although he knew that he would have to contend with the lasting impression of Gielgud's *Ages of Man:*

Of course, there have been one-man shows about Shakespeare before me. Some very distinguished, like John Gielgud's *Ages of Man.* . . . A very celebrated actor recapping some of his great successes, wearing a tuxedo, and talking, very briefly, about the speeches he was going to do. I didn't want to copy that format. I wanted my program to reflect my own feel-ings about Shakespeare, and so I had to start examining what my feelings were about this amazing man who was born four hundred years ago and who was helping me to earn a living at the time (quoted in Hallinan and Andrews 1982:135).

McKellen decided to develop a program that contrasted with the elegant formality of Gielgud's recital and emphasized instead a casualness that encouraged a dialogue with the audience. Unlike John Gielgud, who kept his comments between his selections to a minimum, McKellen filled his show with anecdotal theatrical reminiscences and explications of difficult passages.

Inspired by that first audience's response, McKellen later performed the solo in England at other festivals and subsequently took it to Ireland, Northern Ireland, Israel, and Scandinavia. *Acting Shakespeare*'s first New York appearance was a benefit performance in 1981, while McKellen was performing in *Amadeus* on Broadway. The recital was then videotaped at a CBS studio in Manhattan in November 1981 and eventually aired on PBS in April 1982. McKellen expressed at the time of the taping a dissatisfaction with the television version of the program. He regretted the loss of spontaneity possible only in live performance. His recital, he explained, is shaped by each individual audience:

I make the point during the show that it is with some regret that I have taped it and fixed it. Each time I do the show in a theatre I do like to do it for that specific audience. My timing changes, some thing are omitted, maybe other things are adlibbed and put in so that the audience has the real sense that if they weren't there the performance couldn't be taking place. If I'm asked to do the show again in the theatre, I think I would like to (quoted in Hallinan and Andrews 1982:136).

McKellen received his wish to again perform the show live. On 19 January 1984, *Ian McKellen Acting Shakespeare* opened for its first professional run in New York at the Ritz Theatre. A few days before the New York opening, a *Times* article summarized the usual nature of the program: "*Acting Shakespeare* is a distinctive theatrical experiment—part autobiography, part classroom lecture, part vaudeville show, along with hefty chunks of Shakespearean poetry and drama" (Farber 1984:17).

Dressed in street clothes, McKellen began his recital striding down the auditorium aisle and springing onto the stage. From that "unconventional beginning," one reviewer wrote, "audience and actor were involved together in spontaneous dialogues and other kinds of stage business seldom tried on Broadway" (Robertson

1984:C11). McKellen desired to make Shakespeare accessible and to show him as a man of the theatre. The title of the show, as McKellen has explained, emphasizes the theatrical, not the literary, Shakespeare:

The actual basis for the show is contained in a pun that nobody gets but me. . . . It's called *Acting Shakespeare*, which is indeed an actor acting Shakespeare, but it also means an actor talking not about the philosopher Shakespeare or the poet Shakespeare, but the *acting* Shakespeare, the Shakespeare who was an actor and interested in acting. Except perhaps for the section from *Romeo and Juliet*, everything I do in the show is chosen because it has to do with acting (quoted in Farber 1984:24).

Once on stage, which was bare except for a dark blue backdrop and a high-backed Renaissance-style chair, McKellen began with Jacques's "All the world's a stage" monologue from *As You Like It*. This opening was truly an inspired choice; within the show's first few moments, McKellen not only established his show's theatre motif but acknowledged the memory of Geilgud's performance. The Jacques monologue explicitly stated the McKellen theatre metaphor while implicitly reminding the audience of the Gielgud "ages of man" statement. McKellen's allusion to Gielgud, which also included a parody, was appreciated: "The evening begins with the 'seven ages of man' speech as if McKellen were courting comparisons between his own solo turn and John Gielgud's legendary *Ages of Man* recital. Not long after that, Mr. McKellen is doing a mischievous and funny impersonation of a howling Gielgud Lear" (Rich 1984b:C3). McKellen's tacit acknowledgement and his subsequent parody diffused any possible audience preconception that *Acting Shakespeare* was simply a reiteration of Gielgud's *Ages of Man*. Widely different in its tone, visual aspects, and staging, *Acting Shakespeare* achieved its own success.

Following the opening selection from *As You Like It*, the first act of McKellen's program moved to scenes from *Henry V, Hamlet, A Midsummer Night's Dream, Henry VI Part 3, Henry IV Part 1*, Sonnet 20, and concluded with *Romeo and Juliet*. McKellen chose scenes to illustrate the central theme of the theatre but also (as Gielgud had done) to permit himself to return to roles he had succeeded in earlier in his career. Moving about the stage, dangling his legs from its apron, and bounding up and down the aisles of the auditorium, McKellen liberally interjected commentary throughout the program. "This is a *tour de force* with footnotes," said the review in the *Christian Science Monitor,* "personal reminiscences, historical references, exchanges with the audience, and those theatrical anecdotes that nobody tells better than an actor" (Beaufort 1984:21). Audiences felt free to respond to McKellen and even joined him on the stage for some impromptu ensemble acting.

The second part of *Acting Shakespeare* began with a powerful performance of Richard II's "hollow crown" speech. McKellen then moved into a comic sequence. He characterized Samuel Pepys's and Bernard Shaw's caustic comments on actors and the theatre and "impersonated" a florid David Garrick performance. This comic segment then segued into the recital's recognized dramatic highlight, McKellen's interpretation of the "Tomorrow, and tomorrow, and tomorrow" soliloquy from *Macbeth*. Starting with an impersonation of Richard Burbage (the first Macbeth) in a heavy Scottish accent, McKellen ultimately moved to his own interpretation:

> But the highspot—in the one naughty thunderbolt of intellectual virtuosity—comes when he has the calm nerve, and the nerve had all evening been coming up to this climax, to interpret, line by line, phrase by phrase, thought by thought, image by image, Macbeth's "Tomorrow and tomorrow" speech.
>
> Then he places the speech he has analyzed into the full context of his Macbeth. He starts encased in a cone of light—then he moves forward and strikes Shakespeare to the quick instant (Barnes 1984a: 389-90).

After this dramatic climax, McKellen closed the program with Prospero's "stuff as dreams" monologue from *The Tempest*. The final moments belonged to those brave audience members who joined the actor on stage for impromptu ensemble acting.

For all its apparent informality, *Acting Shakespeare* is clearly a thoughtfully arranged script, complete with dramatic structure and comic relief. McKellen's causal tone was as calculated for its effect as was Gielgud's elegant formality. Seemingly so different from each other, *Acting Shakespeare* and *Ages of Man* were finally comparable in their essential function as showcases for an actor's virtuosity: "[F]or all the adulterated charm and professional bonhomie, the key to the evening is whenever (and it is most of the time) McKellen shoughs off his cloak of being a regular fella, and becomes what becomes him most, a consummate Shakespearean" (Barnes 1984a:389).

Despite his recognized success in *Acting Shakespeare*, McKellen has expressed no intention of developing another solo. "I certainly don't want to become," he has said, "one of those actors who are known for their one-man shows" (quoted in Robertson 1984:C11). He has since returned to other stage work.

ALEC MCCOWEN'S *St. Mark's Gospel*

John Geilgud and Ian McKellen restored the Shakespeare recital to a position of distinction it had not enjoyed since the days of Fanny Kemble and Charlotte Cushman. Yet their success, while remarkable, is not totally surprising. Both men were brilliant Shakespearean actors with established reputations at the time they first performed their solos and Shakespeare, as a dramatist, had never lost his popularity on the English-speaking stage. As a public entertainment form, the Bible recital seemed far less likely to succeed within the contemporary theatre. Attendance at mainstream American churches had been declining since midcentury and it was not until the 1980s that the resurgency of Christian fundamentalism was fully recognized. So when Alec McCowen first presented his solo performance based on the Gospel according to Saint Mark in the 1970s, few people would have predicted its popular success. The church and the theatre, as we have already discussed in relation to the Victorian period, have often shared an enmity. The theatre's roots are pagan and its practitioners are known for their licentious lifestyles. On closer examination, however, we discover that the church and the theatre have actually worked together. Richard Finley Ward, in an intensive study (1987), shows us how performance effectiveness played a critical role in the early church. Medieval mystery and miracle plays brought drama directly into the church. Today, both the elaborate Roman Catholic/high church Protestant rituals and the spartan but emotional Evangelical sermons possess undeniable theatrical appeals. Thus McCowen's success in appealing to both the theatre and the Christian communities is not quite as startling as initially imagined. It is true that McCowen's solo had been pre-dated by Charles Laughton's Bible readings, but Laughton primarily presented miscellaneous programs of secular literature. Alec McCowen was the first contemporary performer to achieve great success in a solo devoted wholly to Scripture.

"I have always wanted to be an entertainer rather than an actor," admitted McCowen in his book *Double Bill,* "and idolized the great performers who can hold an audience on their own. . . . I have got more tingling excitement from watching a great entertainer than from watching any straight actor" (1980:118). With such an inclination, it seems logical that McCowen eventually turned to solo performance. An *actor* in a play must relate to other actors; an *entertainer,* however, must know how to relate directly with an audience. In this regard, a solo performer in any genre is more akin to the entertainer than the actor. Because of the insistent performer-audience relationship and the absence of other actors with which to work, even the best actors find the one-person show form daunting. Jason Robards, originally cast in Paul Shyre's Mencken solo, left the show, feeling overwhelmed by the lack of other actors on stage (Poschman 1982:31). McCowen, far from being put off by the intense one-to-one relationship with the audience, cherished the prospect.

The beginnings of McCowen's *St. Mark's Gospel* date back to his youthful admiration of Ruth Draper, whom he acknowledged on stage as an inspiration.[12] Many years later, when he started to consider developing his own one-person show, he began by reading the Bible, which he felt had been neglected theatrically. McCowen read through the Gospels, as he explained in an interview: "I began with John, but he is a great intellectual and his prose is too difficult to be spoken aloud. Matthew is too long, and Luke is a bit flowery for my taste. So I started to work with Mark, who has a blunt, straightforward style and is of a good theatrical length" ("Alec McCowen" 1978:32). McCowen also discovered that Mark's Gospel possessed a compelling dramatic structure, complete with a powerful "first act" climax (at chapter 9, verse 1) and a final catastrophe worthy of a great tragic play. Having selected St. Mark's Gospel as his text, McCowen quickly decided to use the King James Version. His own Shakespearean training attracted him to the seventeenth-century prose, which he found ideally suited to be spoken aloud.

McCowen first performed *St. Mark's Gospel* professionally in New Castle, England, in 1977. After slowly building a reputation, the show eventually moved to the Mermaid Theatre in London and eventually to London's West End. *St. Mark's Gospel* opened in New York on 7 September 1978, for a limited run at the Marymount Manhattan Theatre and later played on Broadway at the Playhouse Theatre. The show was the unexpected hit of the season. "The unlikeliest evening in town this fall," wrote Walter Kerr in the *New York Times*, "was one of the most provocative and most riveting" (1978:54).

McCowen entered the stage wearing informal clothes: a tweed jacket, brown pants, an open-necked shirt or a turtleneck. His setting consisted of a table (with a glass and water pitcher) and three straight-backed chairs. The mode of the performance was distinctly presentational. The chairs occasionally served as transformational objects, suggesting in performance variously the seats of the money changers at the temple, the stern of a boat, or a mountain peak. Working with his minimal setting, McCowen used considerable movement on the stage, allowing certain areas to suggest different geographical locations. He elaborated on his use of the stage areas:

The scenes in the houses, the ships, and the temple are played in the center of the stage near the table; the scenes in the street are in front of that; the scenes by the sea are events further forward; and the scenes by the mountains are at the back. Then, there are one or two confidential passages—such as when James and John ask Jesus for preferential treatment—when I come very far down front and will need the kind of spot you use in a music hall ("Alec McCowen" 1978:32).

The actor's movement, while considerable, remained "always a directional response to the text" (Beaufort 1978b:177). The true focus of the production was unmistakably the oral delivery of the Gospel. "As delivered by McCowen," wrote *Time*, "Mark is a triumph of the human voice and the English language" (Porterfield 1978:100).

Reviewers often noted the journalistic and reportorial style of McCowen's interpretation. The actor consciously worked for a spontaneity of delivery, creating in the process the persona of an excited eyewitness storyteller: "The operative word for McCowen is tell. He tells Mark's story, he does not intone it. He clears away the ponderousness and singsong preachiness of centuries of Bible reading to discover the urgent, living voice of a man who is recounting nearly contemporary events, many of them derived from eyewitness accounts" (Porterfield 1978:100). Eunice Ruth Eifert has thoughtfully analyzed McCowen's assumption of the storyteller persona in *St. Mark*. Eifert posits that McCowen created a "fictional" persona in response to the implied author of the text:

The persona is assumed to be the author Mark, but it would be more accurate to say that the persona is someone who heard about and witnessed some remarkable events and is now telling others about them. It would be impossible to re-create a historically accurate St. Mark. . . . So McCowen has chosen to accent the qualities of the storyteller rather than the outer accouterments of a first century Mark. . . . The persona is derived more from the study of the work of literature (i.e., an imaginative character) than from a study of first-century history (1984:137–38).

McCowen gradually assumed the persona of the modern storyteller in performance throughout his introductory comments to the audience. This introduction, conversational in tone and adapted for the current location of a given performance, set the mood for the entire production. McCowen's chosen persona of a modern-day storyteller was entirely appropriate for his desired goal. He wanted to give the Gospel an immediacy and vitality: his choice of persona, of which his "costume" of informal contemporary clothes was an extension, effectively cleared away the centuries separating the audience and St. Mark. The audience of the show did not move back in time, as they did in *Emlyn Williams as Charles Dickens,* nor would it be quite accurate to say that St. Mark moved forward into the twentieth century. If McCowen wanted a fully contemporized Mark, he could have easily selected a more recent translation as his text. As it is, however, McCowen's *St. Mark* existed in a kind of time warp: first-century events, seventeenth-century language, and twentieth-century persona and audience. Remarkably, the combination of time periods did not detract from the performance. Instead, the cumulative effect was perhaps the most desirable, giving the overall impression of universal timelessness.

While working against any sense of strict historical time, McCowen also minimized the presence of the written manuscript. In *Ages of Man,* John Gielgud emphasized the authorial presence by having both a lectern and a book on his stage; those two props served as reminders to the audience of the text's existence in print form. McCowen, on the other hand, chose to emphasize the qualities of immediacy and orality. In sixteen months, McCowen memorized the complete Gospel; in performance, the printed text functioned marginally. As reported by the *New York Times,* McCowen walked out on stage and "place[d] a pocket St. Mark's Gospel on a table and, with a glance above, wryly observe[d], 'Just in case,' and, without faltering, immerse[d] himself and the audience in the fabulous story" (Gussow 1981:C21). Perhaps McCowen's reference to the pocket text of the Gospel was honest; maybe its sole intended function was to comfort the performer simply by its presence should a mental block occur. In actuality, however, McCowen's sly "Just in case," helped to create the impression that the performance was a simple, straightforward, unadorned, and unaffected event. Like Ian McKellen in *Acting Shakespeare,* Alec McCowen in *St. Mark's Gospel* worked to encourage the audience to perceive the performance as spontaneous and casual; in doing so, both actors had to underplay the fact that their performances were carefully conceived and calculated affairs by expert players. *St. Mark's Gospel* was clearly an actor's *tour de force,* and yet such terminology betrays the essential simplicity of McCowen's performance: "It is the sort of feat that inevitably is called a tour de force; yet a tour de force is precisely what it is not. The performance, quietly magnificent as it is, nevertheless is purged of all bravura. It is compelling theater that is at the same time nontheatrical" (Porterfield 1978:100). McCowen avoided all bombast in his delivery, presenting even the most dramatic moments (such as the Cruxifiction) in a restrained, straightforward manner. By working against audience expectations at the key climatic scenes, McCowen achieved the greatest impact.

The general tone of *St. Mark's Gospel* was typically joyful and proclamatory, emphasizing, as the actor pointed out in his introduction, that *gospel* means "good news." The performance was clearly an actor's interpretation. McCowen stressed the narrative and his characterizations. He brought to life the scribes and Pharisees, the Disciples, and Jesus Christ—who emerged as the central presence in the performance. McCowen, as he recently wrote in his book *Personal Mark,* focused on the human qualities of Jesus:

I am going to examine the actions of Jesus, and think about the life of Jesus, as if he was an ordinary human being. I do not want a virgin birth, or voices from heaven, or supernatural powers. They diminish his triumph. I want to present—through Mark—a fallible man; sometimes tired, hungry, irritable. Sometimes humorous, cynical, sarcastic, often compassionate, often unreasonable. Always ahead of us. Unpredictable. Unbelievably brave. Understandably frightened (1985:14).

McCowen's interpretation of Jesus was central to his performance as a whole. By emphasizing the human elements, he consequently minimized the divine. And this choice of interpretation cannot be removed from his own religious beliefs: during his introduction to the Gospel, McCowen stated on stage that he was not a believer in Jesus Christ as the son of God. This disclaimer informed the entire production and altered the audience's experience with the text in performance and its relation to McCowen's stage persona. "[H]e's like a delightful English uncle," wrote Jack Kroll and Katrine Ames in *Newsweek,* "who doesn't really believe that Jesus was the son of God but certainly knows a ripping good story when he sees it" (1978:66).

The review continued with a cogent discussion concerning McCowen's de-emphasis of the divinity of Jesus Christ:

The lack of the divine element is felt most strongly in the second half. McCowen's Jesus, agonized in Gethsemane, expresses human pathos but not the ultimate terror that only he of all creatures faced. McCowen is a fine actor, who has chosen not to imagine the Gospel's supreme tension between faith and doubt. It's that tension which transfigures this story into an ultimatum that must be accepted or rejected, not simply enjoyed. McCowen has told the story well, but he hasn't fleshed out the passion, which is the story's soul (1978:66).

Kroll and Ames's criticism raises important issues concerning the responsibility to the text in a performance of Scripture. Are the solo performer's individual beliefs appropriate concerns of the audience? Do those beliefs impact on the performance as an aesthetic experience? McCowen chose to make his religious beliefs public in an explicit statement preceding the Gospel. Tom Key, who performs *The Revelation of John,* a solo based on the last book of the Bible and similar in concept to McCowen's *St. Mark,* felt that McCowen's disclaimer diminished the experience for him. "That detached me," Key has said, "from what was to come" (quoted in Crouch 1986a:3B). Key was left admiring the literature but ultimately unmoved by the performance. Would the impact of the performance be changed if McCowen had refrained from including his disclaimer? For particularly sensitive viewers, the overt disclaimer merely confirmed what was implicit throughout the performance. Those who agreed with Jack Kroll and Katrine Ames found that the absence of the divine element in McCowen's interpretation effectively removed the major purpose of the entire Gospel. Yet many other people were greatly moved by McCowen's performance (even with the disclaimer) or the show would never have met with its outstanding success. Some may argue that the solo succeeded as a theatrical but not as a religious event. This is purely speculative, for we have no way of gauging a distinction between the audience's aesthetic and spiritual responses.

Although we cannot conclude by arguing whether or not only true believers should perform the Bible, we do learn that the performer's beliefs are a concern in the performance of Scripture and those beliefs have important ramifications for the audience. Whereas performers of secular literature are typically expected to maintain a faithfulness to the text, the performers of sacred works take on additional responsibilities and expectations of a different kind of *faith*fulness to the text of a far greater dimension. As for McCowen himself, his own religious convictions stand between believer and agnostic. At the time of his New York engagement in 1978, he told the *New Yorker:* "I certainly don't describe myself as a Christian, though I'd be very flattered if somebody else described me as one. . . . But I do believe that Mark wrote the Gospel, and I do believe that Peter saw the events he described. You may quarrel about the Gardarene swine or one or two other peculiar episodes, but there's no getting away from the fact that something—to use Mark's word—'astonishing' happened two thousand years ago in Galilee" ("Alec McCowen" 1978:33). Several years later, McCowen's views moved even closer to belief, as indicated by the closing comments of his book *Personal Mark:*

> Jesus believed that he had a father in heaven.
> He believed that—if we choose—you and I have a father in heaven.
> What a ridiculous idea! but also . . .
> What a beautiful idea!
> . . . and a necessary one (ellipses in original, McCowen 1985:236).

Alec McCowen's performance in *St. Mark's Gospel* received a Tony award nomination for Outstanding Actor in a Play. Since the show's initial New York engagement, McCowen had toured *St. Mark* internationally and returned to New York for another run in 1981. The demand for *St. Mark's Gospel* superseded McCowen's availability and, in response, he has since directed other actors in the recital.

CONTEMPORARY MONOLOGUISTS

Moving from Alec McCowen's *St. Mark's Gospel* to the performances of contemporary monologuists is literally moving from the sacred to the profane. The startling contrast in language—the crystalline poetry of the King James Version and the coarse, often obscene speech of the character sketches by comic monologuists—indicates the diversity of texts in current one-person shows. The fact that these widely different shows succeed also indicates the flexibility and eclecticism of the contemporary theatregoing public: they enjoy the beauty of sacred texts in seventeenth-century English as well as the obscene mouthings of the characters frequently presented by monologuists.

The earlier placement of Spalding Gray within the discussion of biographical one-person shows may have struck some readers of this study as erroneous; his work, despite its links between biography and autobiography, appears more closely related to that of the standup comedians. His social commentary links him to a tradition that currently includes such diverse performers as Bill Cosby, George Carlin, Robin Williams, Eddie Murphy, Steve Martin, Richard Pryor, and Johnny Carson. Yet when considered within the context of the standup comedians, Gray's work is more complex. His performances move us beyond laughter and a slap on the knee. More significantly, Gray's performances claim a position as legitimate theatre, whereas the comedians remain within the boundaries of the nightclub and the cabaret. This does not mean that Gray inhabits the nebulous zone betwixt and between standup comic and solo actor alone. Other solo performers share this liminal region, most notably Lily Tomlin, Whoopi Goldberg, and Eric Bogosian. All three of these talented soloists, like Spalding Gray, show an interest in social commentary, yet their work, unlike Gray's, takes the form of character sketches. Whereas Gray favors the epic mode and the role of the storyteller, Tomlin, Goldberg, and Bogosian favor the dramatic mode and the role of the character actor. They are the contemporary inheritors of the monologuist tradition already brought to a position of preeminence in this country by Ruth Draper.

LILY TOMLIN

The monologues of Ruth Draper were inspirational for young Lily Tomlin. Early in her career, "when Lily Tomlin was doing impressions in a coffeehouse in Detroit an incidental comment by a stranger directed her to the Ruth Draper recordings, and she was, in her own words 'totally inspired' by the possibilities of the monologue and was from that day committed to the form" ("Centennial" 1985:26). As Tomlin's career progressed, her work with the monologue form became more complex. Her short character sketches of Ernestine and Edith Ann on the popular television comedy *Laugh-in* won her a following. Later she successfully moved on to her own television specials and one-woman shows. In 1977 her solo production *Appearing Nitely* opened on Broadway. The show, essentially a series of unconnected character sketches, was well received by critics and audiences and won Tomlin a special Tony award but, in retrospect, *Appearing Nitely* was simply a foretaste of the more complex solo work Tomlin was to undertake for her second show, *The Search for Signs of Intelligent*

Life in the Universe. "As in her 1977 Broadway production, *Appearing Nightly* (*sic*)," wrote the *New York Times,* "this one is a cavalcade of characters. But this time they are not self-contained skits. This time, each character is like a chapter in a book, each a small part of the overall parable" (Fein 1985:1). Act 1 of *The Search . . .* opened with the character of Trudy, an eccentric bagwoman on the streets of New York, who served as the show's narrator and whose sensibility unified the entire script. Tomlin then moved into various characters, male and female, while remaining in the same outfit of black pants and blouse. Her performance drew notices typical of many soloists adept at portraying multiple characters purely through their change of voice and physical bearing:

Miss Tomlin puts on new faces, voices, personalities with the ease and know-how of the consummate psychic quick-change artist she is. Whether she portrays a bag woman philosophizing about her contact with extraterrestrials, a bevy of early Women's Libbers, a pair of New York hookers, an affluent young California working mother who has it all . . . or several other characters crisscrossing the stage . . . she is always in canny, trenchant command (Simon 1985:64).

Initially the characters in *The Search . . .* seemed unconnected but as the show progressed, the script developed links between them. The unsuspecting audience member, who thought he or she was just seeing a recital of monologues, was hoodwinked and suddenly realized that the show stood as a dramatic whole and was, in a word, a play.

Act 2 included the show's most provocative material. While the entire script offered social commentary, Act 2 presented what has often been cited as the highlight of the play: a compressed history of the feminist movement. As stated by the *New York Times:* "The play . . . is a compact history of the modern women's movement, from the 1960s to the summer of Geraldine Ferraro. As if it weren't exciting enough to watch Miss Tomlin whip in and out of this saga's various roles, we're also treated to a trenchant view of social history that few other mass entertainers in any medium would dramatize with such sophistication and ideological evenhandedness" (Rich 1985a:5). *The Search* . . . for all its success with a general theatregoing public, was clearly feminist art and as such represents a milestone. As noted in *Ms.* magazine, *The Search* . . . "is the first work . . . that simply takes it as a given that a mass audience will accept feminist attitudes, that proceeds on the assumption these attitudes are shared, and that therefore does not lecture, hector or even underline" (French 1986:34).

Whether dramatizing the women's movement or satirizing would-be political activists, much of *The Search* . . . was biting, cynical social commentary and, according to the *Times*, "the most subversive comedy to be produced on Broadway in years." Toward the end of the play, however, once the character plot lines converged in "a series of rapid-fire Dickensian coincidences," the script's "tone turns abruptly sentimental" (Rich 1985a:5). Tomlin and her playwright Jane Wagner wanted the show to end optimistically, although they both feared the New York critics might think that they had "gone soft" (Young 1988:459). In a 1987-released film (simply titled *Lily Tomlin,* which chronicles the development of the script and performance), Wagner admitted that she was concerned that the ending might become "corny." Despite any misgivings, however, both the playwright and the performer agreed to go ahead with the optimistic ending. "I think more of a hard edge is in vogue today," said Wagner in a magazine interview, "But we know all the negative stuff. You have to say it and go beyond." Tomlin concurred: "You embrace the darkness. . . . You acknowledge it. But you glorify the light" (Young 1988:456).

The script's unabashed upbeat closing moments did bring some sharp criticism, as did a perceived unevenness in Wagner's writing, but overall *The Search* . . . earned excellent reviews, won several awards for both the writer and the performer, and quickly became one of the most successful productions of the 1985–86 Broadway season. Tomlin's performance was especially praised for excellence. In the category of Best Actress in a Play, she won the Tony, Drama Desk, and Outer Critics' Circle awards. *Variety* noted "Tomlin's artistry has deepened since her last Broadway outing in a hit limited run in 1976–77 [for *Appearing Nitely*], and now had advanced to the legend-worthy stratosphere" (Humm 1985:152).

WHOOPI GOLDBERG

Whoopi Goldberg, which opened on Broadway in 1984, established its performer-creator as a major new talent. Like Lily Tomlin, Goldberg's impressive ability to quickly change characters with minimal assistance from costuming or properties drew special attention. Frank Rich commented in the *New York Times:* "With only a simple pants-and-shirt costume, a few props and an empty stage . . . Miss Goldberg can instantly transform herself from a jivey, feral black male drug addict to a whiter-than-white 12-year-old Los Angeles Valley Girl" (1984c:C17). Many reviewers noted the similarities in talents possessed by Goldberg and Tomlin as well as their shared interest in social commentary. A comparison of Goldberg's show with Tomlin's *The Search . . .* (which opened the following season) demonstrates, however, clear distinctions both dramatically and technically.

The Search . . ., although performed on a nearly empty stage, was polished visually and technically. Tomlin used few set pieces: two chairs, a stool, and a freestanding series of steps, all of which were of a slick contemporary design. The stage itself was draped in black; a black cloth covered the floor. Tomlin wore a blouse and black pants. Adding to the look of contemporary polish were the show's considerable technical elements. The show includes a series of complex lighting and sound cues that served to signal a change in character, to set a mood, or to establish an environment for a character (such as music for an aerobics class). Goldberg's show, in contrast, was visually much coarser. The stage was literally bare and lighting cues were kept to a minimum. Even Goldberg's single costume was coarse in comparison to Tomlin's. In short, although both shows aimed at a kind of minimalist stage picture, thus emphasizing the talents of the lone performer, the look for *The Search . . .* may be called "minimalist hi-tech slick" whereas Goldberg's was clearly "minimalist street rough." Some readers may find this discussion of staging elements to be unnecessary. The point is that so many one-person shows use minimal staging effects that it becomes easy to dismiss them as simple equivalents and to overlook the distinct nonverbal messages a specific production's technical effects impress on an audience. Goldberg's show stands as a case in point. The coarse appearance of

Whoopi Goldberg helped maintain at least a semblance of the underground or nonestablishment roots of the performer and her material. Although transferred from experimental performance clubs to a major Broadway theatre (the Lyceum), the production attempted to play against the traditional Broadway expectations of glitz and glamour and emphasized a fidelity to Goldberg's texts. Ultimately a strange dichotomy resulted from the contrast between the coarseness of the staging, the costuming, and the language of Goldberg's show, and the opulence of the auditorium and lobby of the Lyceum Theatre. Try as they might to create the sense of an intimate Off-Broadway counterculture cabaret, the producers could not overcome the permanent features of the Lyceum, which bespeak tradition and establishment. Sensitive reviewers noted the tension between the Lyceum Theatre space and the Goldberg performance:

What she seeks to achieve with her audiences is an intimacy that is possible only in a relatively confined space, where she can mingle with and, if she chooses, actually reach out and touch members of the audience; on the broad, old-fashioned proscenium stage of the Lyceum, when she bends down to seize the hands of people in the first row the gesture becomes, under the circumstances, an artificial one, working against her intentions instead of with them (Gill 1984:155).

Dramaturgical differences also exist between *Whoopi Goldberg* and *The Search.* ... Goldberg's script, a collection of unconnected character sketches, lacked the structural and thematic complexities of *The Search* ... and was actually closer in structure to Tomlin's earlier *Appearing Nitely.* Goldberg's characters included:

Fontaine: a black male drug addict who experiences an epiphany when visiting Anne Frank's hideout in Amsterdam.
Valley girl: a thirteen-year-old white Los Angeles teenager who deals with an unwanted pregnancy.
Deformed cripple: a cripple who finds romance. This character speaks one of Goldberg's most often quoted lines: "Normal is in the eye of the beholder."
Jamaican woman: a woman brought to the U.S.A. by a wealthy eighty-five-year-old American male who dies on her during intercourse.

Unbeknownst to her, the old man left her millions of dollars in his will.

Young black girl: nine years old, she dreams of becoming a white, blond television star. By the end of the sketch, she accepts her blackness.

Bowery bum: who returns panhandled quarters from the audience.

Whereas some theatre critics were disturbed by the combination of satiric social commentary and optimistic sentimentality in *The Search . . .*, their reactions were even more divided when reviewing *Whoopi Goldberg*. "Whoopi Goldberg is a slight, sprite-like comic actress," wrote Mel Gussow in the *New York Times*, "whose mind and body are inhabited by some of the drollest and most touching characters one is ever likely to encounter in a Broadway theatre or on a city street." Gussow continued his sanguine praise of Goldberg's talents: "Her monologues are not anecdotes but complete short plays with a twist or two at the ending. . . . She is, simultaneously, an actress, dramatist, clown, and social critic—a detonation of comic virtuosity" (1984a:5). Countering such praise were critics who left the theatre unmoved by Goldberg and, in the case of John Simon, hostile to the overt sentimentality and moral lessons implicit in her sketches. "Whoopi Goldberg," said Simon, "is a phony as a three dollar bill." Simon did go on to acknowledge Goldberg's performance skills, which he found hindered by her inferior material: "Miss Goldberg . . . is an accomplished nightclub comedienne with good timing, lively facial expressions, considerable flexibility in her impersonations, and real skill with accents. What she doesn't have is material worth doing in a better cabaret, let along as a full evening on Broadway" (1984:74). Less adulatory than Gussow's praise and less vicious than Simon's attack, Frank Rich's review of Goldberg's show is the most valuable of the three for its seemingly objective critique of the performance's flaws. According to Rich,

Miss Goldberg, much like Lily Tomlin, wants to make us laugh, cry and think. Yet her jokes, however scatalogical in language, can be mild and overextended, and her moments of pathos are often too mechanically ironic and maudlin to provoke. . . . .[N]early all [the sketches] follow the same primitive dramatic formula. The sketches usually start out friskily and then lurch toward a sentimental trick ending. Sometimes the sentimental ending is downbeat . . . but more often it is uplifting. . . . The epiphanies that soon result [on the part of the characters] . . . are no less platitudinous for being declared in earnest. . . . By repeatedly shifting from diffuse clowning to omniscient preaching, she vitiates her characters' spontaneity and manages to make even her deepest feelings sound contrived (1984c:C17).

Despite the mixed reaction to Goldberg's material, her performance made the show a success. As a vehicle and as a showcase, Goldberg could not have asked for more. The show brought her "overnight" celebrity, landed her the plum role of Celie in the motion-picture adaptation of *The Color Purple,* and effectively launched her film career. Goldberg is currently developing a new solo, *Living on the Edge of Chaos,* in which she returns to several characters from her Broadway show and extends their life stories. We wait with interest to see her future development as a solo performer.

ERIC BOGOSIAN

No critic has accused Eric Bogosian, the third member of this talented triumvirate of contemporary monologuists, of sentimentality. Of his most recent one-person show, *Drinking in America,* one reviewer wrote that it is "as astringent as iodine on a scratch" (Humm 1986:158). Looking for recurring motifs in the reviews of his work, we find that Bogosian is unanimously hailed as a performer of considerable skill in characterization and as a writer of uncompromising, caustic social commentary. The reviewers contrasted Bogosian's work with that of Whoopi Goldberg and Lily Tomlin: "[W]hile Miss Goldberg turns her vignettes into little homilies and even Miss Tomlin ends her current Broadway show with a feel-good salute to the audience, Mr. Bogosian leaves his edges raw. He aims less at getting laughs than at outraging his audiences, trying to shock them into a moral response" (Freedman 1986:5). His monologues expose the underside of the American dream. Whether satirizing upwardly mobile businessmen or strung-out drug addicts, Bogosian focuses on the moral depravity in contemporary America. His characters, writes Frank Rich, "are gluttons for power, money and sex as well as for chemical stimulants; they have pigged out on the American way" (1986b:C15). Bogosian's commentary goes beyond individuals to American society as a whole and its media-hyped materialism. Speaking of his latest solo performance, Bogosian has said:

Drinking in America is a meditation on power in the American context . . . and it uses drinking as a catalyst, a striking stone, something to play off. "Drunk with power" is a phrase that comes to mind. The way booze and drugs can be abused is the way power can be abused, too. Intoxication is very central to our society now. There's no question we're in a decadent phase in our country. I don't provide any answers to that, but I do know something's missing and we're rushing to replace it with booze or drugs or power or money (quoted in Freedman 1986:30).

A review in *Variety* spoke further on the thematic issues in *Drinking in America:* "The enormous chasm that separates the media-peddled images of the good life in the U.S. and the reality of the hungers and desperation of most of the society is Bogosian's prominent theme. It's embodied in several routines in *Drinking,* most poignantly in his black heroin addict mumbling his devotion to the needle, in eerie half-darkness. It's a memorable image of passive despair, tough-minded and unsentimental" (Humm 1986:158). This last comment is particularly relevant to our discussion on contemporary monologuists, for our understanding of Bogosian's work is deepened when we specifically contrast his stark and disturbing portrayal of the black heroin addict with Whoopi Goldberg's "Fontaine." Goldberg's character—like Bogosian's—is a black drug addict but there the comparison ends. Fontaine, foulmouthed and arrogant as he is, possesses a vital charisma and a storyteller's talent that draws the audience to him. In Goldberg's monologue, Fontaine eventually describes his trip to Amsterdam, where he visited Anne Frank's hideout apartment. There he reads the famous words, "In spite of everything, I still believe that people are really good at heart," which move him to an epiphany about human nature. Bogosian's black drug addict has no such charisma nor a storyteller's penchant for personal narrative. Instead, Bogosian's character presents a bleak portrait of an addict absorbed in the one thing that gives his life meaning: heroin. There is no warmhearted epiphany for this character. The epiphany, if any occurs, is the audience's realization that the same drive for the good life in America that turns some of us into oily hardsell salesmen sends others of us who cannot seem to "make it" to escape in narcotics.

As bleak and as grim as Bogosian's vision of life in the United States may be, hope may still be found by the end of *Drinking in America*. Although avoiding both Goldberg's explicit moral lessons and Tomlin's upbeat salutations to the audience, his performance "does not leave us in despair" (Honan 1986:6). With a reference to the character who closes Bogosian's show (a wino who reaches out to the audience asking for spare change), William H. Honan spoke of the cumulative effect of *Drinking in America:*

The effect is stunning. We have been taunted, offended, solicited and finally seized by the notion—the magnificent, liberating, hope-filled notion of community. For we have been reminded that the society which cast this derelict down, is also, perhaps more than any other in history, characterized by the inseparability and interdependence of its members. Like it or not, the wino is telling us, we are our brothers' keepers (1986:6).

After initially playing in Boston and throughout Great Britain, *Drinking in America* opened at the American Place Theatre in New York on 20 January 1986. The show is his most recent as well as most successful. His previous solo performances, *Men Inside* and *FunHouse,* were also collections of character sketches dealing with the darker aspects of American life. In retrospect, these two early pieces appear as precursors to *Drinking in America,* which marked Bogosian's full maturity as a major solo performer. Since *Drinking,* Bogosian has appeared in both the play and film versions of *Talk Radio,* a multiactor script of his own composition. His plans for the future include a new solo titled *The New Americans (Between a Rock and a Hard Place).* Bogosian is aware that his increasing fame and following may tempt him to change the cynical tone typical of his past successes in order to appeal to mainstream theatregoers. He is determined, however, to avoid the urge to compromise his material, as he explained in a recent article in the *New York Times:* "Now that I've got a larger audience, my big challenge for this year is trying to keep the tone of my material as dark as it used to be. [*The New Americans*] is a return to the aggressive stance that I was taking when I first starting (*sic*) doing these solos" ("1988: Previews from 36 Artists" 1988:30).

Bogosian's early background includes work not only in the theatre but also in performance art. Unable to support himself as an actor, Bogosian felt alienated from traditional theatre. Along with his financial problems, he felt artistically repelled from mainstream Broadway: "I was having doubts about legitimate theater; what saved me, I guess, was discovering other things going on, especially in SoHo: performance art, video art and so-called experimental theater. I learned about 'artists,' people who didn't wait for a director, casting agent, acting coach or cabaret owner to get work. They just did it, and I wanted to, too" (Bogosian 1987:5). His experience in performance art continued to influence his current work. One reviewer commented that Bogosian is "less a writer or actor than a mixture of stand-up comic and performance artist" (Freedman 1986:5). Eventually, Bogosian blended his backgrounds in theatre and performance art to create a new form. He represents, therefore, multiple performance traditions incarnate in one person: the monologuist, the stand-up comic, and the performance artist. When speaking about the opening of *Men Inside,* Bogosian commented on the liminal position of his work, the reactions of purists, and his own conclusions on the subject of genre classification:

"People from theater came [to the performance] and said, 'That's not theater,'" he sighed. "Performance artists came and said, 'That's not performance art.' But I don't really care what you call it. That's not important. What's important is effect" (quoted in Arkatoy 1985:2).

Bogosian offered sound advice to other solo performers in those few words. Rather than attempting to work within one pure tradition of performance genre, creative artists must seek their own forms regardless of labels. Ultimately truly superior artists, and Bogosian is among them, will succeed with critics and audiences despite confusions in nomenclature. Great artists in any of the arts generate new forms that can initially perplex viewers-listeners-audience members, but eventually they are responsible for moving the arts forward and enriching the very tradition that they have seemingly disregarded.

NORTH LIGHT REPERTORY
By Arrangement with
ARTHUR CANTOR
Presents

EMLYN WILLIAMS

as

CHARLES DICKENS

*A solo performance of scenes
from the novels and stories*

OCTOBER 27 - NOVEMBER 8, 1981

Program cover for *Emlyn Williams as Charles Dickens*. Collection of the author.

Photograph of Emlyn Williams portraying Charles Dickens.
Photograph by Bryan Heseltine. Reprinted courtesy of Arthur Cantor,
Inc.

left: Photograph of Emlyn Williams in *The Playboy of the Weekend World*. *right:* Emlyn Williams in *Dylan Thomas Growing Up*. Photographs by Bryan Heseltine. Both reprinted courtesy of Arthur Cantor, Inc.

Announcement for Hal Holbrook in *Mark Twain Tonight!* Collection of the author.

Photograph of Hal Holbrook in *Mark Twain Tonight!* Collection of the author.

Julie Harris in *The Belle of Amherst*. Reprinted courtesy of the Theatre Collection, Museum of the City of New York.

Advertisement for *Gertrude Stein Gertrude Stein Gertrude Stein* with Pat Carroll. Collection of the author.

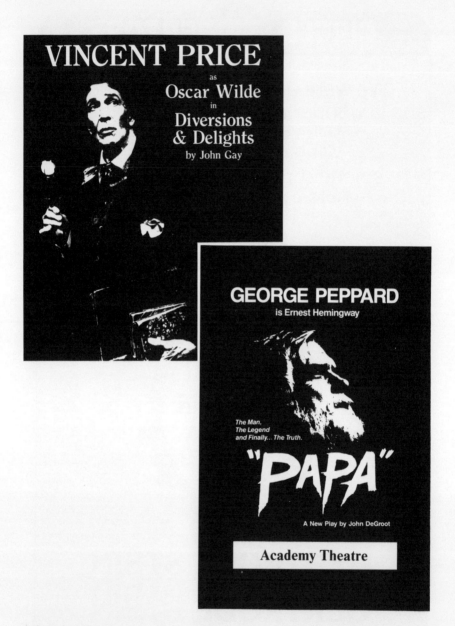

left: Advertisement for Vincent Price as Oscar Wilde in *Diversions & Delights. right:* Program cover for *Papa* with George Peppard. Both, collection of the author.

Playbill cover for *Will Rogers' U.S.A.* with James Whitmore. Courtesy of the Paul Shyre Papers, Mugar Memorial Library, Boston University.

above: Celeste Holm as Janet Flanner in *Paris Was Yesterday. below:* Celeste Holm with Janet Flanner in February 1978. Both photographs by Suzanne Karp Krebs, reprinted courtesy of the Paul Shyre Papers, Mugar Memorial Library, Boston University.

Paul Shyre as H. L. Mencken in *Blasts and Bravos*. Reprinted courtesy of the Paul Shyre Papers, Mugar Memorial Library, Boston University.

Publicity photograph of Spalding Gray. Photograph by Nancy Campbell.
Collection of the author.

Advertisement for the film version of Spalding Gray's
Swimming to Cambodia. Collection of the author.

Publicity photograph of Quentin Crisp. Collection of the author.

Program cover for John Gielgud in the *Ages of Man* at the Theatre Royal. Reprinted courtesy of the Billy Rose Theatre Collection, New York Public Library at Lincoln Center, Astor, Lenox and Tilden Foundations.

Lily Tomlin in *The Search for Signs of Intelligent Life in the Universe*.
Photograph by Norman Seeff, reprinted courtesy of the Billy Rose
Theatre Collection, New York Public Library at Lincoln Center, Astor,
Lenox and Tilden Foundations.

PLYMOUTH THEATRE

A Shubert Organization Theatre

Gerald Schoenfeld, *Chairman*   Bernard B. Jacobs, *President*

TOMLIN AND WAGNER THEATRICALZ

presents

LILY TOMLIN in

The Search for Signs of Intelligent Life In The Universe

Written by

JANE WAGNER

production supervised by
CHARLES BOWDEN

NEIL PETER JAMPOLIS
scenery and lighting

OTTS MUNDERLOH
sound

JANET BEROZA
production stage manager

associate producer
CHERYL SWANNACK

produced by
LILY TOMLIN

directed by
JANE WAGNER

AUGUST 25, 1986

23

Title page from the program for *The Search for Signs of Intelligent Life in the Universe.* Collection of the author.

Cover of the *Playbill* for Whoopi Goldberg at the Lyceum Theatre.
Collection of the author.

presents:

ERIC BOGOSIAN

NEW AMERICANS
(Between a Rock and a Hard Place)

left: Cover of the program for Eric Bogosian in *New Americans (Between a Rock and a Hard Place),* presented on 5–6 February 1988 at the Institute of Contemporary Art, Boston. Collection of the author. *right:* Eric Bogosian in *Drinking in America.* Photograph by Paula Court, reprinted courtesy of the Billy Rose Theatre Collection, New York Public Library at Lincoln Center, Astor, Lenox and Tilden Foundations.

THE POETRY CENTER

JOHN MALCOLM BRINNIN, Director

presents

DYLAN THOMAS

reading from

"King Lear" "Dr. Faustus" and other Elizabethan
and Jacobean dramas as well as his own new work

THURSDAY EVENING, MAY 15, 1952 at 8:40

ADM. $1.50   For reservations call TRafalgar 6-2366

or make check payable to the YM-YWHA and mail to the Poetry Center

YM-YWHA   •   Lexington Ave. at 92nd Street   •   New York 28

357

above: Announcement for Dylan Thomas's 15 May 1952 reading
at the Poetry Center, 92nd Street YM-YWHA, New York City.
Reprinted courtesy of the Archives of the 92nd Street YM-YWHA.
below: Dylan Thomas reading at the Poetry Center, 1952.
Photograph reprinted courtesy of Rollie McKenna.

Covers of the humanities guides for recent seasons of the Great Plains Chautauqua. Collection of the author.

LIGHTS! CURTAIN! ACTION!

POE
IN PERSON
with Conrad Pomerleau

Mark Stevenson in
A Visitation
from John Keats

FINAL·CURTAIN

WRITTEN & PERFORMED
BY
NADINE STERNE

THEATRE LEGENDS
ENCORE!

NATALIE ROSS AS
Emily Dickinson

The Belle of Amherst
by WILLIAM LUCE

The Wilde
Spirit

As the
Wind
Rocks
the
Wagon

True stories of the Oregon Trail
from the diaries of pioneer women

Shedding
Light
on
Shakespeare

LIVING
Literature

Cover art from the 1988 season brochure of "Living Literature," a company
of solo performers managed by Mark Stevenson. Collection of the author.

Publicity photograph of Mark Stevenson as John Keats, taken at Keats House, Hampstead, England. Collection of the author.

VIRTUOSO PERFORMANCE

in

Blake

*"Stage veteran Campbell gives
a riveting portrayal"*
London Free Press, Nov./82
by Elliott Hayes
Directed by Richard Monette
Designed by Debra Hanson
Lighting by Robert Bosworth-Morrison

Third Stage: June 18 to August 13

One of Canada's foremost actors introduces us to the
visionary poet and painter William Blake and explores
both serious and light-hearted moments in a life of
dramatic intensity.

in

DAMIEN

*"Gordon gives a remarkable
performance...a prodigious
feat of acting"*
Syracuse Post-Standard, Aug./82
by Aldyth Morris
Directed by Guy Sprung
Designed by Barbra Matis
Lighting by Steven Hawkins

Third Stage: June 19 to August 5

Acclaimed at Stratford last summer, the distinguished
Canadian actor stars in this factual story of a young
priest's struggle to help his outcast parishioners attain a
measure of human dignity.

in

When that I was...

*"A two-hour burst of solo versatility...
audience sat in awe"*
Canadian Press, Feb./82
by John Mortimer and Edward Atienza
Original design by Sue LePage
Music by Alan Laing
Lighting by Louise Guinand

Third Stage: July 7 to September 3

The renowned author of *Voyage Round My Father* and the
television series adaptation of *Brideshead Revisited* joins
forces with a superb classical actor in presenting an
astonishing array of Shakespeare characters from Juliet
to King Lear.

*"Just possibly the
greatest actress
in the world"*
Walter Kerr

in

Letters of Love and Affection
Third Stage: July 9, July 16.
...from the famous and obscure reflecting every aspect of
the human condition.

Venus and Adonis
by William Shakespeare
Edited by Irene Worth
Third Stage: July 12, July 20
...a passionate narrative work written in
Shakespeare's youth.

Ulysses and Mrs. Dalloway
Third Stage: July 15, July 22
...a celebration of James Joyce and Virginia Woolf.

"Virtuoso Performances," from the 1983 season brochure of the Stratford
Festival in Ontario, Canada. Collection of the author.

Whether considered monologuists, performance artists, or standup comedians, Tomlin, Goldberg, and Bogosian have already made important contributions to American solo performances. The tone of their material may vary—from the astringency of Bogosian to the sentimentality of Goldberg—but they each possess the talents of insightful social critics as well as of virtuoso character actors. As commentators, their voices represent our collective social conscience. Often choosing derelict characters (e.g., Tomlin's Trudy, Goldberg's Fontaine, Bogosian's wino) to serve as prophets who speak hard truths, these artists are able to suspend, if only momentarily, our individual distinctions and to help us recognize our common humanity and cultural bonds. What Stephanie Koziski, a popular culture scholar, said of the role of comedians in our society, ably applies to Tomlin, Goldberg, and Bogosian: "[They have] taken the place, in our present culture, of the story teller in primitive cultures—the grandfather or grandmother who could relate an experience through a story or tribal myth to communicate cultural knowledge" (1984:73).

CONTEMPORARY WRITER-PERFORMERS IN "THE AGE OF THE READING"

Writers have remained important figures throughout the history of solo performance. As we have already seen, biographical one-person shows usually center on writers because many of them not only present interesting personalities and life stories but they also have the added advantage of offering a volume of literary work to draw upon (Gussow 1984b:C22). However, it is not only through actors' recreations that writers appear on the stage or on the platform. Many of the greatest names in this history have been writers. It is hardly surprising, then, to turn to the current period and to find that writers are continuing to make important contributions as solo performers. Nor is it startling to discover that along with the resurgence since the early 1950s of one-person shows in the theatre, a concurrent renaissance is occurring for authors' readings. So significant is this "great revival of spoken poetry" (Billington 1980:204), that one scholar recently dubbed the current era "The Age of the Reading" (Wojahn 1985:266).

Dylan Thomas

When examining the latter half of the twentieth century, one writer-performer looms above all others, one whose platform work set a standard for those who have followed. Dylan Thomas remains the only twentieth-century figure whose remarkable talents both as a writer and as a performer place him in comparison with Charles Dickens:

[T]he typical Thomas poem is a performance, and Thomas as he found himself as a poet found himself as a performer. Not an actor: he was not plastic or impersonal enough. Not a dramatist: he had not the gift of the seeming-objective and had a sense of situation but not of action. Not a rhetorician, though his poems have been called rhetorical: he did not persuade or attempt to persuade. He was a special kind of performer, the showman of the one-man show—like Dickens. Not the poet in the theatre but the poet on the platform (Blissett 1956:55).

The comparison between Thomas and Dickens goes beyond their mutual possession of exceptional literary and histrionic talents. Other similarities do exist. As writers, they share certain characteristics. Dylan Thomas, said Roger Mitchell, "brought poetry back almost singlehandedly to the nineteenth century: to sentiment, the family, the romantic child, even to popularity" (1980:2). In other words, Thomas's writings have many qualities we consider Dickensian, qualities which were particularly true of the pieces Dickens chose from his canon to perform publicly.

As platform readers, both men demonstrated strong talents, although they ostensibly claimed that their motive for reading in public was simply financial. Thomas, like Dickens and Thackeray and so many other nineteenth-century British literary figures, saw in America his chance for monetary aggrandizement. Thomas's words on the subject, in fact, sound remarkably like Thackeray's quoted earlier. About his American tour, Thomas told his tour manager, John Malcom Brinnin, that he wanted "to return to England with some dollars in my pocket" (quoted in Brinnin 1955:31). Yet for all the financial advantages his tours offered, Thomas, like Dickens, invested a tremendous energy in his readings, which indicated that performing filled a deeper need. Indeed, just as some scholars have claimed for Dickens, the extreme emotional stresses of his performances and tours probably hastened Thomas's death. Most Thomas studies support the view that Thomas sought in his American tours and his performances a means of escape from his life in England. If his public readings can be blamed for assisting in his early death, Thomas was an eager accomplice. He actively pursued ways of coming to the United States for years preceding Brinnin's offer in 1949 for a reading tour to begin the following year: "Dylan was not seduced into first crossing the Atlantic; he had been trying to do so for five years. No victim ever went more willingly to his gregarious death by strangers" (Sinclair 1975:140).

Whatever creative fulfillment Thomas's readings brought him, appearing in public habitually filled him, according to Brinnin, with a "bone-chilling anxiety" (1955:22). Thomas would cope with his extreme stage fright by drinking, and consequently, he often performed less than sober. Remarkably, his drinking did not diminish his ability once on the platform and his performances, particularly his resonant voice, quickly made Thomas a reading legend. Brinnin described Thomas's first American reading at the Kaufmann Auditorium of the YM-YWHA Poetry Center in New York City on 23 February 1950:

[A]t the appointed time, he walked out on stage . . . and proceeded to give the first of those performances which were to bring to America a whole new conception of poetry reading. The enormous range and organ-deep resonance of his voice as he read from Yeats, Hardy, Auden, Lawrence, MacNiece, Alun Lewis and Edith Sitwell gave new music to familiar cadences and, at times, revealed values in the poems never disclosed on the page. When he concluded the evening with a selection of his own works—encompassing both tenderly lyrical and oratorical passages with absolute authority—it was difficult to know which gave the greater pleasure, the music or the meaning (1955:23–24).

The excited reception of his reading was accepted by Thomas with humorous understatement and self-effacement. In an interview with the New York Times, Thomas summed up his own estimation of his abilities as a performer: "I'm afraid," he said, "it's second-rate Charles Laughton" (quoted in Breit 1950:19). Thomas's self-deprecation extended to his writings. He enjoyed reading from the work of other writers more than from his own and frequently performed not only from the writers listed in Brinnin's account of the first American reading but also selections by Shakespeare (from *King Lear*), Webster (the mad scene from *The Duchess of Malfi*), and Marlowe (quite stirringly, the final soliloquy from *Dr. Faustus*). Of reading his own works, Thomas wrote Brinnin, "An hour of me aloud is hell, and produces large burning spots in front of the mind" (quoted in Brinnin 1955:31). Thomas typically closed his program with selections from his own work, which most often included "Fern Hill," "A Refusal to Mourn," "This Side of Truth," "Do Not Go Gentle Into That Good Night," "And Death Shall Have No Dominion," "In My Craft," and "Poem in October." Although favoring certain selections, Thomas never formally scripted a performance anthology (as did Emlyn Williams). Instead, Thomas would take a full collection of possible text choices up with him to the lectern and in performance spontaneously choose selections, as he said, "according to the 'feel' of the audience" (quoted in Ferris 1977:239–40).

Whether reading from his own or others' work, Thomas was "a true medieval minstrel" (Sinclair 1975:38); his voice was able, some critics contended, to give a greatness to works even of lesser merit. The *New York Times* observed that: "It has often been said of Dylan Thomas, as a verse reader, that he could read anything to make it sound like Something. The same dangerous facility, the same unremitting Golden Voice (a gold that can shade into peach into rose into ham) is the primary component of his poetry; thought, emotion and eye are secondary compared with it" (MacNiece 1953:1). This last comment explains an enduring suspicion about Thomas's readings and about poetry readings in general. For the literary audience, as distinguished from the theatre audience, excellence in performance is not greeted without reservation. Writers who perform well are suspected of masking weak writing or overwhelming the literature with an awareness of themselves as performers. Emily Ellison, author of *First Light,* commented during a discussion after a reading from her novel that the danger lies in "the person becoming bigger than the work" (interview, 17 Oct. 1985). This may indeed be said of Dylan Thomas. He brought to poetry a wider audience, he demonstrated the power of spoken poetry, but in the wake of his own celebrity and performance ability (again, particularly the famous voice), he can be accused of superseding the supposed main focus of any reading: the meaning of the literary text. One biographer wrote: "His rich voice overcame any problems of meaning. People frequently said that Thomas' way of reading made them understand poems for the first time; but it may be that under the influence of his voice, the literal meaning of a poem became irrelevant" (Ferris 1977:233). If we accept the idea that an audience may be seriously moved without fully understanding the meaning of what is being spoken, what does a reader like Dylan Thomas bring to a poetry reading? Before answering this very real question regarding the value of poetry readings, we need to recognize that a good reader (and Thomas, by all accounts, was an excellent one) *does* give at least some members of the audience a greater understanding and appreciation of the literature performed. Beyond this, there are elements of a poetry reading by a celebrated writer that are undeniably extraliterary. A large part of the audience excitement at a Thomas reading was not concerned with the literature but—going back to Ellison's comment—with the person. A well-known writer—whether or not a capable performer—brings a celebrity, an ethos so strong to the platform that it surpasses all other concerns and remains the raison d'être for the reading. John Ciardi called this aspect of solo readings "a platform charge": "I suspect there will always be an audience for a man who can bring dramatic personality into a lecture-hall, but the question of poetic merit is not the question there. Thomas happened to have both merit and showmanship (plus legend). . . . Thomas could give even the ignorant a platform-charge, but that charge was incidental to poetic merit" (quoted in Wray 1961:253). The element of "platform charge" was strong in Thomas's performances. In a cyclical pattern, he brought to his readings a celebrity and his readings, in turn, augmented that celebrity. Audiences are "persuaded" to attend an event, and Thomas's multifaceted ethos was an important appeal. In a Dylan Thomas reading, three kinds of ethos were responsible for his success: first and most important, his position as a major writer of the day; second, his reputation as a fine dramatic reader; and third, his notorious persona. This persona—that of a self-destructive, hard drinking, womanizing genius—should not be underestimated as a reason for his platform success. Thomas himself was aware of his personal reputation and may have, at least in part, consciously pursued and created it. When asked why he drank so much, he answered: "Because they expect it of me" (quoted in Sinclair 1975:67). His public readings were both a celebration of and a means to further his legend. Unmistakable echoes exist with other individuals in this study who were able to use solo performance as a way to invent a public persona.

Thomas's reading tours in America from 1950 to 1953 had an effect on the literary community similar to those of Charles Dickens a century earlier. Authors' readings as we have seen, became widely popular in the late nineteenth century following Dickens's tours. Today, readings are again a standard part of the literary world. Thomas's readings, those combinations of literary and histrionic talent and celebrated persona—or as Donald Hall refers to them, combinations of "excellence and freak show" (1984/85:65)—established the contemporary poetry reading movement:

Dylan Thomas on his three American tours drew attention to poetry readings. Surely some of this attention was legitimate: he sang other poets' poems as well as his own, read beautifully, and traveled not only as the Poet himself but as the Voice of Poetry, rhapsode and reciter. Also, of course, he was notorious. . . . Because he was the fashionable college poet of his day . . . contemporary poetry started to be identified with the poetry reading. Because the phenomenon was both good and bad—excellence and freak show—Dylan Thomas provides both starting point and emblem. For it was right after his successful tours that poetry readings began to multiply (Hall 1984/85:64–65).

THE BEAT POETS AND BEYOND

Dylan Thomas is indeed emblematic of the contemporary poetry reading movement: he is representative of the celebrated writer-performer who is credible and recognized for both aspects of that dual identity. He brought to twentieth-century authors' readings a renewed interest, a heightened prestige, a respect for an effective delivery, and a broadened appeal. Yet without diminishing Thomas's significance in this history of solo performance, we need to recognize the contributions of other poet-performers who took to the platform soon after Thomas's death in 1953. The Beat poets democratized the poetry reading; they transformed the reading platform from an altar reserved for literary luminaries to a forum for new and emerging voices. These new voices of the "Beat generation" included Allen Ginsberg, Jack Kerouac, Gregory Corso, Phil Whalen, Lawrence Ferlinghetti, Gary Snyder, LeRoi Jones Baraka, and other writers belonging to the San Francisco Renaissance, the New York Scene, and Black Mountain College. Whereas Dylan Thomas may be said to have set a standard against which readings by celebrated writers may be measured, the writers of the Beat generation, particularly Allen Ginsberg, are credited with popularizing readings and largely instigating the current "great revival of spoken poetry" (Billington 1980:204).

The event most scholars consider the beginning of the Beat movement is the Six Gallery reading in San Francisco in the autumn of 1955. It was at that reading that Ginsberg first performed *Howl,* which became the manifesto (along with Kerouac's *On the Road*) of the movement. Lawrence Ferlinghetti explained in the *Chicago Review* how the new Beat poetry broke with the poetry of the literary establishment:

There are all kinds of poets here, writing very dissimilar types of poetry. . . . But I should say that the kind of poetry which has been making the most noise here is quite different from the "poetry about poetry," the poetry of technique, the poetry for poets and professors which has dominated the quarterlies and anthologies in this country for some time and which of course is also written in San Francisco. The poetry which has been making itself heard here of late is what should be called street poetry. For it amounts to getting the poet out of the inner esthetic sanctum where he has too long been contemplating his complicated navel. It amounts to getting poetry back into the street where it once was, out of the classroom, out of the speech department, and—in fact—off the printed page. The printed word has made poetry so silent. But the poetry I am talking about here is spoken poetry, poetry conceived as oral messages. It "makes it" aloud. Some of it has been read with jazz, much of it has not. A new "ashcan" school? Rock and roll? Who cares what names it's called. What is important is that this poetry is using its eyes and ears as they have not been used for a number of years (1958:4).

Ferlinghetti's assessment was astute; time has proven that one of the most important contributions of Beat poetics to contemporary literature was its renewed emphasis on the oral/aural dimension. "The aural *sound* of language of poetry," wrote Lee Hudson concerning the Beats, "was revived, a dimension of poetic art frequently ignored" (1977:72). Politically, the Beat poets reacted against the commercial establishment of postwar America; poetically, they broke with the academic establishment of obscure, dense poetry associated with the modern poets such as T. S. Eliot and Ezra Pound. The platform reading, by nature communal, was an extension of the Beat poetics and politics. The reading events became a forum for persuading listeners and changing minds, for exorcising the demons of the American establishment, and for celebrating counterculture values:

> The Beat movement encouraged, and practiced, public performances of poetry—coffee house readings, poems recited in bars to a jazz beat, group word-fests of those high on pot or wine, as well as more *outre* (and sometimes nude, mystical or belligerent) use of the poetic. Those who did not see these sometimes quite effective performances can recognize from the published remains that the real effort was not towards what we usually consider the literary object but to the half-verbal occasion for ritualism, therapy, curse, exhibition or celebration (Widmer 1970:165–66).

The Beat poets blasted any remaining notions that poetry readings were elocutionary delights for ladies' garden clubs or dry, egghead entertainments for academics. The Beat poetry reading featured language that was coarse, common, and frequently vulgar. Indeed, the obscenity trial regarding Ginsberg's *Howl* was a media event central in popularizing the Beat movement across the nation. The Beats demonstrated the power of spoken poetry as a political tool that could be wielded to persuade outsiders and to stimulate supporters. The civil rights groups of the 1960s (and beyond) have followed the example of the Beat poets. "Activists in the movements," wrote Katharyn Machan Aal in her study of contemporary poetry and fiction readings, "for Black rights, women's rights, gay rights, animal rights, and nuclear disarmament, for example, all currently use readings as one means of reaching the public and (more realistically) further bonding their adherents" (1984, vol. 1:130). Thus the political use of the poetry reading continues to flourish today, as demonstrated by Adrienne Rich, a writer very much in demand as a reader and one who owes a significant part of her audience appeal to the political nature of her poetry.

There are, of course, nonpolitical reasons motivating contemporary writers to give readings. Like most soloists, many writers-performers typically claim that money is the main incentive. A closer examination, however, reveals reasons that move beyond the financial to the social and the artistic. Aal innumerates the major reasons behind a writer's appearance on the public platform; they include: "[F]ees, recognition as a writer, the 'making public' of their work, communication, incentive and method for revision, desire for community, appreciation of the actual sound of their language, generation of 'energy' and obligation and generosity" (1984, vol. 1:138). An individual writer, as Aal points out, may actually perform for a combination of reasons or for different reasons at different times. Whatever the motives behind the decision for writers to turn to public performance, poetry readings are, as David Wojahn states, "an important aspect of American culture" (1985:266). Today the most sought after writer-performers include not only Ginsberg and Rich, but also many other major names in contemporary literature: James Dickey, Denise Levertov, Alan Dugan, Galway Kinnell, Judy Grahn, Carolyn Forché, Maya Angelou, Diane Wakoski, Gwendolyn Brooks, Ted Hughes, Tom Gunn, and Richard Wilbur. The mid-1960s brought the founding of the National Endowments for the Humanities and the Arts (and subsequently the state agencies), which established easier access for funding poetry readings. Thereafter, the poetry reading movement accelerated. Throughout the 1970s and 1980s, audiences have attended poetry readings at numerous academic and community locations.

THE GREAT DEBATE: THE PAGE VERSUS THE STAGE

The proliferation of poetry readings has not been greeted by the literary community with unanimous approval. Several recent publications examine writers' arguments for and against the practice of reading in public.[13] Those who argue in favor of readings claim they broaden the audience for literature, enhance audience understanding and appreciation, provide income and recognition for the writer, and encourage the revision of the texts being performed. The arguments against readings typically relate to the main thesis that public performance by its very nature emphasizes showmanship above literary merit: writers may achieve a following because they are good performers, not good writers; public performance tends to require accessible texts (which, in turn, usurp the place of more complex—and perhaps superior—work); writers may become too concerned with entertaining the audience and resort to cheap gimmicks in performance; performance is transitory, writing is permanent, therefore writing is the superior endeavor; good writers may be bad performers, bad writers may be good performers. The tension between the artist's *identity* as a writer and his or her *activity* as a performer cause some to aschew the word *performance* altogether and to claim that a reading is not a performance. "That word 'performance,'" states Jack Anderson, "is anathema to many poets, who regard it as synonymous with 'falsity' or 'insincerity'" (in Ziegler et al. 1978:9).

Writers, therefore, are divided on the topic of readings—some merely tolerating them as "an onerous duty" (Kostelanetz 1981:79) or avoiding them altogether and others strongly supporting them as an important part of their artistic life. Katharyn Machan Aal labeled the two "camps" in the literary community: the "pagers" and the "stagers":

There are those who believe poetry and fiction are best experienced in silent reading in the privacy of a quiet room—the "pagers." And there are those who believe poetry and fiction are best experienced orally and aurally in the company of others—the "stagers." A military metaphor is appropriate, for some members of each aesthetic group express hostility and contempt for the preference of the other. Many people are moderates in that they say they are open to both approaches, enjoying whichever works best for a given piece of literature; however, most actually do have a preference for one aesthetic or the other (1984, vol. 1:112–13).

The argument for the page against the stage (and, conversely, for the stage against the page) has manifested itself in a variety of ways throughout this study. The same conflict underlies all the theatre critics' reviews which claim that any given performance is not really theatre—it is just a reading of a book that belongs in the library. The only difference is that theatre critics, as opposed to literary critics, clearly prefer the stage over the page and resent undramatic literature's encroachment on territory rightly claimed by drama. The page versus the stage argument is also at the heart of those debates among elocutionists during the early decades of the twentieth century.[14] Clearly those performers who favored subdued interpretive readings emphasized the text, or to continue with our present terminology, the page, whereas those who argued for impersonation preferred the stage. After considering all the arguments for either critical perspective, we are left with one truly rational choice. Page and stage should not be perceived as competitors or opponents. They are, instead, complements—each offering advantages that the other lacks.

In this discussion of writer-performers, I have focused on artists who define themselves foremost as writers. Their role as performers remains incidental, simply a means to an end: the sharing of the *literary text* whose primary place is in print. Whether the text is published or unpublished, the written form remains paramount. In his essay "The Poem as Object," Ted Pearson clarifies the distinction between a writer's performance and a performer's performance of a text by emphasizing the literary artist's tacit agreement with the audience:

When the writer of poems written to be read on the page is involved in such a presentation [a public reading], it is "understood" that he or she is in fact reading *from* a text *to* audience and is not giving a performance *of* a text *for* an audience. It is further "understood" that the text as such is complete in itself and is neither dependent on such presentation for its existence nor intended to serve as an element in a matrix of elements coherent in the term and act of performance (1981:319)

Pearson's discussion is useful because he points out that the actual performance act as an objective event may not visibly differ whether a writer or a performer is on the stage; what changes is the audience perception of the event and the tacit agreement with the artist regarding the primary location of the text.

Although helpful, Pearson's analysis does limit our understanding by setting up an unfortunate dichotomy. Many writers, as we have already seen, are favorably predisposed toward performance and view it as an integral part of their creative life. How do we account for the differences in opinion between the "pagers" and the "stagers"? And what of those artists who create their own texts *for* performance? Spalding Gray and Eric Bogosian have had their performance texts published as books—do we just divorce Gray and Bogosian from Thomas and Ginsberg? In short, how can we distinguish between writer-performers and performer-writers while maintaining an understanding of their relation to each other? Adapting Katharyn Machan Aal's "pager-stager" terminology, we can develop a continuum that charts the movement of artist's attitudes towards the acts of writing and performance (see figure 2). The continuum not only accounts for the two "camps" within the literary world, the "pagers" and the "stagers," but goes beyond to indicate their relation with those artists more appropriately termed "performer-writers," artists who create their own texts especially intended for solo performance.[15] Whereas writer-performers believe the performance aspect of their work is incidental, most performer-writers perceive the writing process as a means to an end: the end for them being the shared *performance event* with a live audience.

FIGURE 2

High Value				High Value
Placed on	"The Pagers"	"The Stagers"	"The On-	Placed on
Writing	(Writer-	Those Artists	Stagers"	Performing
	Performers)	Equally Valuing	(Performer-	
		Writing and	Writers)	
		Performing		
		(Writer-Performers *or* Performer-Writers)		

Although many writers are made uncomfortable by the word *performance* and prefer instead *reading,* many performer-writers shun the word *reading.* I've interviewed one performer-writer whose publicity material explicitly renounces the term *reading* as descriptive of his performance.[16] The word *reading* obviously has negative connotations for some people—connotations such as pedantic, academic, dull, etc.—just as *performance* has for others. As stated, for many performer-writers, writing is simply a necessary step to performing. The act of writing is clearly the writing of

a script. Whether eventually published and silently read as literature or not, the text is intended as a performance phenomenon.
Just as with a play, the solo performance text undergoes constant
revision in rehearsal and in early performances with audiences.
The written document—the text in print—then becomes an artifact; an artifact considered by the performer-writers to be inferior
to the text in performance. Eric Bogosian expresses this opinion
in his introduction to the published collected texts of *Drinking in
America, FunHouse,* and *Men Inside:* "They [the texts] live in my
world, are made for my voice and temperament. They were meant
to be performed and never seen again. To work off the audience. I
hope you can get the sense of the voices from the printed page"
(Bogosian 1987:18).

Whether writer-performer or performer-writer, the duality of
writing and performance—of page and stage—often results in the
artist's internal conflict, or what one critic said in reference to Bogosian, "a tug-of-war" (Nemy 1986:C2). When speaking of his
own experience as a performer and a writer for *Drinking in America,* Bogosian said, "The actor in me just wants to entertain. He
hears people laughing and would keep ad libbing if left alone. The
writer has a point in mind that he wants to make and he's damned
if he's going to let the actor screw it up" (quoted in Nemy
1986:C2). Nearly forty years ago, Dylan Thomas confronted the
same tension between the page and the stage. His conclusion, as
reported by Brinnin, is a fitting closure to our discussion on contemporary poetry readings:

About the reading of poetry, he [Thomas] felt that only perusal of
the printed page—or perhaps the interior or critical monologue, or private discussion—could give to each poem the full concentrated time that
any poem is justified in asking for the assessment of its success or failure
to demonstrate its own hypothesis. In public, only the poem itself can be
presented, and there its effect depends upon the immediacy with which
the hypothesis, the moment and motive of inspiration, can affect the
reader through his ear. In other words, and as he was later fond of saying, the printed page is the place in which to examine the works of a
poem, the platform the place in which to give the poem the works
(1955:126–27).

CONCLUSION

The preceding chapters dealing with the Victorian age and the first half of the twentieth century examined the cultural context of the one-person show mode. Distance in time often allows for a greater clarity when considering the effects of major cultural forces; proximity, on the other hand, tends to obscure what will become apparent to the generations that follow. The years after 1950 have seen the one-person show form enjoy a vogue reminiscent of that of platform performances during the Victorian age. The current ascendancy in popularity may be due to a convergence of complex social forces that will require a greater distance to comprehend fully. We may, however, at least speculate as we begin to understand the renaissance of the one-person show.

At least part of the renewed popularity of one-person shows stems from our recovery from the fevered anti-Victorianism of the early part of this century. By the time Emlyn Williams and Hal Holbrook re-created the Victorian platform appearances of Charles Dickens and Mark Twain, a movement counter to the post–World War I anti-Victorianism was underway. "Nothing did more to rehabilitate the Victorians," wrote Richard D. Altick, "as a society worthy not only of study but of deep respect than, for instance, the discovery that Dickens, far from being the mere popular entertainer he had been tagged by previous criticism, was a great artist" (1973:304). Whereas earlier in the twentieth century audiences may well have found Williams's *Dickens* recital ridiculously stodgy and sentimental, by 1950 attitudes had changed enough to enjoy the performance as a quaint yet cultural and educational experience. The rehabilitation of the reputations of Victorian writers and a new interest in Victoriana prepared the way for the many one-person shows based on the lives of nineteenth-century figures.[17]

Changes within the American theatre have greatly influenced the one-person show. The current vogue of solo performance is dependent on the concurrent theatrical experiments in presentational plays produced during the same period. The roots of Western presentational drama go back to the Greek plays that included direct audience address. Throughout the history of the theatre, some periods have favored the presentationalism whereas others preferred representationalism. The nineteenth century brought representational realism to its zenith and its emphasis on psychological drama paved the way for the intense examination of the single persona in one-person shows. During the hundred years between 1850 and 1950, stage realism was the dominate production style. Since midcentury, however, theatrical innovations in presentational staging have challenged the strictures of proscenium realism. Twentieth-century experiments in presentational staging date back to the early 1900s and the work of Russia's Vsevolod Meyerhold. Meyerhold's comment that he sought a theatre that "concentrated on the *act* of acting not on acting as representing some kind of reality" (Schmidt 1980:xiii) stands as the philosophical statement behind the twentieth-century presentational performances that eventually blasted the equation of theatre with realistic drama. The influence of presentational plays on the one-person show form has been at times surprisingly direct. Ruth Draper had seen *The Yellow Jacket* (a Chinese theatre piece), and its presentational aesthetics both inspired her work and helped convince her to turn professional ("The Interview" 1954:23). At other times, the influence of presentationalism is less direct but more pervasive: the theatrical experiments of Bertolt Brecht and the Absurdist playwrights created an atmosphere in which various kinds of performances could find an audience and could be accepted as legitimate theatre.

In America, Thornton Wilder's *Our Town* proved a seminal production. Frederick Lumley, in *New Trends in 20th-Century Drama*, points to Wilder's play as a landmark: "No single dramatic work in the American theatre has had a greater influence on both sides of the Atlantic than Thornton Wilder's *Our Town*, produced in New York in 1938" (1972:333). When reviewing a 1987 revival of *Our Town*, Mel Gussow of the *New York Times* wrote of the enduring impact of the play:

Stylistically and thematically, *Our Town* was, and is a pioneering work of experimental theatre. In its original production, it broke the Broadway proscenium and encouraged the proliferation of thrust and arena-style staging. . . . It was Wilder's belief that "the box-set staging stifles the life in drama" and "militates against belief." Informally engaging the audience in simulated conversation, shattering suspense by introducing the dead before we know about their lives, the play challenges traditions of stage time, characterization and scenic design (1987:36).

Wilder explained his reasons for debunking the conventions of representational theatre in his now famous preface of *Our Town:*

I became dissatisfied with the theatre because I was unable to lend credence to such childish attempts to be "real." I began writing one-act plays that tried to capture not verisimilitude but reality. . . . Our claim, our hope, our despair was in the mind—not in things, not in "scenery." Moliere said that for the theatre all he needed was a platform and a passion or two. The climax of this play [*Our Town*] needs only five square feet of boarding and the passion to know what life means to us (1976:x-xi).

Wilder not only stripped away the illusionistic artifice of nineteenth-century proscenium scenery but also employed direct audience address through the use of a "Stage Manager" who functioned as a narrator and controller of the action. The use of narrative on the stage, whether it be embodied in one central narrator, immersed in character soliloquy, or divided among a full cast who may directly address the audience as a chorus, has roots that harken back to the drama of classical Greece and Rome and Elizabethan England. Wilder recognized his debt to dramatists of earlier epochs in his preface: "I am not an innovator but a re-discoverer of forgotten goods and I hope a remover of obtrusive bric-a-brac" (1976:xii). Wilder's words are a reminder that the renaissance of the one-person show is actually part of the larger renaissance in the theatre, one in which ancient conventions that date back to the oral storytellers have been rediscovered and adapted. Since Wilder, presentational devices have again become common, if not standard, in the American theatre. *Don Juan in Hell* and *John Brown's Body,* both produced in the 1950s, proved again the effectiveness of nonillusionistic, presentational staging. More recently, *Equus, Evita, Amadeus,* and David Edgar's adaptation of *The Life and Adventures of Nicholas Nickleby* have been among Broadway's most successful productions; they all used presentational staging.[18] All of these performances share with one-person shows the use of performers who directly addresses the audience. Presentational plays and one-person shows have, in effect, prepared their audiences for each other: an audience that accepts the presence of a narrating figure in a play can accept the presence of a narrating figure alone.

As the twenty-first century approaches, one-person shows may achieve an even more prominent position within the American theatre. Theatre historian Milly S. Barranger suggests that solo performers may become preeminent: "What if the new direction of theatrical experiments? Who are the new faces of the 1980s? Some have conjectured that the new wave is led by the *performer* (rather than the *actor* who pretends to be someone else) whose method is the monologue. In an inflated economy, money has been a large factor in the attraction of solo performances. One-person shows naturally cost less" (1984:462). Certainly the relatively small budgets of one-person shows place them at an advantage in the American theatre. The astronomical production costs of mounting plays have simply made them unattractive to producers who are unwilling to take major risks. This, then, is yet another instance of the fortunes of the theatre influencing the contemporary one-person show: as production costs rise, one-person shows flourish. Pragmatists within the theatre have typically agreed with a financial interpretation of the one-person show's success, claiming that economic motives lie behind the proliferation of one-person shows solo performances: "Once novelty items, such [one-person] shows are now a theatrical staple, even cliché. The species, characterized by low production budgets, seems to have proliferated in inverse proportion to a shrinking economy. Money, not art, is the stimulus here" (Jenner 1981:4). Although I would argue that a more complex set of cultural factors lies behind the success of one-person shows in recent years, the economic realities are undeniable. The *London Observer,* in an article announcing the opening of Rhombus Productions (a theatre company specializing in one-person shows), stated that "in times of recession the one-man show flourishes" (Colvin 1981:28). Such a thesis is certainly supported by the startling growth of one-person shows in the 1970s.

Throughout this chapter, several other cultural issues have already been suggested as possible causes for the rise of one-person shows. Certainly our hunger for celebrities has had an enormous impact on the success of contemporary one-person shows. All solo performances by established artists fulfill a desire to see a celebrity in person; whether that artist is an actor, a writer, or a comedian, the "platform charge" that John Ciardi spoke of is an undeniable attraction for audiences. Our celebrity-hunger parallels the movement Sennett refers to as "the fall of public man" as private lives become public property. Biographies and autobiographies have emerged since midcentury as important popular forms of literature. These forces converge on the entertainment world and one result is the proliferation of one-person shows that are celebrations of a single celebrity's virtuosity. Biographical one-person shows such as *The Belle of Amherst* have the advantage of a kind of double dose of "platform charge": a celebrity performer portraying a celebrity historical figure.

If we were to select a cultural force of comparable importance to our age as the advent of the railroads was to the nineteenth century, television would surely be the prime choice. Television became as pervasive after 1950 as the railway system became after 1850. By the 1980s, American homes frequently had more than one television set per family. The pervasiveness of television and our hunger for celebrity often work together, creating media stars faster than live performance, film, or print could ever hope to. The celebrities created by television became potential central characters around which to build one-person shows. How long will it be, I wonder, before a one-person show is based on the life of Oliver North? Television aids solo performance in other ways. The intimate camera close-ups of television and film have made the heightened focus on a single character and direct audience address on stage in a one-person show entirely plausible. Even more directly, television has brought taped solo productions in American homes on commercial, cable, and public networks. Today, you may even rent or purchase videotapes of successful one-person shows (including authors' readings) and enjoy them long after the production has ended its run.

Television's impact, however, is not all positive for the one-person show as a live event. Needless to say, television is the major entertainment mode and as such distracts potential audience members away from the live stage and platform. But neither television nor film has killed the theatre; live performance ultimately offers a kind of experience in exchange of energy between performer and audience that cannot be duplicated in an electronic mode. Indeed, the innate human impulse for live performance has played an important part in the success of the revived Chautauqua circuits. As surprising as it may seem, Chautauqua is experiencing a revival concurrent with the one-person show. Starting in the 1970s, several states (including North Dakota, South Dakota, Wyoming, Nebraska, Kansas, Minnesota, Utah, and Oregon) have funded nonprofit adaptations of the old Chautauqua circuits through their councils for the humanities and the arts. These new Chautauquas are public outreach programs that bring to local communities a variety of lectures, workshops, and dramatic presentations. Aside from readers theatre presentations, the dramatic offerings are typically solo performances. These Chautauqua one-person shows differ from their Broadway counterparts in their emphasis on the shows' educational content as opposed to their entertainment merit. The performers are not professional actors but humanities scholars who have researched and developed their monologues, usually based on figures from regional history.[19] The Great Plains Chautauqua, for example, offered recently "Writers on the Plains: The Pen and the Plow," in which scholar-performers toured eight communities presenting afternoon workshops in the humanities and evening performances of interpretive monologues in the characters of Sinclair Lewis, Willa Cather, Mari Sandoz, Hamlin Garland, and William Allen White. Why does a Victorian idea like Chautauqua succeed in today's media-sophisticated world? Why don't the audiences just stay home and watch their television sets? Clearly, even four decades of television has not squelched the desire for the unique experience of live performance. And the one-person show, whose history is so tied to that of Chautauqua, has again found itself touring rural America under the big top.

NOTES

1. Emlyn Williams, personal interview, 30 Dec. 1982. Subsequent quotations by Williams are from this interview, which was published in *Literature in Performance* (Gentile 1983a).

2. For a full comparison of Dickens's and Williams's performance texts, see Collins (1975) and Williams, (1953).

3. From a press release during a run of *Dylan Thomas Growing Up* at the North Light Repertory Theatre, Evanston, IL, 21 Dec. 1982–2 Jan. 1982. Williams's omission of Thomas's poetry distressed the poet's widow. In a letter to the *New Statesman and Nation,* Caitlin Thomas wrote of her reaction to Williams's performance: "He [Williams] has deliberately emphasized a certain side, and certain aspects, the less worthy ones I should say, of Dylan's character; and almost omitted the dwarfing shadow (dwarfing to Mr. Williams himself, could it be?) of poetry" (11 June 1955:815).

4. See Holbrook's own discussion of his "double impersonation" (1959:37). For Holbrook's comments regarding his use of the cigar in performance, see Holbrook (1959:38–39).

5. This genre of one-person shows has been called "literary one-person shows." I believe the terminology to be unnecessarily confusing. It suggests that the performance is a reading of literature or that the impersonated persona is always a literary figure. Both suggestions are erroneous. The central persona of these one-person shows, as indicated in the text of this study, are often nonliterary figures and the focus of the great majority of these performances is not on the literary writings but rather on the life of the selected figure. For such reasons, I have chosen to call this genre "biographical one-person shows." For a text that refers to them as "literary one-person shows," see Billington (1980:202).

6. It is historically appropriate for a twentieth-century one-person show to be produced in a theatre named after the lyceum.

7. See Eifert (1984): this study is recommended for readers interested in a fuller treatment of the device of casting the audience.

8. "There's clearly a growing general interest along with a significant shift toward biography (and autobiography) as dominant popular forms and an augmented degree of critical sophistication among readers and reviewers" (Kaplan 1987:24). "One of the notable cultural developments in recent decades is the remarkable flowering of American autobiography, not only as a major mode of literary self-expression, but also as a widely popular form of reading and an important new field for scholars and critics" (Stone 1981:1).

9. The *Spalding Gray Retrospective* eventually included seven autobiographical monologues, several of which were published in a collection with later Gray monologues (see Gray 1986).

10. A recent article offers an insightful analysis of the multiple facets of the Spalding Gray persona created in performance: "[S]everal Spalding Grays are at work. First, the 'observer-of-events,' Spalding Gray the private citizen, works in a nearly reportorial fashion to uncover the [American] system's shortcomings as he lives the life of a privileged middle-class male. The results of the espionage, in turn, are handed over to Gray the artist to create a work offering a critical perspective on the

system. The piece is presented by Gray the *naive* performer, who appears fully incorporated into the system and is unaware of the ironies introduced into his presentation by the artist Gray, who shaped the material reported by the observer Gray. Who is the actual Spalding Gray? ... Gray's onstage work presents material, *seemingly* without comment, in an ironic manner that confronts the ... power structure. ... Thus while Gray's work may *appear* supportive of the status quo, it presents a persona who ironically utilizes an empowered naivety to undermine itself and the authority it seems to uphold." From William W. Demastes, "Spalding Gray's *Swimming to Cambodia* and the evolution of an ironic presence," *Theatre Journal* 41 (March 1989): 86.

11. Quentin Crisp, personal interview, 23 April 1986. Subsequent quotations by Crisp are from this interview, which was published in *Literature in Performance* (Gentile 1988a).

12. Responding to a questionaire, McCowen emphasized his debt to Ruth Draper and also named Emlyn Williams, Julie Harris, Victor Borge, and Maurice Chevalier as influences (Alec McCowen, letter to the author, 13 Oct. 1984).

13. Recent publications dealing with poetry readings include: Aal (1984); Hall (1984/85); Vincent and Zweig, (1981); Wojahn (1985); and Ziegler et al. (1978).

14. See "Impersonation: The Great Debate," in Haas and Williams (1975:43–57).

15. I first presented this continuum as part of an essay at a panel on writing and performance at the 1986 conference of the Speech Communication Association. I presented that essay, "The Performer as Writer," directly following Katharyn Machan Aal's presentation of her essay "The Writer as Performer." At that time I had no appropriate "pager-stager" term for performer-writers on the continuum, and I am indebted to Dr. Aal for her suggestion of "on-stagers." These two essays were subsequently published together; see Aal (1987) and Gentile (1987).

16. In Mark Stevenson's 1983 publicity material for his show on John Keats, he directly stated that the performance "certainly isn't just a poetry reading."

17. For a discussion of the anti-Victorian reaction and the recovery, see Altick (1973:299–309).

18. Along with plays using presentational staging, recent Broadway seasons have included numerous productions that are, like *Nicholas Nickleby,* presentational adaptations of nondramatic literature, see HopKins and Bouldin (1983:697–717), and Beggs (1982).

19. For more information about the revival of Chautauqua as public humanities programs, see Curry (1982) and Gentile (1988b).

Conclusion:
The Performer's Perspective

The topic of one-person shows continues to raise many questions for discussion. During my years of studying the genre, several professionals working in the area of solo performance offered their opinions and I have found their thoughts provocative and informative. Their answers are culled from personal interviews and letters as well as from published sources.

Occasionally critics disparage one-person shows by referring to them as "stunts" or "cabaret acts" and have thus diminished their contributions as theatre. How do the performers react to such criticism? Alec McCowen found such a position insupportable and simply responded that his reaction was, to use his word, "unprintable" (letter to the author, 13 Oct. 1984). Arthur Peterson (*Robert Frost: Fire and Ice*) also disagreed with the critics, arguing that history contradicts them. "Since time immemorial," responded Peterson, "we have had storytellers" (letter to the author, 24 July 1984; subsequent quotations are from this letter). Peterson's argument reminds us that the one-person show goes back to the ancient art of storytelling, which is also the origin of drama and literature. If we learn anything from the preceding pages, we learn that literature, drama, and solo performance all grow out of the same impulse towards language and performance. Whereas literary critics have typically perceived a distinction separating the printed word from the spoken word and theatre critics have seen a distinction between "true theatre" and solo performance, history has shown us that as art forms these manifestations of language and performance are in a constant, dynamic, creative interplay.

Why do performers enjoy solo performance? What makes a one-person show more attractive to a performer than an ensemble performance? Enid Nemy suggests a possible answer: "In the world of the theatre, the one-man show is perhaps the closest thing to having it all, a supreme test of assurance and ability, of magnetism and charisma. The format is both seductive and frightening; there's no one to play against, to lean on, to share the criticism. But, for an actor, the prize at the end of a successful solo performance is not only applause but also acclaim—unshared" (1984a:19). Do the performers agree? I have spoken to several and their comments are illuminating. Frank Galati, actor, director, and professor at Northwestern University's Department of Performance Studies (a department that emphasizes the solo performance of literary, folkloric, and personal texts) has performed a one-person show based on Valdimir Nabokov's *Pale Fire*. Galati feels that: "For some people 'vanity production' is appropriate. It [the one-person show] inevitably features the virtuosity of the performer and keeps in the audience's mind how difficult and dazzling it is to sustain a piece over a length of time" (interview, 17 Oct. 1982). William Norris, an actor, director and formerly artistic director of Chicago's Beacon Street Playhouse, whose own experience in solo performance includes the writing and performance of *His Satanic Majesty: A Portrait of Lord Byron* and the performance of *The Hitler Masque*, agrees with Galati. According to Norris, "Anyone that tells you that it [appearing in a one-person show] isn't an ego trip is lying" (interview, 10 March 1983). Alec McCowen, as quoted in the *New York Times*, concurs with Galati and Norris: "I love a one-man show because of reasons of vanity, I suppose, but it's not good to do it too long," he said, "The actor gets too remote and conceited, having things all his own way" (quoted in Nemy 1984a:C3). Not all actors, however, agree that the major benefits lie in self-gratification. Arthur Peterson believes that solo performance is uniquely suited to bringing literary works alive, a belief rooted in his early experience as an undergraduate in an oral interpretation class in 1931 at the University of Minnesota. To Peterson, the true benefit of solo performance is "an accomplishment of being as true to the material as possible and so help prolong the life of the writer as a literary heritage." Emlyn Williams saw no special vanity in solo performance: "I mean it's like saying that to play Hamlet is a form of vanity perhaps" (interview, 30 Dec. 1982).[1] Williams did, however, believe that the control offered to the actor by the one-person show makes the form appealing; Williams preferred solo performances because "You do not have to depend on other actors." Quentin Crisp's response reverses Williams's feelings; Crisp believes that the true benefit of solo performance is not having other actors depend upon him. Crisp told me that: "When you act with a group you have to worry a bit whereas on stage by yourself you don't have to worry at all. I mean I've been known to say things like, 'Oh, I forgot what I was going to say' or 'Where was I?' or things like that. It only makes the audience laugh more. Whereas on the stage [in a play] you've got the others to think of" (interview, 23 April 1986).[2] Spalding Gray's response echoed those of Williams, McCowen, and Crisp: "CONTROL. I can make all the choices" (letter to the author, 27 Feb. 1983).

Artistic freedom and control are characteristic advantages offered the solo performer by the one-person show. *Playbill* recognized these particular advantages in its March 1978 feature article "Monodrama":

There isn't an actor who's done a monodrama who doesn't groan about the loneliness; the absence camaraderie during rehearsal; the backstage whoop-de-do. But give them a moment and . . . they're talking about power, control, the joy that total responsibility brings (subtext: and no one stealing the show, that extra bow). Michael MacLiammoir [said]: "I have nothing on stage with me but a sofa and a bunch of lilies. They can't misuse or slap you on the back at the wrong time" (Cohn 1978: n.p.).

Yet the freedom offered by the one-person show is both a blessing and a danger for the solo performer. The possibility for performer self-indulgence is never far removed from the one-person show. Steven Rumbelow, a former member of the Bristol Old Vic and the Royal Shakespeare Company, has directed a biographical one-person show centered on Joan of Arc. Speaking from the director's point of view, Rumbelow believes that solo performance can actually be damaging for the performer's artistic development: "It's as if the performer has passed a barrier once he has appeared in a one-person show. There is an amount of ego fulfillment in performing alone on stage that can not be achieved in any other performance modality. There's an old adage in the business that once an actor has appeared in a one-person show he is unemployable" (interview, 25 Jan. 1983; subsequent quotations are from this interview). Although Rumbelow qualified his words by recognizing that the best solo performers can move freely between solo and group performance, his thoughts remain sobering. Continuing with his misgivings on the one-person show concept, Rumbelow believes that too often a solo performance grows out of "an actor's bad economic situation and a faith in oneself."

Whoopi Goldberg's comments in an interview appearing in *American Film* indicate that she agrees with Rumbelow. When asked about the intention of her solo Broadway show, Goldberg simply answered: "To get to work. That was my biggest intention. [Laughs.] That show grew out of desperation" (quoted in Kearney 1985:26). Eric Bogosian agrees with both Rumbelow and Goldberg; he also reminds us that one-person shows have the natural advantage of being relatively inexpensive to mount. Bogosian's turn to solo performance came when he realized that, as he put it, "It was time to get practical" (1987:16). He continued to say: "I was out of money, so I had to make work cheap. Solos were the answer. No rehearsal space had to be rented, no actors paid, no costly sets, costumes, or lights. And the stuff was portable. Which meant I could tour and instead of losing money, I could make it" (1987:16). Mark Stevenson, an actor currently touring in his one-person show *A Visitation from John Keats* as well as managing a company of solo performers called "Living Literature," confirmed Rumbelow's assessment in a personal interview. Stevenson, however, qualified his words by adding that the actor "almost has to develop a one-person show as a matter of survival" (interview, 20 April 1983; subsequent quotations are from this interview). For Collene Dewhurst, her solo *My Gene* centered on Charlotte Monterey (O'Neill) is her security as she moves into her sixties. As explained in the *New York Times:*

Embarking on her 60th year, she [Dewhurst] decided a while ago that it would be useful to have an annuity, a popular and durable performance piece that could tour regional theatres and colleges for a long time.

"Millie Dunnock said to me one time, 'Colleen, what you have to do is get a one-woman show, about an hour or something, some woman you like. . . . And you go out and they're wonderful to you.' She said, 'You know they fly you first class and meet you with the limo. They take you to the suite. You lie around. You go out and do it. You answer questions. You get back on the plane, the check is in your hand'" (Dudar 1987:3).

What is the future of one-person shows in America? Speaking particularly about the biographical genre, Mark Stevenson felt that changes in American education have created real dangers for its survival:

I see that what we've gone through is the deheroization of human life over the last twenty-five, thirty years. I think war provides great heroes, they're easy to recognize. Then when you don't have any wars, you get a few politicians, perhaps. But it has come to the point that no one is really respected for what they've done. I mean, everything is just sort of thrown away, it seems. And this is a real danger for the one-person show because one of the reasons you go [as an audience] is to become knowledgeable about someone who you respect as a hero or is famous for doing something. And this, along with the desintegration of classical education in this country ever since the 1960s when the students took power as well as the loss of respect for things that happened in the past, I think makes it very hard for a performer to select a figure that hasn't either been done before or no one has heard about. But as long as there's an interest in biography . . . it may survive because as people read less, I could see one-person shows that are stories told about people—I mean, instead of reading a biography, see the show about so-and-so. [In that case], the performer, I believe, has a responsibility to be very faithful to the truth about the life of the character.

Stevenson's comments are provocative; they refer to deficiencies in American education that have been indentified in the best-selling books *The Closing of the American Mind* by Allan Bloom and *Cultural Literacy* by E. D. Hirsch. Stevenson, after years of visiting our colleges and universities, believes that the malaise affecting American education has major implications for the future of one-person shows. Stevenson's belief derives from his experience as a solo performer which has been marked by a difficulty in finding knowledgeable audiences for his show on John Keats. Along with a disregard for history, our insatiable preoccupation with the private lives of famous people also results in diminishing our heroes. If we are losing our heroes as well as our appreciation of history, then the reserve of material on which to develop a one-person show—particularly the biographical kind—may simply become depleted. The result may be the emergence of autobiographical shows, such as Spalding Gray's monologues and other kinds of autoperformances, as the dominant genre of the future.

Have one-person shows already reached their zenith and will they, like the platform readers of the late nineteenth century, now recede into the past? At this writing there is no abatement in sight. Many of the shows discussed in the previous chapter have appeared on Broadway and on tours for second and third runs during the 1980s. Our appreciation of the contribution that one-person shows have made to the American culture is further increased when we recognize the fact that these productions are not limited to Broadway. They are exemplary of a national (indeed international) performance movement. The Smithsonian Institution's National Portrait Gallery in Washington, D.C., for example, has sponsored for the past several years a series of solo performances entitled "Portraits in Motion." The annual Spoleto Festival in Charleston, South Carolina, and the Edinburgh Festival in Scotland routinely feature one-person shows among their many dramatic presentations. The Shakespeare Festival at Stratford, Ontario, recently offered a full season of "Virtuoso Performances," a repertory of one-person shows including Douglas Campbell in *Blake,* Lewis Gordon in *Damien,* Edward Atienza in a Shakespeare recital *When That I Was...,* and Irene Worth in recitals of *Venus and Adonis, Ulysses and Mrs. Dalloway,* and *Letters of Love and Affection.* One-person shows—biographical, autobiographical, character sketches, and poetry readings—are today seen at a variety of academic and community locations: theatres, recital and concert halls, colleges and universities, secondary schools, literary and dramatic societies, coffee houses, bookstores, cafés, bars, libraries, museums, prisons, medical centers, private parties, lofts, fine and performing arts institutions, town parks and squares, and other locations hospitable to group gatherings. Recent years have even seen the revival of the Chautauqua circuits, which, along with the original Chautauqua Institution in New

York State, again present one-person shows. History has brought us full circle.

What are the hopes for the future? Mark Stevenson offered a vision of possible decline; Emlyn Williams spoke more optimistically. He returns us to the basics of any performance: "I think it will go on, yes. I think it will never supersede plays. It would be dreadful if it does, wouldn't it? Any more than plays shouldn't stifle one-man performances. If they are good and hold an audience."

NOTE

1. Subsequent quotations from Williams are from this interview, which was published in *Literature in Performance* 4 (Nov. 1983): 78–84.

2. The interview with Quentin Crisp was published in *Literature in Performance* 8 (Nov. 1988): 78–86.

Bibliography

MATERIALS IN PRINT

Aal, Katharyn Machan. "The Writer as Performer: A Study of Contemporary Poetry and Fiction Readings, Based in Ithaca, New York." 2 vols. Ph.D. diss., Northwestern University, 1984.
———. "The Writer as Performer." *American Institute of Discussion Review* 3 (1987):21–30.
Abarbanel, Jonathan. Review of *One Perfect Rose*, by Elizabeth Garry. *Chicago Reader*, 18 May 1984, sec. 2:50–51.
"Acting Company Plans to Return." *Chautauquan*, Fall 1982, 1.
Adams, Hazard. *The Contexts of Poetry*. Boston: Little, Brown, 1963.
Adler, Anthony. Review of *Kerouac: The Essence of Jack*, by Vincent Balestri. *Chicago Reader*, 17 Dec. 1982, sec. 2:42.
Alden, Jerome. *Bully! An Adventure with Teddy Roosevelt*. New York: Crown, 1979.
"Alec McCowen." *New Yorker*, 18 Sept. 1978, 31–33.
Alford, Cora W. "The Reading Platform: S. H. Clark." *Werner's*, April 1896, 351–53.
Allen, Frederick Lewis. *The Big Change: America Transforms Itself, 1900–1950*. New York: Harper, 1952.
Allen, Hervey. *Israfel: The Life and Times of Edgar Allan Poe*. 2 vols. New York: Doran, 1926.
Altick, Richard D. *The English Common Reader: A Social History of the Mass Reading Public 1800–1900*. Chicago: Univ. of Chicago Press, 1957.
———. *Victorian People and Ideas*. New York: Norton, 1973.
Anderson, John. "Miss Cecilia Loftus." *Harper's Bazaar*, June 1938, 115.
Aristotle. "Poetics." *Critical Theory Since Plato*, edited by Hazard Adams, 48–66. New York: Harcourt, 1971.
Arkatoy, Janice. "Bogosian's One-Man Bunch: Bouncing Ideas off *FunHouse* Walls." Review of *FunHouse*, by Eric Bogosian. *Los Angeles Times*, 5 April 1985, sec. 6:2.

Armstrong, Margaret. *Fanny Kemble: A Passionate Victorian.* New York: Macmillan, 1938.

Athayde, Roberto. *Miss Margarida's Way: Tragicomic Monologue for an Impetuous Woman.* Garden City: Nelson Doubleday, 1977.

Atkinson, J. Brooks. "Dorothy Sands, in One-Woman Show, Gives *Styles in Acting.*" Review of *Styles in Acting,* by Dorothy Sands. *New York Times,* late ed., 4 April 1932, 13.

———. "Dorothy Sands in *Our Stage and Stars.*" Review of *Our Stage and Stars,* by Dorothy Sands. *New York Times,* late ed., 13 Nov. 1933, 20.

———. "Theatre: *Ages of Man.*" Review of *Ages of Man,* based on an anthology by George Rylands. *New York Times,* late ed., 29 Dec. 1958, C21.

———. *Broadway.* New York: Macmillan, 1974.

Austin, Mary. "The Town that Doesn't Want Chautauqua." *New Republic,* 7 July 1926, 195.

B., J. "Portrays Henry VIII's Wives." Review of *The Wives of Henry VIII,* by Cornelia Otis Skinner. *New York Times,* late ed., 16 Nov. 1931, 22.

B., R. C. "Mark Twain on the Platform." *Critic,* 25 April 1896, 286.

Bacon, Wallace A. "The Elocutionary Career of Thomas Sheridan (1719-1788)." *Speech Monographs* 31 (March 1964):1–53.

———. "Afterword: From Interpretation to Performance Studies." In *Festschrift for Isabel Crouch: Essays on the Theory, Practice, and Criticism of Performance,* edited by Wallace A. Bacon, 71–78. Las Cruces, NM: New Mexico State University, 1987.

Bahn, Eugene, and Margaret L. Bahn. *A History of Oral Interpretation.* Minneapolis: Burgess, 1970.

Bailey, Eleanor June. "Frances Anne Kemble and the American Audience." Master's thesis, Texas Technological University, 1971.

Barnes, Clive. "Theatre: 1-Man Show of Shows." Review of *Dylan Thomas Growing Up,* by Emlyn Williams. *New York Times,* late ed., 13 Oct. 1976, 34.

———. "Williams Offers a Dazzling 'Weekend.'" Review of *The Playboy of the Weekend World,* by Emlyn Williams. *New York Post,* 17 Nov. 1978, 31.

———. "Ian Breathes New Life into the Bard." Review of *Ian McKellen Acting Shakespeare,* by Ian McKellen. *New York Post,* 20 Jan. 1984. Reprint, *New York Theatre Critics' Reviews* 44 (1984a): 389–90.

———. "Overloading the Stage with One-Person Shows." *New York Post,* 28 Jan. 1984b, 13.

Barranger, Milly S. *Theatre Past and Present: An Introduction.* Belmont, CA: Wadsworth, 1984.

Barry, James J. "Ralph Brownell Dennis, Lecturer, Interpreter, and Dean of the School of Speech." Master's thesis Northwestern University, 1947.

Beaufort, John. "Edwardian 'Once Upon a Time . . .'." Review of *The Playboy of The Weekend World,* by Emlyn Williams. *Christian Science Monitor,* 22 Nov. 1978a, 20.

———. "Gospel Brought to Stage." Review of *St. Mark's Gospel,* by Alec McCowen. *Christian Science Monitor,* 8 Sept. 1978. Reprint, *New York Theatre Critics' Reviews* 39 (1978b): 176–77.

———. "A Masterly Escorted Tour Through Shakespeare with Ian McKellen." Review of *Ian McKellen Acting Shakespeare,* by Ian McKellen. *Christian Science Monitor,* 1 Feb. 1984, 21–22.

Beckett, Samuel. *Krapp's Last Tape and Other Dramatic Pieces.* New York: Grove, 1960.

Beggs, James Glen. "Paul Shyre's Contribution to the Professional Performance of Non-Dramatic Literature 1954–1981: An Historical Survey." Ph.D. diss. Louisiana State University, 1982.

Benedetti, Robert L. *Seeming, Being, and Becoming: Acting in Our Century.* New York: Drama, 1976.

Bestor, Arthur Eugene, Jr. *Chautauqua Publications: An Historical and Bibliographical Guide.* Chautauqua, NY: Chautauqua, 1934.

Bikle, Lucy Leffingwell Cable. *George W. Cable: His Life and Letters.* 1928. Reprint. New York: Russell, 1967.

Billington, Michael, ed. *Performing Arts: A Guide to Practice and Appreciation.* New York: Facts, 1980.

Blair, Walter. *Native American Humor.* 1937. Reprint. New York: Harper, 1960.

———. "Charles Mathews and His 'A Trip to America'." *Prospects* 2 (1976): 1–23.

Blissett, William. "Dylan Thomas: A Reader in Search of a Poet." *Queen's Quarterly* 63 (1956): 45–58.

Bode, Carl. *The American Lyceum: Town Meeting of the Mind.* New York: Oxford Univ. Press, 1956.

Bogosian, Eric. *Drinking in America.* New York: Vintage, 1987.

Boorstin, Daniel J. *The Americans: The Colonial Experience.* New York: Random House, 1958.

———. *The Americans: The National Experience.* New York: Random House, 1965.

———. *The Americans: The Democratic Experience.* New York: Random House, 1973.

Bowyer, Frances Esther. "James E. Murdoch, the Elocutionist." Master's thesis, University of Colorado, 1952.

Breit, Harvey. "Talk with Dylan Thomas." *New York Times*, late ed., 14 May 1950, sec. 7:19.

Brinnin, John Malcom. *Dylan Thomas in America: An Intimate Journal.* New York: Viking, 1955.

Bronaugh, Bob. "The Paramountcy of Becoming Someone Else!" *Performer Magazine* (playbill for Ford's Theatre, Washington, D.C.) 1, no. 7 (1971/72): 1.

Brookshire, Helen. "Typical Programs of the Oral Readers as Reflected in *Werner's Magazine*." Master's thesis, Louisiana State University, 1955.

Brunson, Martha L. "Novelists as Platform Readers: Dickens, Clemens, and Stowe." In *Performance of Literature in Historical Perspectives*, edited by Thompson, 651–82.

Burn, W. L. *The Age of Equipoise: A Study of the Mid-Victorian Generation.* New York: Norton, 1964.

Burr, Agnes Rush. *Russell H. Conwell.* Philadelphia: Winston, 1926.

Butler, John H. *The Light and Life of Lakeside-on-Lake Erie, 1923–1948.* Lakeside, OH: Lakeside Association, 1948.

Canby, Vincent. "Soloists on the Big Screen." *New York Times*, late ed., 22 March 1987, sec. 2:19.

Carroll, Margaret. "Stage Shows Can Be Singular Smashes." *Chicago Tribune*, 27 Jan. 1977, sec. 2:1.

Case, Victoria, and Robert Ormond Case. *We Called It Culture: The Story of Chautauqua.* Garden City, NY: Doubleday, 1948.

"Centennial." *New Yorker*, 14 Jan. 1985, 26.

Chapman, John. "Emlyn Williams' Dickens Recital Is a Fascinating One-Man Show." Review of *Emlyn Williams as Charles Dickens*, by Emlyn Williams. *New York Daily News*, 5 Feb. 1952a, 49.

———. "Skinner's *Paris 1890* Charming." Review of *Paris '90*, by Cornelia Otis Skinner. *New York Daily News*, 5 March 1952b, 49.

"Charles Dickens: His Second Reading." *New York Tribune*, 11 Dec. 1867, 4.

"Charles Dickens: The Story of Little Dombey and the Trial from Pickwick." *New York Herald*, 14 Dec. 1867, 4.

"Chautauqua Drama Wanted." *Lyceum*, Aug. 1922, 27.

Chivers, Thomas Holley. *Life of Poe.* Edited by Richard Beale Davis. New York: Dutton, 1952.

Christon, Laurence. "Through a *FunHouse* Mirror." Review of *FunHouse*, by Eric Bogosian. *Los Angeles Times*, 10 April 1985, sec. 6:1.

Clark, Barrett H. *Professor Clark: A Short Memoir by His Son*. Chautauqua, NY: Chautauqua, 1928.

Clark, S. H. "The New Elocution." *Chautauqua Assembly Herald*, 29 July 1895, 2.

———. "The New Elocution." *Proceedings of the Sixth Annual Meeting of the National Association of Elocutionists [28 June–2 July 1897]*. New York: NAE, 1898, 66b–84. Reprinted in part in *The Study of Oral Interpretation*, edited by Haas and Williams, 30–42.

———. *Interpretation of the Printed Page*. Chicago: Row, 1915. (Revised edition, with Maud May Babcock. New York: Prentice, 1940.)

Clemens, Cyril. *Josh Billings, Yankee Humorist*. Foxcroft, 1976.

Clemens, Samuel. *The Autobiography of Mark Twain*. Edited by Charles Neider. New York: Harper, 1959.

Clement, Clara Erskine. *Charlotte Cushman*. Boston: Osgood, 1882.

Coben, Stanley. "The Assault on Victorianism in the Twentieth Century." In *Victorian America*, edited by Howe, 160–81.

Coben, Stanley, and Lorman Ratner. *The Development of an American Culture*. 2d ed. New York: St. Martin's, 1983.

Cocteau, Jean. *The Human Voice*. Translated by Carl Wildman. London: Vision, 1961.

Cohen, Nathan. "One-Man Shows Can Be Exciting." *Toronto Daily Star*, 21 Nov. 1967, 50.

Cohn, Ellen. "Monodrama: Broadway's Answer to the 'Me Decade'." *Playbill*, Mar. 1978.

Collins, Philip. "Dickens' Public Readings: The Performer and the Novelist." *Studies in the Novel* 1 (1969): 118–32.

———. *Reading Aloud: A Victorian Métier*. Lincoln, U.K.: Tennyson Society, 1972.

———. "Dickens's Public Readings: The Kit and the Team." *Dickensian* 74 (Jan. 1978): 8–16.

———. "'Agglomerating Dollars with Prodigious Rapidity': British Pioneers on the American Lecture Circuit." In *Victorian Literature and Society*, edited by James R. Kincaid and Albert J. Kuhn. Ohio State Univ. Press, 1984.

———. ed. *Charles Dickens: The Public Readings*. Oxford: Clarendon Press, 1975.

———, ed. *"Sikes and Nancy" and Other Public Readings*. By Charles Dickens. Oxford: Oxford Univ. Press, 1983.

Colvin, Clare. "Going Solo." *London Observer*, 2 Aug. 1981, 28.

Corson, Hiram. *The Voice and Spiritual Education*. New York: Macmillan, 1897.

Cowley, Susan Sheever, and Stephen Lesher. "One-Man Showmanship." *Newsweek,* 12 May 1975, 189–90.

Crocker, Lionel. "Charles Laughton on Oral Reading." *Central States Speech Journal* 3 (Dec. 1951): 21–26.

Crouch, Paula. "Actor Tom Key Had a 'Revelation' of His Own." *Atlanta Journal,* 16 July 1986a, 3B.

———. "Crisp's Message Is that Everyone Can Have Style." Review of *An Evening with Quentin Crisp,* by Quentin Crisp. *Atlanta Constitution,* 17 April 1986b, 6C.

Crowder, Richard. *Carl Sandburg.* New York: Twayne, 1964.

Culler, A. Dwight. "Monodrama and the Dramatic Monologue." *Publications of the Modern Language Association of America* 3 (May 1975): 366–85.

Cumnock, Robert McLean, ed. *Choice Readings.* Chicago: McClung, 1929.

Cunningham, Cornelius C. "Trying to 'Pos the Impossible'." *Western Speech Journal* 12 (April 1948): 11–13.

Current, Lucille Mary. "A Study of Solomon Henry Clark as a Teacher of Interpretive Speech." Master's thesis, Northwestern University, 1938.

Curry, Jane. "Chautauqua: On the Road and Doing Fine." *Federation Reports* 6 (Nov./Dec. 1982): 16–20.

Curry, S. S. "The Term 'Elocution': A Symposium." *Talent,* June 1905, 15.

———. *Browning and the Dramatic Monologue.* 1908. Reprint. New York: Haskell, 1965.

Cushman, Robert. "One-Man Shows." *London Observer,* 1 April 1979, 16.

DaBoll, Irene Briggs, and Raymond F. DaBoll. *Recollections of the Lyceum and Chautauqua Circuits.* Freeport, ME: Wheelwright, 1969.

Davis, Ronald L., ed. *The Social and Cultural Life of the 1920s.* New York: Holt, 1972.

Day, Donald. *Uncle Sam's Uncle Josh.* 1953. Reprint. Westport, CT: Greenwood, 1972.

Delgado, Alan. *Victorian Entertainment.* New York: Heritage, 1971.

Detzer, Karl W. "Broadway, R.F.D.: The Rejuvenated Chautauqua Is Bigger and Better than Ever." *Century* 116 (July 1928): 311–17.

Devine, Edward T. "Other Towns that Do Not Want Chautauqua—and Why." *New Republic,* 1 Sept. 1926, 46–47.

DeVoto, Bernard, ed. *Mark Twain in Eruption.* New York: Harper, 1940.

Dickens, Mamie. *My Father as I Recall Him.* Westminister: Roxburghe, n.d.

"Dickens' Readings—Fifth Night." *New York Herald,* 16 Dec. 1867, 5.

Dickens, Sir Henry F. *Memories of My Father.* London: Collancz, 1928.

DiMeglio, John E. *Vaudeville U.S.A.* Bowling Green: Bowling Green Univ. Popular Press, 1973.

Dolby, George. *Charles Dickens as I Knew Him: The Story of the Reading Tours in Great Britain and America, 1866–1870.* London: Unwin, 1885.

Donner, Stanley T. "The Speaking and Reading of Mark Twain." Ph.D. diss., Northwestern University, 1946.

———. "Mark Twain as a Reader." *Quarterly Journal of Speech* 33 (Oct. 1947): 308–11.

Douglas, Ann. *The Feminization of American Culture.* New York: Knopf, 1977.

Doyle, Esther M., and Virginia Hastings Floyd, eds. *Studies in Interpretation.* 2 vols. Amsterdam: Rodopi, 1972–77.

Dudar, Helen. "Colleen Dewhurst Portrays O'Neill's Haunted Widow." *New York Times,* late ed., 25 Jan. 1987, sec. 2:3- 4.

Eames, Millicent. "Creating a New American Art." *Independent Woman,* Oct. 1935, 342–44 +.

Eder, Richard. "Stage: Late Afternoon of Saki." Review of *The Playboy of the Weekend World,* by Emlyn Williams. *New York Times,* late ed., 17 Nov. 1978, C3.

Edgerton, Kathleen. "The Lecturing of Edgar Allan Poe." *Southern Speech Journal* 25 (Summer 1963): 268–73.

Editorial. *Platform World* Jan. 1930, 18.

Edwards, Paul C. "The Treatment of 'Taste' in Selected Elocution and Expression Texts: A Comparative Analysis." Ph.D. diss., University of Texas at Austin, 1980.

———. "The Rise of 'Expression.'" In *Performance of Literature in Historical Perspectives,* edited by Thompson, 529–48.

Eifert, Eunice Ruth. "The Fourth-Wall Shattered: A Study of the Performer-Audience Relationship in Selected Full-Length Monodramas." Ph.D. diss., University of Minnesota, 1984.

Ellerbe, K. Alma, and Paul Ellerbe. "The Most American Thing in America." *World's Work* 48 (Aug. 1924): 440–46.

Ellis, Edward Robb. *Echos of Distant Thunder: Life in the United States, 1914–1918.* New York: Coward, 1975.

Ellwood, Hendrick. *Lewis Miller.* New York: Putnam's, 1925.

Erenberg, Lewis A. *Steppin' Out: New York Nightlife and the Transformation of American Culture, 1890–1930.* Westport, CT: Greenwood, 1981.

Erickson, Steve. "Whoopi Goldberg." *Rolling Stone,* 8 May 1986, 39–42+.

Etty, Anne Shum. "What's Wrong with Chautauqua?" *Drama,* (March/April 1924), 213–14.

Eubanks, Marjorie Harrell. "The Redpath Lyceum Bureau From 1868 to 1901." Ph.D. diss., University of Michigan, 1968.

Fagin, N. Bryllion. *The Histrionic Mr. Poe.* Baltimore: Johns Hopkins Univ. Press, 1949.

Fancher, Pauline. *Chautauqua: Its Architecture and Its People.* Miami: Banyan, 1978.

Farber, Stephen. "Enter McKellen, Bearing Shakespeare." *New York Times,* late ed., 15 Jan. 1984, sec. 2:17+.

Farma, William J. "A Study of Comparative Speech Forms of Delivery with Special Reference to Interpretative Reading." Ph.D. diss., University of Wisconsin, 1946.

Fass, Paula S. *The Damned and the Beautiful: American Youth in the 1920s.* New York: Oxford Univ. Press, 1977.

Fatout, Paul, ed. *Mark Twain Speaking.* Iowa City: Univ. of Iowa Press, 1976.

Fawcett, F. Dubrez. *Dickens the Dramatist.* London: Camelot, 1952.

Fein, Esther B. "Lily Tomlin: Comedy with Bite." *New York Times,* late ed., 22 Sept. 1985, sec. 2:1+.

Fennimire, Keith J. *The Heritage of Bay View, 1875–1975: A Centennial History.* Grand Rapids: Eerdmans, 1975.

Ferlinghetti, Lawrence. "Note on Poetry in San Francisco." *Chicago Review* 12 (Spring 1958): 4.

Ferris, Paul. *Dylan Thomas: A Biography.* New York: Dial, 1977.

Field, Kate. *Pen Photographs of Charles Dickens's Readings.* Boston: Osgood, 1871.

Fitzgerald, Percy. *Samuel Foote: A Biography.* London: Chatto, 1910.

Fitzsimons, Raymund. *The Baron of Piccadilly: The Travels and Entertainments of Albert Smith 1816–1860.* London: Bles, 1967.

———. *Garish Lights: The Public Reading Tours of Charles Dickens.* Philadelphia: Lippincott, 1970.

Fletcher, Robert Huntington. "Browning's Dramatic Monologs." *Modern Language Notes* 23 (April 1908): 108–11.

Fonda, Henry. *Fonda, My Life.* New York: NAL, 1981.

Foner, Eric. "The Televised Past." *Nation,* 16 June 1979, 724–26.

Fraser, G. S. "Artist as Young Dog." Review of *Dylan Thomas Growing Up,* by Emlyn Williams. *New Statesman and Nation,* 11 June 1955, 812.

Freedman, Samuel G. "Echoes of Lenny Bruce, via Bogosian and Reddin." *New York Times*, late ed., 19 Jan. 1986, sec. 2:5.

French, Marilyn. "Women of Excellence—Lily Tomlin." *Ms.*, Jan. 1986, 32–34. (Reprinted in part as Afterword, in *The Search for Signs of Intelligent Life in the Universe*, by Wagner, 219–23.)

Furnas, J. C. *Fanny Kemble: Leading Lady of the Nineteenth-Century Stage*. New York: Dial, 1982.

G., J. "Cecilia Loftus Returns." *New York Times*, late ed., 31 Oct. 1938, 12.

Galey, Mary. *The Grand Assembly: The Story of Life at the Colorado Chautauqua*. Boulder: First Flatiron, 1981.

Gallu, Samuel. *Give 'Em Hell, Harry!* New York: Viking, 1975.

Gans, Herbert J. *Popular Culture and High Culture: An Analysis and Evaluation of Taste*. New York: Basic Books, 1974.

Gardner, Paul. "Shakespeare Program Offered by Gielgud." Review of *Ages of Man*, based on an anthology by George Rylands. *New York Times*, late ed., 15 Apr. 1963, 36.

Garrett, Kurt L. "Palliative for Players: *The Lecture on Heads*." *Pennsylvania Magazine of History and Bibliography* 53 (April 1979): 166–76.

———. "*The Brush for Rubbing Off the Rust of Care* in America." *Southern Speech Communication Journal* 48 (Summer 1983a): 368–77.

———. "The Genesis of Oral Interpretation in Eighteenth Century America: The Unknown Reader of 1769." *Literature in Performance* 4 (Nov. 1983b): 1–7.

Gentile, John S. "Interview: With Emlyn Williams." *Literature in Performance* 4 (Nov. 1983a): 78–84.

———. "The New Interpretation: From 'Interpretation' to 'Performance Studies.'" Paper presented at the annual meeting of the Speech Communication Association, Washington, D.C., 11 Nov. 1983b.

———. "The One-Person Show in America: From the Victorian Platform to the Contemporary Stage." Ph.D. diss., Northwestern University, 1984.

———. "The Performer as Writer." *American Institute of Discussion Review* 3 (1987): 31–37.

———. "Interview: With Quentin Crisp." *Literature in Performance* 8 (Nov. 1988a): 77–86.

———. "The Wyoming Chautauqua's *Contesting the Constitution*." *Literature in Performance* 8 (Nov. 1988b): 57–65.

Gerst, Virginia. "Williams at 76: The Corn Remains Green." *Evanston Review*, 5 Nov. 1981, D3.

Gielgud, John. Foreword. In *The Letters of Ruth Draper, 1920- 1956,* edited by Warren, ix-xi.

——. *Gielgud: An Actor and His Time.* In collaboration with John Miller and John Powell. New York: Potter, 1980.

Gilbert, Douglas. *American Vaudeville Its Life and Times.* New York: Dover, 1963.

Gill, Brendan. Review of *Whoopi Goldberg,* by Whoopi Goldberg. *New Yorker,* 5 Nov. 1984, 155.

Glick, David T. "The Independent Chautauquas Then and Now." *Henry Ford Museum and Greenfield Village Herald* 13.2 (1984): 42–51.

Ginger, Ray. *Age of Excess: The United States from 1877 to 1914.* 2d ed. New York: Macmillan, 1975.

Goffman, Erving. *The Presentation of Self in Everyday Life.* Garden City, NY: Doubleday, 1959.

——. *Forms of Talk.* Philadelphia: Univ. of Pennsylvania Press, 1981.

Golden, Harry. *Carl Sandburg.* New York: World, 1961.

Gould Joseph E. *The Chautauqua Movement: An Episode in the Continuing American Revolution.* New York: State Univ. of New York, 1961.

Gracie, Ruth Sprout. "Six Original Monodramas on Pioneer Women of the West with Technique and History of Solodrama." Ph.D. diss., University of Denver, 1983.

Graham, Donald L. "Circuit Chautauqua, a Middle Western Institution." Ph.D. diss., University of Iowa, 1953.

Gray, Giles Wilkeson. "Some Leaders Teachers and the Transition to Twentieth Century Speech Education." In *History of Speech Education in America,* edited by Wallace, 403–32.

——. "What Was Elocution?" *Quarterly Journal of Speech* 46 (Feb. 1960): 1–7.

Gray, John W. "The Public Reading of Edgar Allan Poe." *Southern Speech Journal* 28 (Winter 1962): 109–15.

Gray, Paul H. "The Origins of Expression: Principle Sources of Samuel Silas Curry's Theory of Expression." Ph.D. diss., Louisiana State University, 1966.

——. "Poet as Entertainer: Will Carleton, James Whitcomb Riley, and the Rise of the Poet-Performer Movement." *Literature in Performance* 5 (Nov. 1984): 1–12.

——. "Preparing for Popularity: Origins of the Poet-Performer Movement." *Literature in Performance* 6 (Nov. 1985): 34–41.

Gray, Spalding. *Swimming to Cambodia.* New York: Theatre Communications, 1985.

——. *Sex and Death to the Age 14.* New York: Vintage, 1986.

Greef, Robert J. "Public Lectures in New York, 1851- 1878." Ph.D. diss., University of Chicago, 1941.

Grimsted, David. *Melodrama Unveiled: American Theater and Culture, 1800–1850.* Chicago: Univ. of Chicago Press, 1968.

Gussow, Mel. "Theatre: Alec McCowen Returns in a Solo *St. Mark's Gospel.* Review of *St. Mark's Gospel,* by Alec McCowen. *New York Times,* late ed., 14 May 1981, C21.

———. "Whoopi as Actress, Clown and Social Critic." Review of *Whoopi Goldberg,* by Whoopi Goldberg. *New York Times,* late ed., 28 Oct. 1984a, sec. 2:5.

———. "Yiddish Musical in Czarist Russia." *New York Times,* late ed., 1 Nov. 1984b, C22.

———. "Theatre: Spalding Gray." Review of *Terrors of Pleasure,* by Spalding Gray. *New York Times,* late ed., 15 May 1986, C19.

———. "A Theatrical Vision Endures." Review of *Our Town,* by Thornton Wilder. *New York Times,* late ed., 20 Dec. 1987, sec. 2:36.

Haas, Richard, and David A. Williams, eds. *The Study of Oral Interpretation: Theory and Comment.* Indianapolis: Bobbs-Merrill, 1975.

Hadley, Dorothy Siedenburg. "Oral Interpretation at the Chautauqua Institution and the Chautauqua School of Expression, 1874–1900." Ph.D. diss., Northwestern University, 1956.

Hall, Donald. "The Poetry Reading: Public Performance/Private Art." *American Scholar* (Winter 1984/85): 63- 77.

Hallinan, Tim, and John F. Andrews. "Ian McKellen on Acting Shakespeare." *Shakespeare Quarterly* 33 (1982): 135–41.

Hamilton, Mary Lucille. "The Lyceum in New Orleans, 1840–1860." Master's thesis Louisiana State University, 1948.

Hanscom, Warren D. *Pioneers in Grease Paint.* Bradenton, FL: Collins, 1975.

Hansen, Harry. *Midwest Portraits.* New York: Harcourt, 1923.

"The Happy Ham." *Time,* 31 March 1952, 62–68.

Harrison, Harry P., as told to Karl Detzer. *Culture under Canvas: The Story of Tent Chautauqua.* New York: Hastings, 1958.

Harrison, John Thornton. "Chautauqua in Iowa." *Iowa Journal of History* 50 (April 1952): 97–122.

Hart, James D. *The Popular Book: A History of America's Literary Taste.* Berkeley: Univ. of California Press, 1963.

Hart, Robert Leonard Jr. "Public Readings in New York City from 1851–1861." Master's thesis Louisiana State University, 1952.

Harvey, Roy L. "An Opportunity—and a Challenge!" *Platform World,* Jan./Feb. 1933, 5.

Hass, Joseph, and Gene Levitz. *Carl Sandburg: A Pictorial Biography.* New York: Putnam's, 1967.

Hawkins, Williams. "Dickens Lives Again in Williams' Readings." Review of *Emlyn Williams as Charles Dickens,* by Emlyn Williams. *New York World-Telegram and the Sun,* 5 Feb. 1952, 12.

Hedges, R. Alan. "Actors under Canvas: A Study of the Theatre of the Circuit Chautauqua, 1910–1933." Ph.D. diss., Ohio State University, 1976.

"Helen Potter Again!" *Talent,* May 1897, 1–2.

Henderson, Bruce Edward. "'In the Public Garden': Marianne Moore Performing and Performing Marianne Moore." Ph.D. diss., Northwestern University, 1983.

Henneke, Ben Graf. "The Playgoer in America (1752–1952)." Ph.D. diss., University of Illinois, 1956.

Herford, Beatrice. *Beatrice Herford's Monologues.* New York: French, 1940.

Hernadi, Paul. *Beyond Genre: New Directions in Literary Classification.* Ithaca: Cornell Univ. Press, 1972.

Heston, Lilla. "Early Graduate Education: Michigan, Northwestern, Wisconsin." In *Performance of Literature in Historical Perspectives,* edited by Thompson, 317–57.

Hewes, Henry. "One Man in His Shakespeare." Review of *Ages of Man,* based on an anthology by George Rylands. *Saturday Review,* 17 Jan. 1959, 74.

Hibschman, Harry. "Chautauqua Pro and Contra." *North American Review* 22 (May 1928): 597–605.

Higham, Charles. *Charles Laughton: An Intimate Biography.* Introduction by Elsa Lanchester. New York: Doubleday, 1976.

Higham, John. "The Reorientation of American Culture in the 1890s." In *The Origins of Modern Consciousness,* edited by John Weiss, 25–48. Detroit: Wayne State Univ. Press, 1965.

———. *Writing American History: Essays on Modern Scholarship.* Bloomington: Indiana Univ. Press, 1970.

Hilde, Norma Viola. "A Study of the Life of Sarah Siddons: An Estimate of Her Ability as Oral Interpreter of Literature." Master's thesis, Northwestern University, 1932.

Hinton, Virginia Claire Cooksey. "The Columbus Enquirer and Literature, 1855–1872." Ph.D. diss., University of Georgia, 1967.

Hipps, Donna Carol. "Charles Dickens as an Oral Interpreter." Master's thesis, University of North Carolina at Chapel Hill, 1975.

Hirsch, E. D. *Validity in Interpretation.* New Haven: Yale Univ. Press, 1967.

Hobbs, Dora M. "The Spoken Art of Mark Twain." Master's thesis, University of Oklahoma, 1945.

Hodge, Francis. "Charles Mathews Reports on America." *Quarterly Journal of Speech* 36 (Dec 1950): 492–99.

Holbrook, Hal, ed. *Mark Twain Tonight! An Actor's Portrait.* By Samuel Langhorne Clemens. New York: Washburn, 1959.

Honan, William H. "The American Dream Moves Center Stage." *New York Times,* late ed., 13 Apr. 1986, sec. 2:1+.

HopKins, Mary Frances, and Brent Bouldin. "Professional Group Performance of Nondramatic Literature in New York." In *Performance of Literature in Historical Perspectives,* edited by Thompson, 697–717.

Horner, Charles F. *The Life of James Redpath and the Development of the Modern Lyceum.* New York: Barse, 1926.

———. *Strike the Tents: The Story of the Chautauqua.* Philadelphia: Dorance, 1954.

Howard, Claud. "The Dramatic Monologue: Its Origin and Development." *Studies in Philology* 4 (1910): 33–88. (Reprint, New York: Johnson, 1963: 1–56.)

Howe, Daniel Walker, ed. *Victorian America.* Philadelphia: Univ. of Pennsylvania Press, 1976.

Hudson, Lee. "Beat Generation Poetics and the Oral Tradition of Literature." Ph.D. diss., University of Texas at Austin, 1973a.

———. "Oral Interpretation as Metaphorical Expression." *Speech Teacher* 22 (Jan. 1973b): 27–31.

———. "Poetics in Performance: The Beat Generation." In *Studies in Interpretation,* edited by Doyle and Floyd, 2:59–76.

Hughes, Linda K. *The Manyfacèd Glass: Tennyson's Dramatic Monologues.* Athens, OH: Ohio Univ. Press, 1987.

Humm. Review of *The Search for Signs of Intelligent Life in the Universe,* by Jane Wagner. *Variety,* 2 Oct. 1985, 152+.

———. Review of *Drinking in America,* by Eric Bogosian. *Variety,* 5 Feb. 1986, 158.

Hurlbut, Jesse L. *The Story of Chautauqua.* New York: Putnam's, 1921.

Hymel, Margaret Cecelia. "Fanny Kemble: Dramatic Reader." Master's thesis, Louisiana State University, 1942.

Inge, M. Thomas, ed. *Handbook of American Popular Culture.* 3 vols. London: Greenwood, 1978–80.

The International Speaker and Popular Elocutionist. Chicago: International, 1895.

"The Interview [with Ruth Draper]." New Yorker, 6 March 1954, 22–23.

Irwin, Alfreda L. *Three Taps of the Gavel: Pledge to the Future.* 3d ed. Chautauqua, NY: Chautauqua Institution, 1987.

James, Henry. "Frances Anne Kemble." In *Essays in London and Elsewhere,* by Henry James, 81–120. New York: Harper, 1893.

———. *The Complete Plays of Henry James.* Edited by Leon Edel. Philadelphia: Lippincott, 1949.

Jameson, Sheilagh S. *Chautauqua in Canada.* In collaboration with Nola B. Erickson. Calgary: Glenbow-Alberta Institution, 1979.

Jaswal, A. J. "Oral Interpretation as a Form of Professional Theatre on the New York Stage from 1945–1965." Ph.D. diss., Michigan State University, 1968.

Jenner, C. Lee. "Singular Sensations." Review of *Women I Have Known,* by Tulis McCall, and *Ten East,* by Kevin Heelan. *Other Stages,* 2 July 1981, 4.

Jenson, John R. "A History of Chautauqua Activities at Lakeside, Ohio, 1873–1970." Ph.D. diss., Bowling Green State University, 1970.

Johnson, Claudia D. "That Guilty Third Tier: Prostitution in Nineteenth-Century American Theaters." In *Victorian America,* edited by Howe, 111–20.

———. *American Actress: Perspective on the Nineteenth Century.* Chicago: Nelson, 1984.

Johnson, Gertrude E., ed. *Studies in the Art of Interpretation.* New York: Appleton, 1940.

Kahan, Gerald. "The American Career of George Alexander Stevens' *Lecture on Heads." Theatre Survey* 18 (1977): 60–71.

———. "Fanny Kemble Reads Shakespeare: Her First American Tour, 1849–1850." *Theatre Survey* 24 (1983): 77–98.

———. *George Alexander Stevens and "The Lecture on Heads."* Athens, GA: Univ. of Georgia Press, 1984.

Kaplan, Justin. "In Pursuit of the Ultimate Fiction." *New York Times Book Review,* 19 Apr. 1987, 1+.

Kasel, Daniel. "Charles Laughton's Techniques of Oral Interpretation." Master's thesis, Indiana University, 1969.

Kearney, Jill. "Whoopi Goldberg: Color Her Anything." *American Film,* Dec. 1985, 25–28.

Kelly, Irene. "Ruth Draper—One Woman Theatre." Master's thesis, University of Michigan, 1951.

Kemble, Frances Anne. *Records of Later Life.* New York: Holt, 1882.

Kent, Charles. *Charles Dickens as a Reader.* Philadelphia: Lippincott, 1971.

Kent, Thomas L. "The Classification of Genres." *Genre* 16 (Spring 1983): 1–20.

————. *Interpretation and Genre: The Role of Generic Perception in the Study of Narrative Texts*. Lewisburg: Bucknell Univ. Press, 1986.

Kerr, Walter. "St. Mark's Gospel." Review of *St. Mark's Gospel*, by Alec McCowen. *New York Times*, late ed., 6 Nov. 1978, 54.

Kesterson, David B. *Josh Billings*. New York: Twayne, 1973.

Kestler, James Allen. *This Is Lakeside, 1873–1973: Ohio's Chautauqua of the Great Lakes*. Lakeside, OH: Lakeside Association, 1973.

Kirkland, Audrey S. "The Elocutionary Theory and Practice of James Edward Murdoch." Ph.D. diss., Wayne State University, 1964.

Kissel, Howard. Review of *The Playboy of the Weekend World*, by Emlyn Williams. *Women's Wear Daily*, 17 Nov. 1978, 24.

Klepac, Richard L. *Mr. Mathews at Home*. London: Society For Theatre Research, 1979.

Kohansky, Mendel. *The Disreputable Profession: The Actor in Society*. Westport, CT: Greenwood, 1984.

Kostelanetz, Richard. *The Old Poetries and the New*. Ann Arbor: Univ. of Michigan Press, 1981.

Koziski, Stephanie. "The Standup Comedian as Anthropologist: Intentional Culture Critic." *Journal of Popular Culture* 18 (Fall 1984): 57–76.

Kroll, Jack, and Katrine Ames. "Mark of Genius." Review of *St. Mark's Gospel*, by Alec McCowen. *Newsweek*, 18 Sept. 1978, 66.

Krutch, Joseph Wood. "Drama." Review of *Emlyn Williams as Charles Dickens*, by Emlyn Williams. *Nation*, 23 Feb. 1952, 189–90.

Kuykendall, R. B. "The Reading and Speaking of Vachel Lindsay." Ph.D. diss., Northwestern University, 1952.

Lanchester, Elsa. *Elsa Lanchester, Herself*. New York: St. Martin's, 1983.

Larson, T. A., ed. *Bill Nye's Western Humor*. Lincoln: Univ. of Nebraska Press, 1968.

Laughton, Charles. "Storytelling." *Atlantic*, June 1950, 71–72.

Leach, Joseph. *Bright Particular Star: The Life and Times of Charlotte Cushman*. New Haven: Yale Univ. Press, 1970.

Lennon, E. James, and William W. Hamilton. "Charles Laughton's Interpretative Readings." *Speech Teacher* 4 (Mar. 1955): 87–88.

Leverett, James. Introduction. In *Swimming to Cambodia*, by Gray, ix-xiii.

Levitz, Gene. *Carl Sandburg: A Pictorial Biography*. New York: Putnam's, 1967.

Lewis, Emory. "Review of *Ages of Man*, based on an anthology by George Rylands." *Cue*, 10 Jan. 1959, 16.

Lindeman, Eduard C. "After Lyceums and Chautauquas, What?" *Bookman* 65 (May 1927): 246- 50.

Lockard, D. Sara Kay. "Public Readings in New York City from 1865–1870." Master's thesis, Louisiana State University, 1965.

Loganbill, G. Bruce. "Cornelia Otis Skinner and Her Art-Form of Monologue-Drama." Ph.D. diss., Michigan State University, 1961.

Long, Linda Sue. "The Art of Beatrice Herford, Cissie Loftus, and Dorothy Sands Within the Tradition of Solo Performance." Ph.D. diss., University of Texas at Austin, 1982.

Longfellow, Henry Wadsworth. *Life of Henry Wadsworth Longfellow.* 1891. Edited by Samuel Longfellow. 3 vols. New York: Greenwood, 1969.

———. *The Complete Poetical Works of Longfellow.* Cambridge edition. Boston: Houghton, 1893.

Longo, Lucas. *Carl Sandburg: Poet and Historian.* Edited by D. Steve Rahmas. Charlotteville, NY: SamHar, 1971.

Lorch, Fred W. *The Trouble Begins at Eight: Mark Twain's Lecture Tours.* Ames: Iowa State Univ. Press, 1968.

Low, Donald R. "The Speeches, Lectures, and Readings of Charles Dickens and William M. Thackeray in the United States, 1842–1868." Ph.D. diss., Northwestern University, 1956.

Lowell, Amy. "The New Manner in Poetry." *New Republic,* 4 March 1918, 125.

Luce, William. *The Belle of Amherst.* Boston: Houghton, 1976.

Lumley, Frederick. *New Trends in 20th-Century Drama: A Survey since Ibsen and Shaw.* London: Barrie, 1972.

"The Lyceum Entertainer in Vaudeville." *Talent,* Jan. 1899, 2.

McArthur, Benjamin. *Actors and American Culture, 1880–1920.* Philadelphia: Temple Univ. Press, 1984.

MacCallum, M. W. *The Dramatic Monologue in the Victorian Period.* 1925; Folcroft, 1970.

McClain, John. "Readings, Talents Don't Justify Price." Review of *Emlyn Williams as Charles Dickens,* by Emlyn Williams. *New York Journal-American,* 5 Feb. 1952, 12.

———. "Mark Twain, via Holbrook Is Delightful." Review of *Mark Twain Tonight!* by Hal Holbrook. *New York Journal-American,* 7 Apr. 1959, 16.

McCowen, Alec. *Double Bill.* New York: Atheneum, 1980.

———. *Personal Mark: An Actor's Proclamation of St. Mark's Gospel.* New York: Crossroads, 1985.

McCown, Robert A. "Records of the Redpath Chautauqua." *Books at Iowa,* 8–23. Iowa City: University of Iowa, 1973.

———. "The Development of the Tent Chautauqua." *Henry Ford Museum and Greenfield Village Herald* 13.2 (1984): 32–39.

Mace, Edward. "The One-Man Bandwagon." *London Observer,* 3 Sept. 1967, 8 +.

McKenna, Timothy. *Blasts and Bravos:* Make-Believe Mencken." Review of *Blasts and Bravos: An Evening with H. L. Mencken,* by Paul Shyre. *Paterson [NJ] News,* 17 Jan. 1975, 32.

MacLaren, Gay. *Morally We Roll Along.* Boston: Little, Brown, 1938.

MacLiammoir, Michael. *The Importance of Being Oscar.* London: Oxford Univ. Press, 1963.

———. *An Oscar of No Importance.* London: Heinemann, 1968.

McManus, B. K. "Literary Comedy to Concert Comedy: The Achievements of Artemus Ward, Petroleum V. Nashby, and Josh Billings." Ph.D. diss., University of Texas at Austin, 1976.

McManus, Kirk. "The Platform Humorists: Comedy in One." In *Performance of Literature in Historical Perspectives,* edited by Thompson, 638–95.

MacNeil, Neil. "Old Cowhand." Review of *Will Rogers' U.S.A.,* by Paul Shyre. *Time,* 28 Sept. 1970, 76.

MacNiece, Louis. "The Strange, Mighty Impact of Dylan Thomas' Poetry." *New York Times,* late ed., 5 Apr. 1953, sec. 7: 1 +.

Manderson, M. Sandra. "The Redpath Bureau, an American Critic: Decision Making and Programming Methods for Circuit Chautauquas, circa 1912 to 1920." Ph.D. diss., University of Iowa, 1981.

Marshall, Dorothy. *Fanny Kemble.* New York: St. Martin's, 1977.

Martin, Loy D. *Browning's Dramatic Monologues and the Post-Romantic Subject.* Baltimore: Johns Hopkins Univ. Press, 1985.

Martin, Marty. *Gertrude Stein Gertrude Stein Gertrude Stein.* New York: Random, 1980.

Martin, Robert Carl. "The Early Lyceum, 1862–1845." Ph.D. diss., Northwestern University, 1953.

Massey, Gerald. "Yankee Humor." *Quarterly Review* 122 (Jan. 1876): 212–37.

Matlaw, Myron, ed. *American Popular Entertainment: Papers and Proceedings of the Conference on the History of American Popular Entertainment.* London: Greenwood, 1979.

Mattern, Grace. "The Biography of Robert McLean Cumnock." Master's thesis, Northwestern University, 1929.

May, Henry F. *The End of American Innocence: A Study of the First Years of Our Own Time, 1912–1917.* New York: Knopf, 1959.

Mazumdar, Maxim. *Oscar Remembered.* Toronto: Personal Library, 1977.

Mead, David. *Yankee Eloquence in the Middle West: The Ohio Lyceum 1850–1870*. East Lansing: Michigan State College Press, 1951.

Mead, David. "1914: The Chautauqua and American Innocence." *Journal of Popular Culture* 1 (Spring 1968): 339-56.

Meisel, Martin. *Realizations: Narrative, Pictorial, and Theatrical Arts in Nineteenth-Century England*. Princeton: Princeton Univ. Press, 1983.

Mello, Edward C. "Mark Twain's Writing on Oral Interpretation." Master's thesis, North Texas State University, 1965.

Meltzer, Milton. *Mark Twain Himself: A Pictorial Biography*. New York: Bonanza, 1960.

Merritt, Francine. "The Entertainments of Mr. Albert Smith, Showman." *Literature in Performance* 3 (April 1983): 25–32.

Miller, Melvin H. "Circuit Chautauqua in Michigan." *Michigan Connection* (Winter/Spring 1984): 6–7.

Millstein, Gilbert. "Applause Fit for a King." *New York Times*, late ed., 4 Jan. 1959, sec. 2:5.

"Mr. Charles Dickens's Farewell Readings." *Scotsman*, 8 Dec. 1868, 2.

"Mr. Dickens as a Reader." *New York Times*, 16 Dec. 1867, 5.

"Mr. Dickens's Third Reading." *New York Tribune*, 13 Dec. 1867, 4.

Mitchell, Roger. Review of *Waiting for the Angel*, by Thomas McGrath. *American Book Review*, July/Aug. 1980, 2.

Mitgang, Herbert. "The One-Man Show, from Dickens to Dotrice." *New York Times*, late ed., 9 Mar. 1980, sec. 2:6+.

———. *Mister Lincoln*. Carbondale: Southern Illinois Univ. Press, 1981a.

———. Writers Go Public, for Love rather than Lucre." *New York Times*, late ed., 27 May 1981b, C20.

Morgan H. Wayne, ed. *The Gilded Age: A Reappraisal*. Syracuse: Syracuse Univ. Press, 1963.

Morley, Sheridan. "Three Is One." *Plays and Players*, March 1969, 32–33.

———. "Have Show, Will Travel." *Punch*, 19 March 1975, 465.

Morrison, Theodore. *Chautauqua: A Center for Education, Religion, and the Arts in America*. Chicago: Univ. of Chicago Press, 1974.

Mowatt, Anna Cora. *Autobiography of an Actress; Or, Eight Years on the Stage*. Boston: Ticknor, 1854.

Mullin, Donald, ed. *Victorian Actors and Actresses in Review: A Dictionary of Contemporary Views of Representative British and American Actors and Actresses, 1837–1901*. Westport, CT: Greenwood, 1983.

Mumford, Charles. "More on the Miscellaneous." *Talent,* Sept. 1902, 5.

Murdoch, James E. *Patriotism in Poetry and Prose.* Philadelphia: Lippincott, 1865.

Murphy, Theresa. "Interpretation in the Dickens Period." *Quarterly Journal of Speech* 41 (Oct. 1955): 243–49.

Murphy, Theresa, and Richard Murphy. "Charles Dickens as Professional Reader." *Quarterly Journal of Speech* 33 (Oct. 1947): 299-307.

Nadel, Norman. "Geilgud Returns in One-Man Show." Review of *Ages of Man,* based on an anthology by George Rylands. *New York World-Telegram and the Sun,* 15 April 1963, 13.

Nelsen, Don. "Cuts, Rehearsals Could Help." Review of *Paris Was Yesterday,* by Paul Shyre. *New York Daily News,* 20 Dec. 1979, 111.

Nemy, Enid. "Four for the Season, Alone in the Spotlight." *New York Times,* late ed., 5 Oct. 1984a, C1+.

———. "Whoopi's Ready, But Is Broadway?" *New York Times,* late ed., 21 Oct. 1984b, sec. 2: 1.

———. "Broadway." *New York Times,* late ed., 14 Feb. 1986, C2.

"Nicolson Sylvan Players Will Present Shakespearian Comedy Tonight." *Chautauquan Daily,* 6 Aug. 1910, 1.

"1988: Previews from 36 Artists." *New York Times,* late ed., 3 Jan. 1988, sec. 2:1+.

Noffsinger, John S. *Correspondence Schools, Lyceums, and Chautauquas.* New York: Macmillan, 1926.

Nolan, Jeannette Covert, Horace Gregory and James T. Ferrell. *Poet of the People: An Evaluation of James Whitcomb Riley.* Bloomington: Indiana Univ. Press, 1951.

Nye, Bill. *The Best of Bill Nye's Humor.* Edited by Louis Hasley. New Haven: College and University Press, 1972.

Nye, Russel Blaine. *Society and Culture in America, 1830–1860.* New York: Harper, 1974.

O'Neill, Eugene. *Before Breakfast.* In *Plays of Eugene O'Neill,* vol. 2. New York: Random, 1954–55.

Odell, George C. D. *Annals of the New York Stage.* 15 vols. New York: Columbia Univ. Press, 1927–49.

Oliver, Leonard P. "Chautauqua and the State Humanities Programs: The Quest for Quality and Audiences." *Michigan Connection* (Winter/Spring 1984): 1+.

Orchard, Hugh Anderson. *Fifty Years of Chautauqua: Its Beginnings, Its Development, Its Message and Its Life.* Iowa: Torch, 1923.

Origio, Iris. "Ruth Draper." *Atlantic Monthly,* Oct. 1958, 57-60.

Palmer, Albert M. "American Theatres." In *1795–1895 One Hundred Years of American Commerce,* 2 vols., edited by Chauncey M. Depew, vol. 1:157–65. New York: Greenwood, 1895.

"The Palmy Days of Fanny Kemble." Review of *Readings from Shakespeare,* by Fanny Kemble. *Boston Herald,* eve. ed., 27 Jan. 1849, 1.

Parrish, W. M. "Elocution: A Definition and a Challenge." *Quarterly Journal of Speech* 43 (Feb. 1957): 1–11.

Pearson, Paul M. "Prominent Platform People, VI: Leland Powers." *Lyceumite and Talent,* Jan. 1908a, 13–15.

———. "Robert McClean Cumnock: An Interpreter of Literature." *Lyceumite and Talent,* Oct. 1908b, 15 + .

Pearson, Ted. "The Poem as Object." In *The Poetry Reading,* edited by Vincent and Zweig, 319- 21.

Pelias, Ronald J., and James VanOosting. "A Paradigm for Performance Studies." *Quarterly Journal of Speech* 73 (March 1987): 219–31.

Pemberton, T. Edgar. *Charles Dickens and the Stage.* London: Redway, 1888.

Phillips, Hazel. "The Chautauqua in American Life." Master's thesis, Northwestern University, 1948.

Porterfield, Christopher. "Telling Triumph." Review of *St. Mark's Gospel,* by Alec McCowen. *Time,* 18 Sept. 1978, 100.

Poschman, William. "An Interview with Paul Shyre." *Readers Theatre News* (Spring/Summer 1982): 19 + .

Potter, Helen. *Helen Potter's Impersonations.* New York: Werner, 1891.

"Program of the Fortieth Assembly." *Chautauquan,* 28 June 1913, 65–72.

Quick, Martha. "Professor Soloman Henry Clark, and His Contribution to the Field of Oral Interpretation." Master's thesis, University of Chicago, 1942.

Ray, Gordon N. *Tennyson Reads "Maud."* Vancouver: Univ. of British Columbia, 1968.

Rein, Lynn Miller. "A Rhetorical Study of Lew Sarett." Ph.D. diss., Northwestern University, 1978.

———. *Northwestern University School of Speech: A History.* Evanston, IL: Northwestern University School of Speech, 1981.

Revell, Peter. *James Whitcomb Riley.* Boston: Twayne, 1970.

"A Reverie." *Talent,* March 1903, 2.

Review of Lew Sarett's performance. (Williston, ND), *Herald* 1 Aug. 1918. Lew Sarett Papers. Northwestern University Archives, Northwestern University Libraries. Evanston, Illinois.

Reynolds, Nydia Jones. "A Historical Study of the Oral Interpretation

Activities of the Circuit Chautauqua, 1904–1932." Ph.D. diss., University of Southern California, 1960.

————. "It Wasn't 'Elocution': Five Professional Oral Interpreters, 1900–1925." *Quarterly Journal of Speech* 47 (Oct. 1961): 244–52.

Rice, Vernon. "The Man Mountain that Is Laughton." Review of *An Evening with Charles Laughton,* by Charles Laughton. *New York Post,* 15 May 1953, 52.

Rich, Frank. "Stage: John Cullum as Whistler in One-Man Show of Artist's Life." Review of *Whistler,* by Laurence and Maggie Williams. *New York Times,* late ed., 7 Dec. 1981, C17.

————. "Stage: Alec McCowen in *Kipling.*" Review of *Kipling,* by Brian Clark. *New York Times,* late ed., 11 Oct. 1984a, sec. 3:19.

————. "Stage: McKellen and Shakespeare." Review of *Ian McKellen Acting Shakespeare* by Ian McKellen. *New York Times,* late ed., 20 Jan. 1984b, C3.

————. "Stage: *Whoopi Goldberg* Opens." Review of *Whoopi Goldberg,* by Whoopi Goldberg. *New York Times,* late ed., 25 Oct. 1984c, C17.

————. "Once Again, Theater Was a Place for Wonder." *New York Times,* late ed., 29 Dec. 1985a, sec. 2:5 +.

————. "The Stage: Lily Tomlin in *Search of Signs.*" Review of *The Search for Signs of Intelligent Life in the Universe,* by Jane Wagner. *New York Times,* late ed., 27 Sept. 1985b, C3.

————. "The Stage: Zoe Caldwell as Hellman in *Lillian.*" Review of *Lillian,* by William Luce. *New York Times,* 17 Jan. 1986a, C3.

————. "Theatre: *Drinking in America.*" Review of *Drinking in America,* by Eric Bogosian. *New York Times,* late ed., 21 Jan. 1986b, C5.

————. "To Play Oneself May Be the Greatest Illusion of All." *New York Times,* late ed., 29 June 1986c, sec. 2:3 +.

Richmond, Rebecca. *Chautauqua, an American Place.* New York: Duell, 1943.

Ricket, William E. "Commercializing Elocution: 'Parlor Books' for Home Entertainments." *Southern Speech Communication Journal* 43 (Summer 1978): 384–94.

Ridgman, Jeremy. "The One-Actor Play in Australian Drama." *Australian Literary Studies* 10 (May 1981): 35-47.

Rintels, David W. *Clarence Darrow.* Garden City, NY: Doubleday, 1974.

Robb, Mary Margaret. "The Elocutionary Movement and Its Chief Figures." In *History of Speech Education in America,* edited by Wallace, 193–97.

————. *Oral Interpretation of Literature in American Colleges and Uni-*

versities: A Historical Study of Teaching Methods. Rev. ed. New York: Johnson Reprint, 1968.

Robertson, Nan. "McKellen Turns Ritz into Globe: The Audience Participates." Review of *Ian McKellen Acting Shakespeare*, by Ian McKellen. *New York Times*, late ed., 24 Jan. 1984, C11.

Robins, Edward. *Twelve Great Actresses*. New York: Putnam's, 1900.

Rogers, Neville. "The Art of Ruth Draper." *Ohio Review* 29 (Winter 1978): 6–23.

Roloff, Leland H. "Performer, Performing, Performance: Towards a Psychologicalization of Theory." *Literature in Performance* 3 (April 1983): 13–24.

Rourke, Constance. *American Humor: A Study of the National Character*. Garden City, NY: Doubleday, 1931.

Row, Arthur William. "Acting in Tents in Chautauqua." *Poet Lore* 36 (Summer 1925): 229–30.

Rushe, Desmond. "Dublin: The Flourishing Trend of One-Man Shows." *New York Times*, 4 Oct. 1971, 52.

"Ruth Draper Warmly Greeted at Recital." *New York Times*, late ed., 15 Jan. 1923, 15.

"*The Sad Shepherd:* Ben Jonson's Pastoral Comedy Presented Tonight." *Chautauqua Assembly Herald*, 25 July 1904, 1.

Saradhi, K. P. "The Theatre of the Mind: Browning's Dramatic Monologues." *Genre* 8 (1975): 322–35.

Schechner, Richard. *The End of Humanism: Writings on Performance*. New York: Performing Arts, 1982.

———. *Between Theater and Anthropology*. Philadelphia: Univ. of Pennsylvania Press, 1985.

Schlicke, Paul. *Dickens and Popular Entertainment*. London: Allen, 1985.

Schmidt, Paul. ed. *Meyerhold at Work*. Austin: Univ. of Texas Press, 1980.

Schooley, Bill Jaye. "Anna Cora Mowatt: Public Reader." Master's thesis, Louisiana State University, 1980.

———. "George Vandenhoff, Nineteenth Century Elocutionist in America." Ph.D. diss., Louisiana State University, 1984.

Scott, Marion. *Chautauqua Caravan*. New York: Appleton, 1939.

Sennett, Richard. *The Fall of Public Man*. New York: Vintage, 1978.

Sessions, Ina Beth. "The Dramatic Monologue." *Publications of the Modern Language Association of America* 62 (June 1947): 503–16.

Shepard, O. L. *The Story of Lakeside*. Lakeside, OH: Lakeside Association, 1923.

Shewey, Don. "A Spinner of Tales Moves into the Mainstream." *New York Times*, 11 May 1986, sec. 2:7–8.

Simon, John. "Fakin' Whoopee." Review of *Whoopi Goldberg*, by Whoopi Goldberg. *New York*, 5 Nov. 1984, 74.

———. "This Lily Spins." Review of *The Search for Signs of Intelligent Life in the Universe*, by Jane Wagner. *New York*, 7 Oct. 1985, 64–5.

———. "Raising Hellman." Review of *Lillian*, by William Luce, and *Drinking in America*, by Eric Bogosian. *New York*, 3 Feb. 1986, 56–7.

Sinclair, Andrew. *Dylan Thomas: No Man More Magical*. New York: Holt, 1975.

Sinfield, Alan. *Dramatic Monologue*. London: Methuen, 1977.

Singer, Kurt. *The Laughton Story: An Intimate Biography of Charles Laughton*. Philadelphia: Winston, 1954.

Skinner, Cornelia Otis. "Monologue to Theatre: An Exponent of a Solo Art Discusses Its Rise from the Ranks of the Amateurs." *New York Times*, late ed., 27 Dec. 1931, sec. 8:4.

Slout, William Lawrence. *Theatre in a Tent: The Development of Provincial Entertainment*. Bowling Green: Bowling Green Univ. Popular Press, 1972.

Smith, Bill. *The Vaudevillians*. New York: Macmillan, 1976.

Smith, G. Paul. "Helen Potter." *Talent*, Jan. 1906, 5–8.

Smoot, James S. "Platform Theatre: Theatrical Elements of the Lyceum-Chautauqua." Ph.D. diss., University of Michigan, 1954.

Snyder, Eldon E. "The Modern Chautauquas: Some Theoretical Perspectives." *Journal of American Culture* 6 (Summer 1983): 15-24.

———. "The Chautauqua Movement in Popular Culture: A Sociological Analysis." *Journal of American Culture* 8 (Fall 1985): 79–90.

Sobel, Bernard. "Saga of the One-Man Show." *Theatre Arts*, Oct. 1960, 24-26+.

Stebbins, Emma, ed. *Charlotte Cushman: Her Letters and Memories of Her Life*. Boston: Houghton, 1878.

Stein, Charles W., ed. *American Vaudeville as Seen by Its Contemporaries*. New York: Knopf, 1984.

Stephens, Ruby J. "Charles Dickens—Oral Reader." Master's thesis, University of Oklahoma, 1942.

Stone, Albert E., ed. *The American Autobiography*. Englewood Cliffs, NJ: Prentice-Hall, 1981.

Strachey, Lytton. *Eminent Victorians*. New York: Harcourt, 1918.

Strine, Mary Susan. "Performance Theory as Science: The Formative Impact of Dr. James Rush's *The Philosophy of the Human Voice.*" In *Performance of Literature in Historical Perspectives,* edited by Thompson, 509–27.

Strong, W. F. "An Analysis of Mark Twain's Oral Interpretation on the Reading Tour of 1884–1885." Master's thesis, North Texas State University, 1978.

Stubblefield, Harold W. "The Idea of Lifelong Learning in the Chautauqua Movement." *Adult Education* 31 (Summer 1981): 199–208.

Sullivan, Dan. "Parlor Call on Emily Dickenson." Review of *The Belle of Amherst,* by William Luce. *Los Angeles Times,* 25 Nov. 1976, sec. 4:1+.

Sutherland, J. A. *Victorian Novelists and Publishers.* Chicago: Univ. of Chicago Press, 1976.

Sutton, William A. *Carl Sandburg Remembered.* Metuchen, NJ: Scarecrow, 1979.

Talmage, T. De Witt. *Sports That Kill.* London: Dickinson, 1875.

Tapia, J. E. "Circuit Chautauqua's Promotional Visions: A Study of Program Brochures, circa 1904 to 1932." Ph.D. diss., University of Arizona, 1978.

Terry, R. C. *Victorian Popular Fiction, 1860–80.* Atlantic Highlands, NJ: Humanities, 1983.

Thackeray, William Makepeace. *The Letters and Private Papers of William Makepeace Thackeray.* 4 vols. Edited by Gordon N. Ray. Cambridge: Harvard Univ. Press, 1945–46.

Thomas, Caitlin. "Dylan Thomas and Emlyn Williams." Letter. *New Statesman and Nation,* 11 Jun. 1955, 815.

Thompson, David W. "Early Actress-Readers: Mowatt, Kemble, and Cushman." In *Performance of Literature in Historical Perspectives,* edited by Thompson, 629–50.

———, ed. *Performance of Literature in Historical Perspectives.* Lanham, MD: University Press of America, 1983.

Thompson, Joseph P. *Theatrical Amusements: A Discourse on the Character and Influence of the Theatre.* New York: Baker, 1847.

Thomsen, Anne Wrightsman. "Original Monodramas Adapted from Biographies Selected by the Institute of Character Research." Master's thesis, University of Southern California, 1938.

Tompkins, Jane P. *Reader-Response Criticism: From Formalism to Post-Structuralism.* Baltimore: Johns Hopkins Univ. Press, 1980.

Topor, Tom. "Checking Out the One-Actor Shows." *New York Post,* 7 Mar. 1980, 31+.

Towns, W. Stuart. "The Florida Chautauqua: A Case Study in American

Education." *Southern Speech Communication Journal* 42 (Spring 1977): 228- 45.

Tozier, Roy Becker. "A Short Life-History of the Chautauqua." Ph.D. diss., University of Iowa, 1932.

Trautmann, Frederick. "Hariett Beecher Stowe's Public Readings in the Central States." *Central States Speech Journal* 24 (Spring 1973): 22–28.

———. "Harriet Beecher Stowe's Public Readings in New England." *New England Quarterly* 47 (1974): 279- 89.

Trelease, Jim. *Read-Aloud Handbook.* Rev. ed. New York: Penguin, 1985.

Turner, Arlin. *Mark Twain and George W. Cable: The Record of a Literary Friendship.* East Lansing: Michigan State Univ. Press, 1960.

———. *George W. Cable: A Biography.* Baton Rouge: Louisiana State UP, 1966.

Van Amerongen, J. B. *The Actor in Dickens.* New York: Appleton, 1927.

Vawter, Keith. Letter to C.A. Peffer et al., 17 Jan. 1929. Keith Vawter Papers. Redpath Chautauqua Collection, University of Iowa Libraries. Iowa City, Iowa.

Vene. "*Evening with Laughton* Contagious Enjoyment on Tour Finale in N.Y." Review of *An Evening with Charles Laughton,* by Charles Laughton. *Variety,* 20 May 1953, 55.

Vincent, George E. "University Extension Drama." *Chautauquan,* 11 Oct. 1913, 120.

Vincent, John Heyl. *The Chautauqua Movement.* Boston: Chautauqua, 1886.

Vincent, Leon H. *John Heyl Vincent.* New York: Macmillan, 1925.

Vincent, Stephen, and Ellen Zweig, eds. *The Poetry Reading: A Contemporary Compendium on Language and Performance.* San Francisco: Momo's, 1981.

Vizetelly, Henry. *Glances Back Through Seventy Years: Autobiographical and Other Reminiscences.* 2 vols. London: Kegan Paul, 1893.

"Vogue of the Vaudeville." *Talent,* Jan. 1900, 5.

Wagner, Jane. *The Search for Signs of Intelligent Life in the Universe.* New York: Harper, 1986.

Wahls, Robert. "The Harris Mystique." Review of *The Belle of Amherst,* by William Luce. *New York Daily News,* 23 May 1976, 4.

Wallace, Karl R., ed. *History of Speech Education in America: Background Studies.* New York: Appleton, 1954.

Ward, Richard Finley. "Paul and the Politics of Performance at Corinth: A Study of 2 Corinthians 10–13." Ph.D. diss., Northwestern University, 1987.

Warren, Neilla, ed. *The Letters of Ruth Draper, 1920–1956: A Self-Portrait of a Great Actress*. New York: Scribner's, 1979.

Watt, Douglas. "Ben Kingsley Doesn't Soar to *Kean* Heights." Review of *Edmund Kean*, by Raymund Fitzsimons. *New York Daily News*, 28 Sept. 1983. Reprint, *New York Theatre Critics' Reviews*, 43 (1983): 177.

Watts, Richard, Jr. "A Happy Evening with Mr. Dickens." Review of *Emlyn Williams as Charles Dickens*, by Emlyn Williams. *New York Post*, 5 Feb. 1952, 25.

Weiss, John, ed. *The Origins of Modern Consciousness*. Detroit: Wayne State Univ. Press, 1965.

Widmer, Kingsley. "The Beat in the Rise of Populist Culture." *The Fifties: Fiction, Poetry, Drama*, edited by Warren French, 155–73. DeLand, FL: Painter, 1970.

Wiggam, Albert E. "Is Chautauqua Worth While?" *Bookman*, June 1927, 399–406.

Wilder, Thornton. *Three Plays*. New York: Avon, 1976.

Williams, Charles. "The 'Decline' of Miscellaneous Readings." *Talent*, Sept. 1902, 5.

Williams, Emlyn. *Readings from Dickens*. London: Folio Society, 1953.

———. *George: An Early Autobiography*. New York: Random, 1961.

Wilson, Donald R. "Double Singles." Review of *The Playboy of the Weekend World*, by Emlyn Williams. *Soho Weekly News*, 23 Nov. 1978, 72.

Wilson, Garff B. *A History of American Acting*. Bloomington: Indiana Univ. Press, 1966.

———. *Three Hundred Years of American Drama and Theatre* 2d ed. Englewood Cliffs, NJ: Prentice-Hall, 1982.

Wilson, Robert S. Introduction. In *Gertrude Stein Gertrude Stein Gertrude Stein*, by Martin, xi–xiii.

Wojahn, David. "'A Kind of Vaudeville': Appraising the Age of the Poetry Reading." *New England Review and Bread Loaf Quarterly* 8 (Winter 1985): 265–82.

Woolcott, Alexander. "The Play: The Return of Ruth Draper." *New York Times*, late ed., 28 Jan. 1921, 16.

Woolf, Virginia. *Collected Essays*. 4 vols. New York: Harcourt, 1967.

Wray, Judith Edworthy. "Theories and Methods of Representative Contemporary Poets as Readers of Their Own Poetry." Ph.D. diss., University of Wisconsin, 1961.

Wright, A. Augustus, ed. *Who's Who in the Lyceum*. Philadelphia: Pearson, 1906.

Wyatt, Edith. *Great Companions*. Freeport, NY: Books for Libraries, 1969.

"The Years of Carl Sandburg." *Life*, 4 Aug. 1967, 50.

Young, Tracy. "Tomlin/Wagner." *Vogue*, Nov. 1988, 396 + .

Zabel, Morton Dauwen. *The Art of Ruth Draper*. London: Oxford Univ. Press, 1960.

Zambrano, Ana Laura. "Dickens and Charles Mathews." *Moderna Sprak* 66 (1972): 235–42.

Ziefler, Alan, et al., eds. *Poets on Stage: The Some Symposium on Poetry Readings*. Kensington: Release, 1978.

Ziff, Larzer. *Puritanism in America: New Culture in a New World*. New York: Viking, 1973.

Zucchero, William H. "An Historical Study of the Proceedings of the National Association of Elocutionists." Master's thesis, University of Michigan, 1953.

Zweig, Ellen Marcia. "Performance Poetry: Critical Approaches to Contemporary Intermedia." Ph.D. diss., University of Michigan, 1980.

Interviews and Unpublished Correspondence

Busch, Charles. Personal interview, 30 Sep. 1982.

Crisp, Quentin. Personal interview, 23 Apr. 1986. Published in *Literature in Performance* 8 (Nov. 1988): 77–86.

Ellison, Emily. Personal interview, 17 Oct. 1985.

Galati, Frank. Personal interview, 17 Oct. 1982.

Gray, Spalding. Letter to the author, 27 Feb. 1983.

McCowen, Alec. Letter to the author, 13 Oct. 1984.

Norris, William. Personal interview, 10 Mar. 1983.

Peterson, Arthur. Letter to the author, 24 Jul. 1984.

Rumbelow, Steven. Personal interview, 25 Jan. 1983.

Stevenson, Mark. Personal interview, 20 Apr. 1983.

Williams, Emlyn. Personal interview, 30 Dec. 1982. Published in *Literature in Performance* 4 (Nov. 1983): 78–84.

Special Collections

Berg Collection. The New York Public Library. New York, New York.

Billy Rose Theatre Collection. Library and Museum of the Performing Arts at Lincoln Center, New York Public Library. New York, New York.

Chautauqua Collection. Smith Memorial Library, Chautauqua Institution. Chautauqua, New York.

Hargrett Rare Book and Manuscript Library. University of Georgia Libraries. Athens, Georgia.

Keith Vawter Papers. Redpath Chautauqua Collection, Special Collections, University of Iowa Libraries. Iowa City, Iowa.

Lew Sarett Papers. Northwestern University Archives, Northwestern University Libraries. Evanston, Illinois.

Paul Shyre Papers. Special Collections, Mugar Memorial Library, Boston University. Boston, Massachusetts.

Redpath Chautauqua Collection. Special Collections, University of Iowa Libraries. Iowa City, Iowa.

Robert McLean Cumnock Papers. Northwestern University Archives, Northwestern University Libraries. Evanston, Illinois.

Theatre Collection. Museum of the City of New York. New York, New York.

Index

A Note on the Author

John S. Gentile received his Ph.D. in Performance Studies in 1984 from Northwestern University. He is presently Assistant Professor of Communications and Performance Studies at Kennesaw State College in Marietta, Georgia, where he teaches courses in performance history, performance methodology, and communication theory. His publications have appeared in *Literature in Performance, Studies in Popular Culture,* and *The American Institute for Discussion Review.* In the summers of 1985 and 1989, he served as a scholar-performer with the Wyoming Chautauqua.